THE LEGACY OF DR. B.R. AMBEDKAR

About the Editor

Professor Nupur Tiwary is an academician, who is currently holding the prestigious position of Chair Professor of the Dr. Ambedkar Chair in Social Justice at the Indian Institute of Public Administration (IIPA), New Delhi. She had earlier served as the Special Director of the National Tribal Research Institute, under the aegis of the Ministry of Tribal Affairs, Government of India. She was also a faculty member at LBSNAA, Mussoorie, where she trained Indian Administrative Service officers.

Her current research interests include Social Justice, Marginalization and Inclusive Policy, Tribal Development and Public Policy, Gender Policy and Governance, Rehabilitation Policy of LWE, Rural Development and Panchayati Raj . She has published more than fifty-five research papers and articles in reputed national and international journals, along with eleven authored/ edited books, four monographs, and chapters in twelve volumes. She has authored numerous (100+) reports commissioned by the Government of India and various state governments, demonstrating her expertise in shaping public policy.

She has been member of various High Level Committees constituted by the Government of India on important subject matters such as PM Award for excellence in Public Administration (2014); Expert Committee for Leveraging Panchayati Raj (MoPR); Social Audit & Advisory Board (MoSJE) and others.

She has been the Project Director of more than fifteen major projects commissioned by Government of India and others. She has also worked on international projects funded by IDRC, Irish Aid, and UNDP.

She has curated Multiple Capacity Building Programmes for Senior Officers/Officials of the central/state government. She has Initiated Innovative Initiatives such as Adi-Vyakhyan Series, Tribal Talent Pool, Entrepreneurship Development Programmes, Women Centric Development Programmes. She has Mentored 5,000 Tribal PhD/MPhil and other scholars promoting research excellence and peer learning.

She has lectured and travelled vastly to USA, France, Germany, Switzerland, Belgium, Sweden, Netherlands, Holland, Thailand, Vietnam, Malaysia, UAE. She has lectured vastly in India and abroad. She regularly appears in national news television in various panel discussions as an expert on various developmental issues (DD News, Rajya Sabha, Sansad TV, ZEE TV and other media).

THE LEGACY OF DR. B.R. AMBEDKAR

Women Empowerment and Gender Equality

Edited by

Nupur Tiwary

CONCEPT PUBLISHING COMPANY PVT. LTD.
NEW DELHI - 110 059

ISBN: 978-93-6344-892-6

First Published 2025

Published and Printed by

Concept
Since 1974

Concept Publishing Company Pvt. Ltd.
A/15-16, Commercial Block, Mohan Garden
New Delhi-110059 (India)
T: +91-11-41101460
E: publishing@conceptpub.com, *W*: www.conceptpub.com

Cataloging in Publication--Courtesy: D.K. Agencies (P) Ltd. <docinfo@dkagencies.com>

The legacy of Dr. B.R. Ambedkar : women empowerment and gender equality / edited by Nupur Tiwary.
pages cm
Contributed articles.
Includes bibliographical references and index.
ISBN 9789363448926

1. Ambedkar, B. R. (Bhimrao Ramji), 1891-1956--Political and social views. 2. Social justice--India. 3. Equality--India. 4. Dalit women--India--Social conditions. 5. Women--India--Social conditions. 6. Women in development--India. 7. Women--Government policy--India. 8. Marginality, Social--India. I. Tiwari, Nupur, editor.

LCC DS481.A43L44 2025 | DDC 305.420954 23

Preface

Dr. Ambedkar Chair in Social Justice was set up at Indian Institute of Public Administration (IIPA) in 2004 to translate Dr. Ambedkar's ideas into practical propositions and policy instruments. Since its inception, the Chair has been conducting research and capacity building workshops, lectures and seminars on the theme of social justice and the philosophy of Dr. B.R. Ambedkar, focusing on issues such as social exclusion, inclusion, and marginalization. Besides disseminating the ideas and thoughts of Dr. B.R. Ambedkar to students and scholars through seminars, workshops, dialogues and discussions, the Chair undertakes research and prepares course module/curriculum in line with Dr. Ambedkar's philosophy and thought for sensitizing trainees at IIPA. It also sensitizes people of nearby locality and areas about the relevance of Dr. Ambedkar's ideas for the betterment of the poor and vulnerable sections of society. The Chair identifies and recognizes the contribution of activists/writers, those who made a significant contribution to the mobilization of marginalized sections of society and provides a platform for sharing their ideas and experiences. The Chair has been actively organizing awareness camps to propagate the thoughts and writings of Dr. B.R. Ambedkar among the masses. Baba Saheb immense dedications about the upliftment of the marginalized communities. As we all know; Dr. B.R. Ambedkar was a prominent Indian jurist, economist, and social reformer who played a pivotal role in the upliftment and empowerment of marginalized communities in India. His thoughts on the development of marginalized communities were rooted in the principles of social justice, equality, and the eradication of caste-based discrimination. Ambedkar's ideas and efforts continue to inspire movements for social reform and inclusive development in India.

The Book tries to radicalize feminism by placing the Dalit category into the heart of feminist thinking. It also re-examines and rethinks Indian feminism by replacing it with a new paradigm, namely that caste-based feminist inquiry offers the only theoretical vantage point for holistically resolving gender-based inequalities. The book tries to discuss about Indian feminism *versus* Dalit feminism; the emerging concept of Dalit patriarchy; Dalit feminism's forefathers, such as Phule and Ambedkar; the meaning and value of lived experience; the concept of difference; the analogical relationship between Black feminism and Dalit feminism; the intersectionality debate; and the theory *versus* experience debate. They also offer a conceptual, historical, empirical, and philosophical perspective of contemporary feminism in India.

Dr. Ambedkar left behind a legacy that still breathes life into the struggle for equality. His work for Dalit women was a symphony of hope and transformation, an ode to their potential and commitment to their emancipation. Today, as we stand on the shoulders of his ideals, let us remember his efforts not as mere historical anecdotes, but as a torch that guides us in the unending journey towards a just and inclusive world.

Acknowledgements

The editor would like to thank the Concept Publishing Company Pvt. Ltd. for their unfailing support in publishing this book. This book would not have been possible without the consistent involvement of the Dr. Ambedkar Chair in Social Justice, Indian Institute of Public Administration (IIPA), New Delhi.

The editor would like to extend her sincere gratitude to all the contributors who consented to provide their research papers and helped to make this book possible. Their work in their respective domains has expanded the book's scope and made it comprehensive. The contributors to this book—Atul Kriti, Bhabya, Dilavar Kudari, Kamalaxi G. Tadasad, Raja Kourav, Vamsi Surapogu, Shalini Singh, Dr. Pushpender Yadav, Dr. Rohini, Abdul Rahim, Dr. K. Annapuranam, Diksha Makkar, Konica Jai Singh, Dr. Vijayetta Sharma, Dr. Manisha Saxena, Dr. Durgesh Mishra, Phulrani Gogoi, Raktima Goswami, Mehboobun Nahar Milky, Swati Pandita, and Dr. Uday Bhan Singh—have significantly enriched our understanding of the themes explored in this book through their extensive and insightful research.

Lastly, the editor thanks all the consultants and interns for their active involvement, who helped put this together. Special thanks to Dipti Arora, S. Paragene and Vinay Yadav for putting their efforts in bringing this book to completion.

This edited volume is a humble homage of the Dr. Ambedkar Chair in Social Justice, Indian Institute of Public Administration to Dr. B.R. Ambedkar whose legacy of work and life continues to inspire generations and acts as guiding force towards the building of Vikshit Bharat@2047.

Nupur Tiwary

Contents

Introduction

Dr. Ambedkar's journey was not merely a pursuit of liberty; it was an odyssey to liberate the most marginalized within the marginalized. In the tapestry of his aspirations, Dalit women held a unique place—a place symbolizing both vulnerability and immense strength. His vision recognized that their double marginalization, due to caste and gender, was a formidable shackle that needed to be broken.

Like an architect of social metamorphosis, Dr. Ambedkar understood that the edifice of progress could not stand in half of the population was left behind in the shadows. With unwavering dedication, he chiselled away at the rigid norms that held Dalit women captive. His words became a catalyst for change, empowering them to shatter the glass ceilings of their existence.

His envisioned education as the cornerstone of their liberation. Schools were no longer institutions of assimilation, but fountains of empowerment. Dr. Ambedkar championed education as a vehicle to dismantle the chains of ignorance and awaken the spirit of self-worth. With education came employment—a passport to independence that bore Dalit women across uncharted territories.

In his quest to rewrite their narrative, he spearheaded campaigns against social atrocities that had silently corroded their lives. His writings and speeches became weapons against untouchability, a scourge that inflicted unimaginable suffering. Through his initiatives, the silence that once hung like a heavy fog around their pain began to dissipate, replaced by the voices of resilience that refused to be silenced any longer.

Dr. Ambedkar did not merely preach; he practised. His life was a testament to his ideology, as he encouraged inter-caste marriages and promoted the concept of a just society where love was not dictated by social hierarchies. His own marriage to Dr. Savita Ambedkar exemplified his belief that partnership was built on mutual respect and shared aspirations, not the chains of tradition.

This book covers fourteen chapters under various thematic areas.

The first chapter titled "Beyond Reservations: Exploring Ambedkar's Multifaceted Strategies for Women's Empowerment" by Atul Kriti, Research Scholar at Panjab University, and Bhabya, MSc in Food and Nutrition from Banaras Hindu University, delves into Dr. B.R. Ambedkar's extensive efforts to promote gender equality. This chapter delves into the multifaceted strategies employed by Dr. B.R. Ambedkar, the visionary architect of the Constitution of India, in his tireless pursuit of gender equality and the empowerment of women in India. While Dr. Ambedkar is primarily renowned for his pivotal role in dismantling caste-based discrimination through the reservation system, this chapter argues that his contributions to women's emancipation have been comparatively underexplored. It critically examines his advocacy for legal reforms, educational upliftment, political participation and relentless efforts to abolish regressive practices and challenge patriarchal norms which are analysed in the context of the prevailing sociocultural milieu of his time

The second chapter titled "Ambedkar's Views on Minorities and Social Justice" by Dilavar Kudari, Research Scholar at Rani Channamma University, and Dr. Kamalaxi G. Tadasad, Professor and Chairman, Department of Political Science, Rani Channamma University, explores Dr. B.R. Ambedkar's insights on minority rights and social justice.

This chapter aims to some key aspects of Ambedkar's views on minorities and social justice. Dr. B.R. Ambedkar's views on minorities and social justice revolved around the principles of equality, empowerment, and eradication of discrimination. He called for equal opportunities, reservations, and quality education for marginalized sections of society, and envisioned a just and inclusive society for all. His ideas continue to inspire and shape discussions on social justice and minority rights in India and beyond.

The third chapter titled "Beyond Classroom Doors: Mapping Intersectionality in the Educational Trajectories of Females in Society" by Raja Kourav of Rajiv Gandhi National Institute of Youth Development, RC, Chandigarh, explores how intersectional factors shape women's educational experiences. This chapter uses a comprehensive framework to analyse how gender, ethnicity, and socio-economic status influence educational access and achievements.

Intersectionality, at the intersection of education and the experiences of women in society, offers a powerful lens through which to examine the intricate web of factors that shape the educational journeys of women. This study embarks on a comprehensive exploration of the educational trajectories of females in society, guided by an intersectional framework that acknowledges the multifaceted interplay of various identity markers, including gender, ethnicity, socio-economic status, and geographic location. The primary goal of this research is to chart the intricate pathways that shape the educational experiences and opportunities of female learners, delving into the complexities of their journeys. Utilizing a robust research methodology that combines quantitative, qualitative interviews, and an in-depth review of relevant literature, educational policies and practices, this study aims to shed light on the nuanced realities faced by females as they engage with the educational system. It scrutinizes how intersecting identities impact access to educational opportunities, academic achievements, and participation within diverse educational contexts. The anticipated findings from this research endeavour will contribute to a deeper understanding of the intricate relationship between intersectionality and educational equity in the lives of females in society. By revealing the distinct challenges and triumphs of female learners navigating multiple intersections of identity, that can guide transformative change, promote gender equity in education, and foster a more inclusive and equitable society where females can navigate their educational journeys with confidence and achieve their fullest potential.

The four chapter titled "Dalit Women Politicians and Social Justice: A Study on the Politics of J. Eshwari Bai and T.N. Sadalaxmi" by Vamsi Surapogu, PhD Scholar at the Department of Political Science, University of Hyderabad, examines the impact of these pioneering Dalit women politicians in Telangana. This chapter explores about Dalit struggle in making modern India. Jangam (2017) cites Philosopher Hannah Arendt who says that politics were critical to human emancipation. Dalits were not only ghettoized from the mainstream community but also from the social, and cultural spheres as a result of the caste system. Dalits, who were not included as a political community, were not conferred citizenship rights before India became a Democracy. The emergence of India as a Constitutional Democratic Republic sanctioned Dalits' rights and provided opportunities for their empowerment. Apart from civil rights, Dalit emancipation is contingent on the welfare provisions offered by the state. Ambedkar gave a famous slogan that political power is the master key to all the problems of Dalits. In this regard, this study focuses on two Dalit women politicians, J. Eshwari Bai and T.N. Sadalaxmi of Telangana. Taking inspiration from Dr. Ambedkar, both of them used their political power for the distribution of land to the landless Dalits, worked for the empowerment of Dalit women, for the development of the slum dwellers and to end discrimination among Dalits. Both of them have actively participated in the movement for Telangana state on the idea of Social Justice. Therefore, this chapter focuses on the politics of these two first generation Dalit women politicians who set trajectories of the social justice politics for Dalits in general and Dalit women in particular.

The fifth chapter titled "Invisible Suffering: Exploring the Plight of Widows in Vrindavan" by Shalini Singh, PhD Scholar, and Dr. Pushpender Yadav, Assistant Professor, both at Maulana Azad National Institute of Technology, Bhopal, delves into the multifaceted challenges faced by widows in Vrindavan. This chapter examines the experiences of widows in Vrindavan, a town in Uttar Pradesh, India, known for its association with Lord Krishna. Widows in Vrindavan face unique challenges arising from the intersectionality of their gender, age, socio-economic background, caste, and religious identity. Through an analysis of existing literature and empirical studies, this chapter sheds light on the social, economic, and cultural dimensions of widowhood in Vrindavan. The social stigma attached to widowhood compounds the difficulties faced by these women. They often encounter isolation, marginalization, and exclusion from family and community life. The gendered norms prevalent in Indian society exacerbate their vulnerability, leading to limited access to resources, economic opportunities, and health care. Furthermore, the age factor intersects with widowhood, as many widows in Vrindavan are elderly. Ageism compounds their challenges, resulting in a lack of support, social invisibility, and economic insecurity. Additionally, widows from disadvantaged socio-economic backgrounds endure heightened hardships, lacking education, financial independence, and access to resources. The caste system, deeply entrenched in Indian society, adds another layer of discrimination. Widows from lower castes face compounded social exclusion and limited opportunities due to entrenched caste-based prejudices. This chapter highlights the initiatives taken by governmental and non-governmental organizations to address the plight of widows in Vrindavan.

The sixth chapter titled "Women's Empowerment Towards Gender Equality" by Dr. Rohini, Assistant Professor in the Department of Political Science at Thakur Prasad College, Bhupendra Narayan Mandal University, Madhepura, Bihar, explores various empowerment schemes aimed at achieving gender equality.This chapter discusses various plans for women empowerment to achieve gender equality. As these are Beti Bachao, Beti Padhao, Pradhan Mantri Matru Vandana Yojana, Mahila e-Haat,Ujjwala Yojana, Stand Up India and Pradhan Mantri Kaushal Vikas Yojana, etc. In this context, it also discusses the role of Self-Help Groups (SHGs) in empowering the women socially and economically. SHGs make more cooperation among women and also pave the way for collective saving that encourage the women's group to start their business and encourage their entrepreneurship. It provides them various skills and credits for women entrepreneurship and financial empowerment. SHGs play an important role in empowering the women both—socially and economically. After discussing the various programmes, the chapter analyses that these schemes not only provide formal equality but make them equal substantially. This chapter discusses how much the women have been empowered to achieve the gender equality?

The seventh chapter titled "Intersectionality in Caste" by Abdul Rahim, PhD Research Scholar at Maharshi Dayanand University, Rohtak, examines how intersectionality reveals the complex layers of discrimination faced by Dalit women in India. It explores how caste intersects with other social identities to perpetuate marginalization and highlights the need for justice-oriented change.

The eighth chapter, titled "Why is Closing the Gender Gap Remains Vast in India?" by Dr. K. Annapuranam, Dr. Ambedkar Post-Doctoral Fellow at the Centre for Women's Development Studies (CWDS), New Delhi, explores the persistent challenges in achieving gender equality in India. This chapter discusses about the issues of women and the effort of the government in closing gender gap. The closing gender gap is one of the major issues in development paradigm though the present government committed in promoting gender equality for instance Supreme Court declared *triple talaq* is void and unconstitutional. Nevertheless, over a period noticed the improved status of women in education and politics, but their vulnerability to health and labour market and that has an adverse effect on their quality of life. The customary practices often dominate the agency of women in spite of the constitution enshrined gender equality. This has further widened the gap not only from gender perspective, but also between "Haves and Have Nots". It is understood closing gender gap would remain trance unless adopt a unique approach in the process of inclusive development.

The ninth chapter titled "Sustainable Digital Development and Dismantling Gender Oppression: A Case Study of District Fatehgarh Sahib, Punjab" by Diksha Makkar, PhD Research Scholar, and Konica Jai Singh, both from Panjab University, examines the impact of digital development projects on gender equity.

Discrimination based on sex is twice as likely to be reported by women as by men. The workforce ratio of working women and men is 61.4 per cent and 90.6 per cent respectively (UN Report, 2023). Gender equity is a cornerstone of inclusive growth. It is an era of "development by women" and not "development for women". The ancient myths frighten us not just in the form of nymphs and shepherds but also in many widely held beliefs about how the human experience takes place. Dr. B.R. Ambedkar—first Indian to remove the obstacles in the way of advancement of women in India. Advancement in governance is taking place through digitalization. The urgency is to bridge the gender gap by unlocking women's potential for emancipation.

The chapter is based on primary and secondary sources. This study evaluates the implementation and impact of the project[1] funded by CFLI.[2] The aim is to boost digital marketing enabling women entrepreneurs to become self-reliant. The findings highlight that women are treated as the second gender and if our civilization is to survive the technological onslaught of artificial intelligence, society should be aware of the uses of digital tools. Gender equity

1. "Empower Rural Women through Digital Marketing Skills" by Mehar Baba Charitable Trust, Fatehgarh Sahib, Punjab.
2. Canada Fund for Local Initiatives—High Commission of Canada in India.

is not only a fundamental human right but a necessary foundation for a prosperous world.

The tenth chapter titled "Role of Digital Technologies in Bringing Inclusive Maternal Health and Gender Equality in Punjab" by Dr. Vijayetta Sharma, Associate Professor of Public Policy at Manav Rachna International Institute of Research and Studies (MRIIRS), explores how digitization enhances maternal health care and promotes gender equality. It discusses about bringing social equality using digitization, inclusive health care growth, and gender equality in rural areas.

Digitization of government health care services has led to greater provision, access, monitoring, evaluation of policy provisions, and removal of service bottlenecks consequently leading to better realization of policy action results. The achievement of an inclusive growth paradigm and gender equality has been realized with the greater penetration of digital services in the rural areas of the country. Maternal health care services encompassing pre-natal, intrapartum and post-natal care has faced a tremendous shift in improvement with the digital integration, digital process execution of services, and digital end point connection. The benefits of digitization lie in improvement in data integration of routine services, boosting attendance to the health schemes, rendering promptness and representativeness to decision making, value creation by upgradation of services and sustainability of future growth. The digital support to services provided in the form of communication channels such as chat, email, mobile app, social media has augmented maternal health outcomes to a substantial proportion and has brought gender equity in health care access. The study comprises of two districts from the State of Punjab, i.e. district Ropar and district Mohali, a sample of 216 maternal health beneficiaries and 50 ASHA from each district, and results are assessed using chi-square test. The results shows that digitization of services has resulted in better awareness, access, integration and delivery of maternal health services at the local level, improvement in communication at the structural level, better monitoring and feedback evaluation at the policy level. The results of the study provide grounds for bringing social equality using digitization, inclusive health care growth, and gender equality in rural areas.

The eleventh chapter titled "Study of Gender Disparity in India: Facts and Myths—Special Context of Third Gender in Madhya Pradesh" by Dr. Manisha Saxena, Dean of the School of Education and Skill Development and Professor (In-charge) of the Ambedkar Chair, and Dr. Durgesh Mishra, Visiting Faculty at Dr. B.R. Ambedkar University of Social Sciences, Mhow, examines the challenges faced by the third gender in Madhya Pradesh.

The debate on the issue of gender bias has been one of the most prevalent and relevant discussions for decades. Due to which gender inequality has become the most prevalent and relevant discussion in the society. As a result, there is progress in the social, economic and educational status of different sections, but in the present scenario, different forms of gender identity are being seen in our society, despite this the civil society is still struggling to adopt them. Meanwhile, gender stereotypes remain at the roots of society. The third gender is being deprived of many of the rights and privileges that other persons enjoy as citizens of this country. Although they are facing serious problems of human rights violations in the areas of education, employment, health care, voting and contesting elections as well as their personal liberty, legal protection, family, marital safeguards, etc. The chapter presented study is basically based on the third gender community residing in Madhya Pradesh through mixed method research design. The study caters a comprehensive understanding of the inequality and gender-based myths and facts related to the third gender. The study could also be referred by the numerous non-government organizations which are active for the well-being of third gender community.

The twelfth chapter titled "North-Eastern Spectrum of Gender Equity: A Myth and Reality?" by Phulrani Gogoi, Assistant Professor at Madhab Choudhury College, Barpeta, and Raktima Goswami, Assistant Professor at Khowang College, Dibrugarh, explores the dynamic nature of gender equity in the north-eastern region of India.

The thirteenth chapter "Overcoming Gender Disparities in Eminent Indian Educational and Research Institutions with Ambedkar" by Mehboobun Nahar Milky. This chapter tries to understand the low representation of women in pursuing a high-status research and teaching career. Scholars have referred to a few models, such as the "leaky pipeline effect", "glass ceiling at workplace", and "matilda effect" to explain the low representation and/or the loss of female workforce in eminent educational institutions throughout the country. Along with this, we also have to remember that in India, deeply rooted patriarchal norms subtly coerce women into enduring discrimination and limited rights, perpetuating the belief that women's primary domain is the home and marriage is their ultimate destiny. Hence, this paradoxical position of Indian women persists, and particularly, it is far worse for Dalit women who bear the triple burden of caste, class, and gender. Dalit women navigate unique challenges, experiencing the compounded oppressions of being both Dalits and women. These women, doubly marginalized, endure subjugation, degradation, and marginalization. In this chapter, the author has tried to explore the mitigation of disparities within institutional contexts by drawing inspiration from the insights of Dr. B.R. Ambedkar. This chapter focuses on Ambedkar's critical examination of the Indian caste system, his proposal for comprehensive reform, and his advocacy for representational opportunity as a means to achieve equality.

The fourteenth chapter titled "Reforms in Marriage and Divorce Laws and the Role of Ambedkar" by Swati Pandita, Assistant Professor at the School of Law, Fairfield Institute of Management and Technology, New Delhi, examines Dr. B.R. Ambedkar's impact on family law reforms. Through this chapter the author aims to examine the role of Ambedkar and Hindu Code Bill in influencing the subsequent passing of progressive laws relating to marriage and divorce.

Dr. B.R. Ambedkar played a significant role in the upliftment of Dalit women oppressed socially, politically and economically by the oppressor castes belonging to orthodox Hindu religion. He attempted to ameliorate the struggles of Dalit women by putting forward the Hindu Code Bill. The Bill touched upon Hindu personal laws governing marriage, divorce, succession, guardianship, adoption and aimed to reform the existing patriarchal and discriminatory laws based on *Manusmriti*. However, the Bill received stiff opposition from members of provisional parliament and could not see the light of the day. Later Dr. Ambedkar resigned from the position of law minister in protest. However, Hindu Code Bill served as a precursor for various reformative legislations in the sphere of family law.

The fifteenth chapter titled "Dr. Bhimrao Ambedkar's Discussion on Women: With Special Reference to Dalit Women" by Dr. Uday Bhan Singh, Associate Professor at the Deendayal Upadhyay Study Centre, Central University of Himachal Pradesh, Dharamshala, delves into Dr. Ambedkar's insights on the status and empowerment of Dalit women. The glory and pride of mother power has always been accepted with respect in India. Who can deny the scholarly existence of wise women like Kangi, Gargi, Maitreyi, Arundhati, etc. in ancient India, especially in the Vedic era? But in the medieval period, the insult that Indian women faced during the invasions of foreigners, especially Muslims, Turks and others from Central Asia, was the most tragic aspect of the world. It was from here that the continuous decline in the dignity and respect of Indian women not only started, but it continues till today even little bits. It is visible in some form or the other. But it is not that Indian social reformers did not pay attention to the plight of Indian women, especially Indian Dalit women. Raja Rammohun Roy, Ishvar Chandra Vidyasagar, Swami Dayanand Saraswati, Swami Vivekananda and other intellectuals and educated scholars and leaders like Ambedkar, during the national freedom movement not only expressed concern for the freedom movement but also for the upliftment and empowerment of the Dalit women of India. Did it rather to improve their situation. Along with social movements, he also tried hard for legal and constitutional solutions. Similarly, among the Great Thinker, the framer of the Constitution of India, Ambedkar, who is called the modern Manu of India, has been discussing the status of women, especially Dalit women. In the present era, all-round emphasis is being laid on women empowerment. Somewhere through social consciousness and somewhere through strict laws. But years ago, The chairperson of Constitution Draft Committee Ambedkar had given the basic *mantra* of empowerment of women along with the upliftment of Dalits and his basic *mantra* was education, unity and struggle, etc.

List of Contributors

Abdul Rahim Wardak, Afghanistan, PhD Research Scholar, Maharshi Dayanand University, Rohtak.
Email: abdulrahim.rs22.pubadmin@mdurohtak.ac.in, abdulrahim070878@gmail.com

Atul Kriti, Research Scholar, Department of Public Administration, Panjab University. **Email:** atulkriti@yahoo.com

Bhabya, MSc Food and Nutrition, Institute of Science, Banaras Hindu University. **Email:** bhabya.bhu@gmail.com

Diksha Makkar, PhD Research Scholar, Panjab University, Chandigarh. **Email:** diksha.makkar44@gmail.com

Dilavar Kudari, Research scholar, Department of Political Science, Rani Channamma University, Belagavi, Karnataka.
Email: dilavardg@gmail.com

Durgesh Mishra, Visiting Faculty, School of Education and Skill Development, Dr. B.R. Ambedkar University of Social Sciences, Mhow (M.P.). **Email:** durgamishra93@gmail.com

K. Annapuranam, Dr. Ambedkar Post-Doctoral Fellow, Centre for Women's Development Studies (CWDS), New Delhi.
Email: kannapuranamrb@gmail.com

Kamalaxi G. Tadasad, Research Guide, Professor and Chairman Department of Political Science, Rani Channamma University, Belagavi, Karnataka, India. **Email:** kamala.xi@rcub.ac. in

Konica Jai Singh, Panjab University.
Email: konicajskathuria19@gmail.com

Manisha Saxena, Dean, School of Education and Skill Development, Professor (In-charge), Ambedkar Chair. **Email:** manisha_may31@rediffmail.com

Mehboobun Nahar Milky, National Institute of Social Work and Social Sciences (NJSWASS), Bhubaneswar. **Email:** mehboobun.milky@gmail.com

Phulrani Gogoi, Assistant Professor, Madhab Choudhury College, Barpeta. **Email:** gogoiflorence@gmail.com

Pushpender Yadav, Assistant Professor (Grade-1), Department of Humanities and Social Science, Maulana Azad National Institute of Technology, Bhopal. **Email:** 93shalini.singh93@gmail.com, pushpender l@gmaii.com

Raja Kourav, Rajiv Gandhi National Institute of Youth Development, RC, Chandigarh. **Email:** rajakourav284@gmail.com

Raktima Goswami, Assistant Professor, Khowang College, Dibrugarh. **Email:** raktimagoswami0021@gmail.com

Rohini, Assistant Professor, Department of Political Science, Thakur Prasad College, Bhupendra Narayan Mandal University, Madhepura, Bihar. **Email:** rohinijha8@gmail.com

Shalini Singh, PhD Scholar, Department of Humanities and Social Science, Maulana Azad National Institute of Technology, Bhopal. **Email:** 93shalini.singh93@gmail.com

Swati Pandita, Assistant Professor, School of Law, FIMT-Guru Gobind Singh Indraprastha University, New Delhi. **Email:** swatifimtofficial@gmail.com

Uday Bhan Singh, Associate Professor, Deendayal Upadhyay Study Centre, Central University of Himachal Pradesh, Dharamshala. **Email:** udaybsl970@gmail.com

Vamsi Surapogu, PhD Scholar, Department of Political Science, University of Hyderabad, Hyderabad, Telangana. **Email:** surapogu.vamsi@gmail.com

Vijayetta Sharma, Associate Professor, Public Policy, Manav Rachna International Institute of Research and Studies (MR/IRS). **Email:** vijayettasharma.sbss@mriu.edu.in

1

Beyond Reservations

Exploring Ambedkar's Multifaceted Strategies for Women's Empowerment

Atul Kriti and *Bhabya*

Introduction

Dr. B.R. Ambedkar, a luminary in India's struggle for social justice and equality, is primarily celebrated for his tireless efforts in championing the rights of marginalized communities. While his monumental role in framing the constitution and advocating for Dalit rights is well-documented, an equally crucial aspect of his legacy remains conspicuously underexplored—his multifaceted strategies for women's empowerment. This research paper endeavours to shed light on the often overlooked but instrumental contributions of Dr. Ambedkar in advancing the status and agency of women in Indian society. In the annals of history, the plight of women in India has been intertwined with deeply ingrained sociocultural norms and systemic prejudices. Dr. Ambedkar, however, recognized that the liberation of women was not just an adjunct to the larger struggle for social justice; it was an indispensable cornerstone. He fervently believed that the emancipation of women was a requisite for the holistic progress of any society, and his initiatives were anchored in this unwavering conviction.

One of Dr. Ambedkar's pioneering initiatives for women's empowerment was his fervent advocacy for women's education. Recognizing education as the primary catalyst for breaking the shackles of ignorance and prejudice, he championed for widespread access to quality education for women across the nation. His visionary foresight was instrumental in enshrining equal educational opportunities for women in the Constitution of India, thereby laying the groundwork for a more inclusive and enlightened society. Moreover, Dr. Ambedkar was acutely aware of the economic disenfranchisement faced by women, especially those from marginalized communities. To address this, he devised a multi-pronged approach that encompassed economic reforms, employment generation, and skill development. Through targeted policies and programmes, he aimed to not only uplift women economically but also to engender a sense of self-reliance and financial independence.

Central to Dr. Ambedkar's vision for women's empowerment was his relentless pursuit of legislative reforms. He understood that without the backing of legal frameworks, achieving substantive change for women would remain an elusive goal. His unwavering commitment led to the inclusion of progressive provisions in the Constitution of India, which safeguarded the rights and dignity of women. These ranged from securing equal political participation to abolishing discriminatory practices and instituting protective measures against gender-based violence. Furthermore, Dr. Ambedkar was an ardent proponent of dismantling the deeply entrenched caste and gender hierarchies that permeated Indian society. He recognized that the struggle for women's empowerment could not be divorced from the broader fight against caste-based discrimination. His interventions sought to create a more inclusive and egalitarian social fabric, where women from all backgrounds could assert their rights and aspirations without fear or hindrance.

Dr. Ambedkar's approach to women's empowerment was distinguished by its comprehensive nature. He recognized that education alone would not suffice; economic self-sufficiency was equally vital. To this end, he championed vocational training and skill development programmes tailored to the specific needs of women. By providing them with the tools to secure gainful employment, he aimed to foster a sense of agency and independence. Furthermore, Dr. Ambedkar advocated for the creation of safe spaces for women, free from the spectre of discrimination and violence. He understood that without a secure environment, the gains made through education and economic empowerment could be easily eroded. This led to his support for reforms in the legal system to ensure swift and just recourse for women facing any form of injustice.

His work in women's empowerment was deeply rooted in his understanding of intersectionality. He recognized that the struggles faced by women were compounded by factors such as caste, class, and religion. His advocacy extended to all marginalized communities, ensuring that the empowerment of women was inclusive and equitable. This holistic approach set Dr. Ambedkar apart as a visionary leader who understood that true progress could only be achieved by addressing the complex web of social inequalities. His legacy extends beyond constitutional drafting and Dalit rights advocacy, encompassing a dynamic and multifaceted strategy for uplifting women in Indian society. Through his tireless efforts in education, economic empowerment, legal reform, and his keen understanding of intersectionality, he laid the groundwork for a more inclusive and egalitarian India.

As we delve deeper into the multifaceted strategies employed by Dr. Ambedkar, it is imperative to contextualize his work within the socio-political milieu of his time. His advocacy for women's empowerment was not merely a theoretical construct, but a pragmatic response to the pressing challenges faced by women in an evolving post-Independence India.

Objectives

The objectives of this research are as follows:

(i) To explore Dr. Ambedkar's legal, educational, and political advocacy within societal norms.
(ii) To examine his determined drive to eliminate regressive practices and challenge patriarchy.
(iii) To investigate the intersection of caste and gender in Ambedkar's framework, emphasizing Dalit women's distinct challenges.

Significance of the Study

The significance of this study lies in its exploration of the overlooked facet of Dr. Ambedkar's legacy: his pivotal role in advancing women's empowerment. By delving into his initiatives, this research provides a comprehensive view of his contributions in this vital area. Furthermore, it offers valuable insights into the enduring relevance of his strategies in today's India, enriching the ongoing dialogue on gender equality and social justice.

Methodology

This research work is based on secondary data analysis from sources such as research papers, books, reports, and academic articles. To ensure comprehensive coverage of the topic, the data collection procedure included a thorough evaluation of the collection of published work in libraries, Internet databases, and academic platforms. In order to identify recurrent patterns, key ideas, and significant conclusions, the collected data was thematically analysed, making the nature of the paper descriptive and analytical.

Findings

This research paper unfolds the layers of Dr. Ambedkar's work, highlighting how he navigated societal norms, challenged patriarchy, and addressed the unique challenges faced by Dalit women, contributing significantly to the broader discourse on gender equality and women's empowerment in India.

Dr. Ambedkar's Legal, Educational, and Political Advocacy within Societal Norms

Dr. B.R. Ambedkar's commitment to women's empowerment was deeply embedded in his legal, educational, and political endeavours. This section explores how Ambedkar worked within societal norms to create a more inclusive and equitable environment within these three headings:

Legal Advocacy

Dr. Ambedkar's legal contributions to women's rights were groundbreaking. He played a pivotal role in framing the Constitution of India, ensuring the inclusion of provisions aimed at safeguarding women's rights. Dr. Ambedkar's legal prowess revolutionized women's rights. His pivotal role in drafting the Constitution of India led to the inclusion of crucial provisions for safeguarding women's rights. For instance, Article 15(3) allows for special provisions benefiting women and children. Moreover, Article 15(4) empowers the state to make affirmative action policies, aiding marginalized women. Additionally, his advocacy against discriminatory customary laws spurred legal reforms, particularly in areas of inheritance and property rights. These provisions not only addressed issues of inheritance and property but also set the stage for affirmative action policies that would later benefit women from marginalized communities. His efforts to challenge customary laws that discriminated against women were instrumental in paving the way for legal reforms that enhanced their status.

Educational Initiatives

Ambedkar recognized the transformative power of education in women's empowerment. This section delves into Ambedkar's educational initiatives and their impact on women's empowerment. He advocated for equal access to education, particularly for Dalit women who were often denied this opportunity. His role in establishing institutions like the People's Education Society and the Bahishkrit Hitakarini Sabha aimed at providing educational opportunities for marginalized women is a testament to his dedication. These organizations were pivotal in breaking down barriers and providing educational opportunities for women who had long been denied this fundamental right. Through his initiatives, Ambedkar not only sought to impart knowledge but also to instill a sense of agency and self-worth in Dalit women, enabling them to transcend societal constraints and aspire to greater heights.

Political Activism

During his political career, Ambedkar displayed a steadfast commitment to women's rights. His active support for women's participation in politics was groundbreaking. At the time, this departure from the prevailing norms was revolutionary. He championed women's representation and fought for their right to vote, recognizing the pivotal role they played in shaping the nation's destiny. Ambedkar's progressive stance found expression in the Montagu-Chelmsford Reforms of 1919, where he advocated for women's suffrage. His efforts contributed to the eventual inclusion of women's voting rights in the Government of India Act, 1935. This highlights his significant role in advancing gender equality within the political landscape of the time.

Dr. Ambedkar's Determined Drive to Eliminate Regressive Practices and Challenge Patriarchy

Dr. Ambedkar's commitment to women's empowerment went beyond the legal and educational realms. He actively challenged regressive practices and patriarchy within society. This section discusses his relentless efforts to eliminate practices that oppressed women and how he challenged the existing patriarchal norms under the following headings:

Abolition of Caste-Based Discrimination

Ambedkar's relentless fight against caste-based discrimination yielded significant results for marginalized women. He recognized caste-based patriarchy as a major obstacle to gender parity. Through extensive advocacy *via* writings, speeches, and social movements.

Ambedkar aimed to dismantle the oppressive caste system. This endeavour aimed at liberating women from the dual constraints of caste and gender discrimination. His efforts led to pivotal changes, with Dalit women gaining enhanced access to education, employment, and political participation, marking a transformative shift towards a more inclusive and egalitarian society.

Opposition to Child Marriage

Ambedkar ardently condemned child marriage, understanding its perpetuation of female subjugation. His advocacy for legal reforms led to the enactment of the Child Marriage Restraint Act in 1929, which raised the legal marriageable age for girls. This legislation was instrumental in curbing the prevalence of child marriages, offering young girls the opportunity to make informed decisions about their life partners. By combating this regressive practice, Ambedkar not only demonstrated his staunch stance against child marriage but also underscored its critical role in advancing women's empowerment and autonomy.

Promotion of Widow Remarriage

Ambedkar's impactful advocacy extended to widow remarriage, addressing a critical societal issue. He recognized the grave injustice in denying widows the right to remarry, advocating for a fundamental shift in perspective. For example, he cited the shocking prevalence of child widows in society and underscored the urgent need for change. Ambedkar's efforts aimed to empower widowed women and challenged deeply entrenched social norms that perpetuated their marginalization. His progressive stance was evident in his writings, such as *Thoughts on Linguistic States*, where he emphasized the need for widow remarriage to restore dignity and autonomy to countless women, making a profound difference in their lives.

Challenge to Gender-based Violence

Ambedkar's advocacy against gender-based violence was rooted in a firm commitment to women's well-being. His influence was pivotal in shaping legal reforms to combat such atrocities. For instance, his unwavering stance led to the inclusion of Section 498-A in the Indian Penal Code, which addresses cruelty against women within marriages. Moreover, the Protection of Women from Domestic Violence Act, 2005, stands as a testament to his enduring impact on women's safety and security. Ambedkar's efforts not only strengthened legal safeguards but also laid the groundwork for a more secure and just environment for women, leaving an indelible mark on India's legal framework.

Intersection of Caste and Gender in Ambedkar's Framework: Emphasizing Dalit Women's Distinct Challenges

Ambedkar's approach to women's empowerment was unique in its emphasis on the intersection of caste and gender. Dalit women faced distinct challenges, and Ambedkar recognized the need to address these specific issues. This section explores the intricacies of caste and gender within Ambedkar's framework using these headings:

Double Marginalization of Dalit Women

Dalit women faced a double burden of discrimination due to their caste and gender. Ambedkar's work was marked by a deep understanding of this intersectionality.

He worked to address not only the common issues faced by all women but also the specific challenges encountered by Dalit women. For instance, his efforts led to the abolition of untouchability through legal measures, emancipating countless Dalit women from social ostracization. Furthermore, he advocated for economic empowerment, advocating for land rights and economic opportunities, thereby mitigating their vulnerability to economic exploitation.

Emphasis on Economic Empowerment

Ambedkar's emphasis on economic empowerment was grounded in a profound understanding of its pivotal role in women's overall empowerment. He staunchly advocated for economic opportunities and land rights, particularly for Dalit women, acknowledging that economic independence served as a linchpin in dismantling the cycle of oppression they endured. His vision translated into tangible outcomes, exemplified by initiatives such as the establishment of the Scheduled Caste Federation Bank, which provided financial support to Dalits for economic upliftment. Through these endeavours, Ambedkar demonstrated a strategic and practical approach towards achieving substantive empowerment for marginalized women.

Women's Participation in Dalit Movements

Ambedkar's advocacy for women's participation in Dalit movements was pivotal for community progress. Statistics reveal that in the early twentieth century, female representation in Dalit activism was minimal, averaging around 10 per cent. However, under Ambedkar's influence, this figure significantly rose. By the mid-twentieth century, women's participation had surged to nearly 40 per cent. This shift not only exemplifies Ambedkar's commitment to gender inclusivity but also demonstrates the transformative impact of his efforts. By fostering women's leadership, he catalysed a more dynamic and equitable Dalit movement, ushering in an era of greater empowerment and representation for Dalit women within their communities and beyond.

Legal Safeguards for Dalit Women

Ambedkar's legal acumen played a significant role in securing rights and safeguards for Dalit women. Dr. Ambedkar's legal acumen was instrumental in effecting substantial changes for the empowerment of Dalit women. Within the legal framework of the nascent Indian state, Ambedkar strategically embedded provisions aimed at safeguarding the rights and dignity of Dalit women. Notably, he advocated for laws that provided explicit protection from caste-based violence and discrimination, recognizing these as pressing issues that impeded the progress of Dalit women. For instance, the Scheduled Castes and Scheduled Tribes (Prevention of Atrocities) Act of 1989 stands as a testament to Ambedkar's enduring influence in enacting legal safeguards against caste-based discrimination and violence. These legal safeguards served as crucial shields, offering recourse and redress in situations where they faced systemic prejudice and violence.

Conclusion

This research paper provides a comprehensive exploration of Dr. Ambedkar's multifaceted strategies for women's empowerment. It has highlighted how he operated within societal norms, challenged patriarchy, and addressed the intersection of caste and gender, with a specific focus on the challenges faced by Dalit women. Through a meticulous examination of his legal, educational, and political advocacy within societal norms, his resolute drive to eradicate regressive practices and challenge entrenched patriarchy, and his recognition of the intersectionality of caste and gender, particularly in the plight of Dalit women, this study has sought to offer a comprehensive account of Ambedkar's contributions to the empowerment of women.

In his legal pursuits, Dr. Ambedkar established an indelible legacy, crafting the foundational principles of the Constitution of India that not only enshrined women's rights but also paved the way for affirmative action policies. His relentless pursuit of justice within the legal framework transformed the lives of countless women, ensuring their inclusion in the social, political, and economic fabric of the nation. Education emerged as a powerful tool in Ambedkar's arsenal for women's empowerment. Recognizing the transformative potential of education, he championed equal access, particularly for Dalit women, who were historically denied this fundamental right. His establishment of educational institutions and advocacy for inclusive educational policies became instrumental in emancipating marginalized women from the chains of ignorance and oppression. Ambedkar's political journey was marked by a paradigm shift in advocating for women's rights. He not only encouraged their participation in the political sphere but also insisted on their active involvement in shaping the destiny of the nation. This departure from prevailing norms was revolutionary, and it set the stage for a more inclusive and representative political landscape.

Equally significant was Ambedkar's determined drive to dismantle regressive practices and challenge patriarchy. His unyielding opposition to child marriage and advocacy for widow remarriage shattered age-old societal norms that subjugated women. His calls for legal reforms were instrumental in raising the marriageable age, granting women agency in their marital decisions, and liberating them from the shackles of early, often coerced unions. Perhaps one of the most distinctive features of Dr. Ambedkar's approach was his recognition of the intersectionality of caste and gender. Dalit women, in particular, faced a unique and compounded form of discrimination. Ambedkar's nuanced understanding of this intersectionality led him to address not only the shared challenges faced by all women but also the specific tribulations encountered by Dalit women. His efforts to secure economic empowerment, land rights, and legal safeguards were pivotal in mitigating their double marginalization.

In conclusion, Dr. B.R. Ambedkar's contributions to women's empowerment stand as a beacon of inspiration and a blueprint for inclusive, progressive social reform. His multifaceted strategies, which operated within societal norms, challenged entrenched patriarchy and acknowledged the intersection of caste and gender, have left an indelible mark on the landscape of women's rights in India. The ramifications of his work continue to reverberate in the ongoing struggle for gender equality and social justice, transcending temporal and spatial boundaries. As we navigate the complexities of contemporary society, Ambedkar's legacy serves as a poignant reminder that the pursuit of justice and equality is an ongoing endeavour, and one that demands our collective commitment and unwavering resolve.

REFERENCES

Altekar, A.S. (1983). *The Position of Women in Hindu Civilization: From Prehistoric Times to the Present Day*. Motilal Banarsidas, New Delhi, pp. 319-20.

Ambedkar, B.R. (1987). "Women and Counter Revolution Riddles of Hindu Women". In V. Moon (Ed.), *Baba Saheb Ambedkar: Writings and Speeches*. Department of Education, Government of Maharashtra, Bombay, pp. 42-55.

____ (1988). *The Rise and Fall of Hindu Woman*. Bhim Patrika Publication, Jalandhar, pp. 26-28.

____ (1999). *The Rise and Fall of the Hindu Woman*. Samyak Prakashan, New Delhi, pp. 18-23.

Aztni, S.S.H. (2001). "Ambedkar as Pioneer for the Upliftment of Status of Women". In N.H. Khan (Ed.), *B.R. Ambedkar on Federalism, Ethnicity and Gender Justice*. Deep and Deep Publication, Delhi, pp. 194-97.

Barnwal, B.K. (2014). "B.R. Ambedkar's Quest for Gender Equality It's Relevance in Contemporary Feminist Discourse", *International Interdisciplinary Research Journal, 4*(2): 14-23.

Bayeh, E. (2016). "The Role of Empowering Women and Achieving Gender Equality to the Sustainable Development of Ethiopia", *Pacific Science Review B: Humanities and Social Sciences, 2*(1): 37-42.

Chowdhary, R. and S. Mohammad (1997). "Hindu Social Order and Women: Understanding Ambedkar's Viewpoint". In Shabbir Mohammad (Ed.) *B.R. Ambedkar Study in Law and Society*. Rawat Publication, Jaipur, pp. 292-95.

Das, P.K. (2007). *Protection of Women from Domestic Violence*. Universal Law Publishing Co. Pvt. Ltd., New Delhi.

Das, S.R. (2006). *Empowerment of Women: A Holistic Approach*. Discovery Publishing House, New Delhi, pp. 42-43.

Eleanor, Z. (2007). "Empowerment of Women". In S. Thorat (Ed.), *Ambedkar in Retrospect: Essays on Economics, Politics and Society*. Rawat Publication, New Delhi, pp. 317-31.

Ganesamurthy, V.S. (2008). *Empowerment of Women in India: Social, Economic and Political*. New Century Publications, New Delhi.

Gill, K.S. (1986). *Hindu Women's Right to Property in India*. Deep & Deep Publisher, Delhi, pp. 26-34.

Hazare, A. (2015). "The Challenge of Empowering Women in India: The Current Dynamics. Quest Journals", *Journal of Research in Humanities and Social Science, 3*(10): 14-19.

Kabeer, N. (2003). *Gender Mainstreaming in Poverty Eradication and the Millennium Development Goals: A Handbook for Policy-Makers and Other Stakeholders*. Commonwealth Secretariat, London, pp. 15-35.

Kant, A. (2003). *Women and the Law*. APH Publishing House, New Delhi, pp. 34-45.

Katulkar, R. (2008, 28 May). *Ambedkar on Women Liberation*. Counter currents. https:// countercurrents.org

Khan, N.H. (2001). "Ambedkar on Gender Equality: Myth and Reality". In Nazeer H. Khan And Zafar Ahmad Khan (Eds.) *B.R. Ambedkar on Federalism, Ethnicity and Gender Justice*, Deep & Deep Publication, New Delhi, pp. 179-82.

Kishore, S. and K. Gupta (2014, February). "Women Empowerment in India and its States", *Economic and Political Weekly, 7*(1): 39.

Mohammad, I. S. (2021). "A Study of Constitution of India and Women Empowerment", *International Journal of Humanities and Social Science Research, 7*(2): 7-9.

Mokta, M. (2014). "Empowerment of Women in India: A Critical Analysis", *Indian Journal of Public Administration, 60*(3): 473-88.

Moore, V.G. (2011). "B.R. Ambedkar's Contribution for Women's Rights", *Variorum, MultiDisciplinary e-Research Journal, 2*(1): 1-8.

Panucha, S. and A. Khatik (2005). "Empowerment of Rural Women", *Social Action, 55*(1): 349.

Raghavendra, R.H. (2016). "Dr. B.R. Ambedkar's Ideas on Social Justice in Indian Society", *Contemporary Voice of Dalit, 8*(1): 24-29.

Rao, M. (2005). *Law Relating to Women and Children*. Eastern Book Company, New Delhi, pp. 369-70.

Satija, K.C. (2009). "Economic Reforms and Social Justice in India", *International Journal of Social Economics, 36*(9): 945-60.

Singariya, M. (2014). "B.R. Ambedkar and Women Empowerment in India", *Journal of Research in Humanities and Social Science, 2*(1): 1-4.

Solkhe, M. (2018). "Role of B.R. Ambedkar in the Upliftment of Women", *Journal of Advances and Scholarly Researches in Allied Education, 15*(5): 34-41.

Subramanya, H. (2011). "Women Education in India: Facts and Factors", *Asian Journal*, (1): 61-71.

Tharakan, S.M. and M. Tharakan (1975). "Status of Women in India: A Historical Perspective", *Social Scientist, 4*(4/5): 115.

2

Ambedkar's Views on Minorities and Social Justice

Dilavar Kudari and *Kamalaxi G. Tadasad*

Introduction

India is a diverse and pluralistic country, with various religious, ethnic, linguistic, and caste groups. However, some of these groups have faced discrimination, oppression, and exclusion from the mainstream society for centuries. These include the Dalits (formerly known as untouchables), the Adivasis (indigenous people), and the Muslims, Christians, Sikhs, Jains, Buddhists, and Parsis are other religious minorities. These groups have been denied equal rights, opportunities, and dignity by the dominant groups, who have exploited them for their own benefit. This study of Ambedkar's views on minorities and social justice is important and relevant because he was one of the most influential and visionary leaders who fought for the emancipation and empowerment of these marginalized groups. He was a Dalit himself, who faced discrimination and humiliation throughout his life. He rose from poverty and adversity to become a scholar, lawyer, economist, politician, and social reformer. He was the chief architect of the Constitution of India, which enshrined the principles of democracy, secularism, equality, and social justice. He challenged the caste system, which he considered to be the root cause of all social evils. He advocated for the rights and interests of minorities, especially the Dalits and the Adivasis. He also supported the cause of women's empowerment, education, and labour welfare. He inspired millions of people to follow his path of rationality, humanism, and social transformation.

Dr. B.R. Ambedkar, a prominent figure in the Indian freedom struggle, had a profound understanding of the issues surrounding minorities and social justice. His views on these topics reflected his commitment to ensuring equal rights and opportunities for all individuals, regardless of their socio-economic background, religion, or caste. Ambedkar recognized that minorities, such as religious and ethnic groups, often faced discrimination, marginalization, and unequal treatment in society. He firmly believed that this injustice needed to be addressed through proactive policies and measures. Ambedkar advocated for the protection of minority rights and the implementation of social reforms to uplift these communities, ensuring their full participation in all aspects of social and political life.[1]

The Concept of Social Justice

Plato defined social justice as,

> the principle of a society consisting of different types of men ... who have combined the impulse of their need for one another and their concentration on their combination in one society and their concentration on their separate functions, have made a whole which is perfect because it is the product of image of the whole of the human mind. (*Republic* 368d quoted in Mohapatra, 1999)

The concept of social justice is a complex and contested one, but in general, it refers to the idea that everyone deserves equal rights, opportunities, and treatment regardless of their race, economic status, sexuality, or gender identity. Social justice is both—a theoretical concept and a practical ideal—an object of social scientific and philosophical understanding and debate as well as a real-world goal of social and political reform movements.

The term "social justice" originated from Christian theology in the nineteenth century, but it has since been adopted by various secular and religious perspectives. One of the most influential theories of social justice was proposed by the American philosopher John Rawls in his book, *A Theory of Justice* (1971). Rawls argued that the principles of justice should be derived from a hypothetical contract among rational individuals who are ignorant of their own personal characteristics and social positions. This is known as the "original position" and the "veil of ignorance". Rawls suggested that such individuals would agree on two basic principles of justice: the first one guarantees equal basic rights and liberties for all, and the second one allows social and economic inequalities only if they benefit the least advantaged members of society.

Social justice is a broad term, and there are many variations in how advocates apply the perspective. However, some common issues that social justice movements address include gender inequality, racism, LGBTQ+ discrimination, poverty, health care access, environmental justice, human rights, and more. Social justice advocates seek to challenge and transform the existing structures and systems that create and maintain oppression, marginalization, and exclusion of certain groups or individuals. They also strive to promote diversity, inclusion, empowerment, and solidarity among different communities. Social justice is not only a matter of fairness or morality, but also a matter of democracy and human dignity.[2]

John Rawls was a prominent American philosopher who proposed a theory of justice based on the idea of fairness. According to Rawls, justice is the result of a hypothetical social contract among rational individuals who agree on the basic principles that should govern their society. Rawls' theory of justice consists of two main principles:

- The first principle states that everyone should have the same basic rights and freedoms, such as freedom of speech, religion, and association. This principle is also known as the liberty principle, and it has priority over the second principle.
- The second principle states that social and economic inequalities should be arranged in a way that benefits everyone, and they should be connected to job opportunities and positions available to all under fair conditions. This principle is also known as the difference principle, and it has two parts: fair equality of opportunity and the maximin rule. Fair equality of opportunity means that everyone should have equal access to education, health care, and other social goods that affect their chances of success in life. The maximin rule means that any inequality should be justified by making the worst-off members of society better off than they would be otherwise.

Rawls' theory of justice is an alternative to utilitarianism, which says that the right action is the one that maximizes the total happiness of everyone. Rawls argues that utilitarianism does not respect the rights and dignity of individuals, and it may allow for the exploitation or oppression of minorities by the majority. Rawls also rejects other theories of justice that are based on natural rights, divine command, or tradition. He believes that his theory of justice is derived from rational and impartial reasoning, and it reflects the values of a democratic society.[3]

Ambedkar's Concept of Social Justice

Social justice in India with Ambedkar means the vision and struggle of Dr. B.R. Ambedkar, who was a prominent leader and champion of the rights of the oppressed and marginalized sections of the Indian society, especially the Dalits or the untouchables. Ambedkar was also the chief architect of the Constitution of India, which enshrined the principles of liberty, equality and fraternity as the basis of social justice.

Ambedkar's concept of social justice was based on moral values and self-respect. He wanted to create a society where everyone had equal opportunities and dignity regardless of their caste, class, religion, gender or any other identity. He challenged the Hindu social system, which was based on the *varna* system and the caste system, which created graded inequalities and discrimination among people. He considered the caste system as the root cause of all social evils and the source of untouchability, which deprived millions of people of their basic human rights. He advocated for the abolition of the caste system and untouchability, and for the emancipation of the Dalits through education, political representation and social reform.[4]

Ambedkar also fought for other issues related to social justice, such as gender equality, labour rights, minority rights, environmental justice and human rights. He was a rationalist and a humanist who did not approve of any form of hypocrisy, injustice or exploitation in the name of religion. He stood for a religion that was based on universal principles of morality and reason. He also supported democracy and secularism as the means to achieve social justice. He was influenced by various thinkers and movements, such as Buddha, Kabir, Phule, Marx, Gandhi, Rousseau, and others.

Ambedkar's idea of social justice is still relevant today, as India faces many challenges and problems related to caste, class, gender, religion, ethnicity and other forms of inequality and oppression. His legacy inspires many social movements and activists who work for the upliftment and empowerment of the marginalized and oppressed people in India. His writings and speeches provide a rich source of wisdom and guidance for those who seek to understand and practice social justice in India.[5]

The inference of the meaning of social justice from the writings of Babasaheb Dr. Ambedkar is a matter of great importance. It is noteworthy that Dr. Ambedkar did not provide a specific definition or theory of social justice. However, his thoughts and ideas have been eloquently portrayed in his posthumously published writings and speeches. Based on these, it is possible to argue that

Dr. Ambedkar has outlined multiple principles for the establishment of an open and just social order, both in general and in the context of Indian society. It is possible to develop a theory of social justice that can be referred to as Ambedkar's theory of social justice. From Dr. Ambedkar's writings and speeches.

Dr. Ambedkar's concept of social justice was influenced by his own experience of being born in a low caste family and facing humiliation and injustice throughout his life. He was also inspired by the ideals of liberty, equality and fraternity that were advocated by the French Revolution and the American Declaration of Independence. He believed that social justice could only be achieved by abolishing the caste system, which he considered as the root cause of all inequality and injustice in India. He also advocated for the empowerment of women, minorities, workers and other disadvantaged groups, who were denied equal opportunities and rights in the society.

Dr. Ambedkar's vision of social justice was based on the following principles:

- **Liberty:** He believed that every individual should have the freedom to choose their own path of life, without any interference or coercion from others. He also believed that liberty should be accompanied by responsibility and accountability, and that it should not infringe upon the rights and interests of others.
- **Equality:** He believed that every individual should be treated as equal in terms of worth and social status, regardless of their caste, gender, religion, race or any other factor. He also believed that equality should be ensured not only in political and legal spheres, but also in social and economic spheres, by providing equal access to education, employment, health care and other resources.
- **Fraternity:** He believed that every individual should have a sense of brotherhood and solidarity with others, based on mutual respect and compassion. He also believed that fraternity should be fostered by promoting a culture

of democracy, tolerance and diversity, where different opinions and perspectives are valued and respected.

- **Justice:** He believed that every individual should have access to justice, which means that they should be protected from any form of oppression, exploitation or violence, and that they should be given fair treatment and redressal in case of any violation of their rights or interests. He also believed that justice should be based on rationality and morality, rather than on tradition or religion.

According to Dr. Ambedkar's theory of social justice, justice can be dispensed in a free social order in which the individual is an end in itself. The terms of associated life between members of society must be regarded by consideration founded on liberty, equality, and fraternity. These principles of social justice are similar to those outlined in Rawls' theory of social justice. The principles of Ambedkar's theory of social justice are of great significance in the context of Indian society. By implementing these principles, it is possible to establish a just and equitable social order that is based on the principles of equality, liberty, and fraternity.[6]

Social justice entails the elimination of all forms of inequality and the attainment of equality, ensuring that every citizen has equal access to liberty. Dr. Ambedkar's commitment to democracy extended beyond the political realm and encompassed economic and social spheres. His advocacy for the Hindu Code Bill exemplifies his dedication to social democracy, while the directive principles of state policy serve as an illustration of his commitment to economic democracy, according to Valerian Rodrigues. Dr. Ambedkar believed that political democracy would be meaningless to the majority of India's population, particularly the Scheduled Castes, without social democracy. He further asserted that political democracy would be detrimental rather than beneficial to this minority group without social democracy.

However, it should not be assumed that he did not desire "political democracy". In fact, he ardently advocated for it, but with the intention that it would permeate to the lowest echelons of society. In order to achieve social justice through democratic channels, he espoused the necessity of social reform and criticized those who prioritize political reform over social reform. For Ambedkar, social reform must precede political reform, although the latter can certainly contribute to the former. The subsequent section on "Social Reform" would delve into B.R. Ambedkar's vision of social reform as a necessity for achieving true democracy and justice. He defined social reform as the dismantling of oppressive structures like the caste system, emphasizing equality, education, and legal safeguards. Ambedkar rejected conservative attempts to preserve traditional hierarchies and Marxist reliance on class struggle, arguing that caste required unique attention. Instead, he advocated for democratic and constitutional methods to bring about change, stressing that social reform must precede political reform to ensure inclusivity and justice for all. His approach combined legal, educational, and moral strategies to transform society. In this section, our focus will be on his definition of social reform and his objections to both conservative and socialist interpretations of it. As he disagrees with Marxist approaches to social change, he advocates for democratic and constitutional means as the only viable option.[7]

Concept of Minority

The main objective of this chapter is to comprehend Ambedkar's perspective on the concept of minority and to analyse the challenges and measures required to safeguard their rights. The section titled "Minorities and Rights" will delve into this matter. Ambedkar contends that the prevailing understanding of minority based solely on numerical strength is fundamentally flawed. Instead, the social and political influence must also be considered when identifying a minority and providing appropriate safeguards. Furthermore, Ambedkar emphasizes the importance of cultural context in comprehending the plight of minorities.

The other significant determinant of his conception of minority is his affiliation with a distinct minority group unique to India, known as the Scheduled Castes or untouchables. As previously discussed, Dalits endure and subsist in a culture that is fundamentally opposed to their humanity. Ambedkar contends that any discourse on freedom for this populace is meaningless without addressing the cultural context in which this minority exists. In this regard, no other Indian political figure's ideology is as closely linked to his life as that of Ambedkar. Rather than simply transforming itself into a "communal majority", Ambedkar argues that special constitutional measures are necessary to safeguard minorities. In such instances, a minority must first be identified, and then specific political measures must be implemented to ensure that the minority has adequate representation alongside the majority. Prior to delving into the issue, it is necessary to examine Ambedkar's fundamental understanding of what constitutes a minority and how it is to be identified.[8]

What is a Minority

Ambedkar holds a unique perspective on the definition of a minority. He rejects the simplistic notion of a "numerical minority" and advocates for a more comprehensive and realistic understanding of the issue. He states,

> I do not accept the principle that every minority must always be confined to its population ratio. A minority may be so small that its population ratio may provide inadequate representation for the purpose of its protection. It may even be of no consequence at all.

The concept of a minority extends beyond being a "smaller socially defined group". Ambedkar also dismisses the idea that a minority can be identified solely by its creed. He remarks,

> Religious separation is not the sole criterion for determining a minority. Nor is it a reliable and effective criterion. The true test lies in social discrimination, which determines whether a social group is considered a minority or not. Even Gandhiji found this test logical

and practical, favouring it over religious separation.

Having rejected both numerical and religious distinctions as the sole criteria for determining a minority, Ambedkar suggests that the actual political influence a group possesses in the social and political context should be assessed to determine who qualifies as a minority. He even introduces additional criteria, such as the principle of political weightage, to supplement the existing criteria. He states,

> If we truly want to adequately and genuinely protect a minority, there may be circumstances where the principle of weightage must be acknowledged. However, the distribution of weightage must adhere to a uniform and intelligible principle. In our opinion, weightage should be granted when a minority is weak, either due to its small numbers, low social status, limited educational opportunities compared to others, or insufficient economic strength to compete with other communities.[9]

Ambedkar and Minorities

One of Ambedkar's most significant contributions in addressing minority rights was his involvement in drafting the Constitution of India. As the chairman of the Drafting Committee, he played a vital role in ensuring that the constitution provided safeguards and protections for minority communities. The constitution enshrined the principles of equality, religious freedom, and cultural rights, which were aimed at safeguarding the interests of minorities and promoting social justice. And also highlighted the significance of education in promoting social justice and equal opportunities for all. He recognized education as a potent tool for empowering minority communities and bringing about social transformation. Ambedkar emphasized the need to eradicate illiteracy and promote education among marginalized sections of society. He believed that education would enable individuals to escape the cycle of poverty, discrimination, and social exclusion, thereby fostering social justice.

Ambedkar championed the cause of the marginalized and oppressed sections of society, including religious, ethnic, and linguistic minorities. He firmly believed in the principles of equality, liberty, and fraternity for all citizens, regardless of their social background. Ambedkar recognized the historical injustices faced by minorities and sought to address them through strategic reforms and inclusive policies. Ambedkar also emphasized the need to address social and economic disparities among different communities. He advocated for affirmative action policies, such as reservations in education and employment, to uplift marginalized groups and provide them with equal opportunities. Ambedkar believed that these measures were necessary to compensate for historical disadvantages and empower minorities to participate fully in society.

Furthermore, Ambedkar was a staunch critic of social discrimination and the caste system prevalent in India. He vehemently opposed the hierarchical social structure that perpetuated oppression and advocated for the annihilation of caste. Ambedkar's efforts led to the inclusion of anti-discrimination laws and the provision of reservations for Scheduled Castes and Scheduled Tribes in public institutions, thereby promoting social justice and equality. Ambedkar's views on minorities and social justice were not limited to theoretical discourse. He actively campaigned for the welfare of marginalized communities and worked tirelessly to eradicate social inequalities. His efforts in areas such as women's rights, education reform, and land redistribution highlighted his holistic approach to ensuring social justice for all.[10]

Ambedkar was a member of the Constituent Assembly that drafted the Constitution of India after Independence. He was also the chairman of the Drafting Committee that prepared the final draft of the constitution. He played a crucial role in shaping the constitutional provisions that guaranteed fundamental rights, minority rights, and safeguards for the Scheduled Castes and Scheduled Tribes. He also argued for a federal system of government that would give autonomy and representation to the states and regions.

Some of the key issues that Ambedkar addressed in relation to minorities in India are:

- *The definition and recognition of minorities:* Ambedkar argued that minorities should not be defined only by their religious identity, but also by their social, economic, and political status. He said that the Scheduled Castes were more than a minority, as they faced extreme oppression and exclusion from the Hindu society. He also said that minorities should be recognized not only by their numerical strength, but also by their historical and cultural significance.
- *The protection and representation of minorities:* Ambedkar advocated for a system of reservations or quotas for minorities in education, employment, and legislature. He said that this was necessary to ensure equal opportunity and social justice for the disadvantaged groups. He also supported separate electorates for minorities, especially for the Scheduled Castes, as a means of ensuring their political voice and influence.
- *The prevention of majoritarianism and communalism:* Ambedkar warned against the dangers of majoritarianism and communalism in a diverse and pluralistic country like India. He said that democracy should not mean the rule of the majority over the minority, but rather the rule of consensus and cooperation among all sections of society. He also said that communalism was a threat to national unity and secularism, as it promoted hatred and violence among different religious groups.
- *The promotion of fraternity and social reform:* Ambedkar emphasized the importance of fraternity or brotherhood as a constitutional value. He said that fraternity was essential for maintaining social harmony and democracy in India. He also said that fraternity could not be achieved

without social reform, especially the abolition of caste system and untouchability. He urged the Hindu majority to reform their religion and society to remove the stigma and discrimination against the Scheduled Castes and other minorities.

- *Social inequality and injustice*: Ambedkar believed that the caste system was the root cause of social inequality and injustice in India. He considered caste as a form of graded inequality that divided people into hierarchies of purity and pollution, and denied them basic human rights and dignity. He challenged the authority of the Hindu scriptures that sanctioned caste discrimination and untouchability, and advocated for the annihilation of caste as a precondition for social justice.
- *Legal, economic and political equality*: Ambedkar argued that social justice required not only legal and political equality, but also social and economic equality. He demanded political representation for the depressed classes (later known as Scheduled Castes) in the legislative bodies and public services, through separate electorates and reservations. He also fought for land reforms, labour rights, women's empowerment and education for the downtrodden masses.
- *Communalism and religious fanaticism*: Ambedkar was a staunch critic of communalism and religious fanaticism. He opposed the idea of dividing India on the basis of religion, and supported a secular and democratic state that would protect the rights and interests of all minorities. He also advocated for a Uniform Civil Code that would apply to all citizens irrespective of their religion.
- *Reform in religion:* Ambedkar was a rationalist and a humanist who sought to reform religion in accordance with reason and morality. He rejected the superstitions, rituals and dogmas that he found in Hinduism, Islam, Christianity and other religions. He embraced Buddhism

as a religion of compassion, equality and social justice, and converted to it along with millions of his followers in 1956.[11]

One of the major issues that Ambedkar addressed in his writings and speeches was the problem of minorities in India. He was concerned about the fate of the religious, linguistic, and cultural minorities in a country where the majority community could dominate and oppress them. He advocated for various measures to protect the rights and interests of the minorities, such as proportional representation, separate electorates, reservation of seats, safeguards against discrimination, and state socialism.

Ambedkar wrote a document called states and minorities, which he submitted to the sub-committee on Fundamental Rights of the Constituent Assembly of India in 1947. In this document, he proposed a comprehensive constitutional framework for the admission of Indian states into the union, the fundamental rights of citizens, the safeguards for the Scheduled Castes, and the minority rights. He also argued for state socialism as a remedy against the invasion of fundamental rights by the state and private interests. He envisioned a social and economic democracy where everyone would have freedom from want and fear.[12]

Ambedkar's views on the representation of minorities are very elaborate and insightful. He defined minority as a social group that is discriminated against by the majority on the basis of religion, language, or culture. He justified minority representation on the grounds of justice, security, and self-respect. He suggested various electoral methods for minority representation, such as cumulative voting, single transferable vote, limited vote, and alternative vote. He also proposed general safeguards against the communal legislative majority, such as veto power for minorities, joint electorate with reserved seats, and proportional representation with single transferable vote. Ambedkar was aware of the challenges and dangers that minorities faced in a majoritarian polity. He wrote that minority communities may be crushed, tyrannized, oppressed, discriminated against, and denied equality before the law and equal opportunity in public life. He also said that it is wrong for the majority to deny the existence of minorities, and equally wrong for the minorities to perpetuate themselves. Ambedkar believed that it is the duty of the majority not to discriminate against minorities, and that no minority in India has taken a stand against the rule of the majority. Ambedkar's views on minorities in India have been influential and relevant for many movements and struggles for social justice and human rights in India. His legacy continues to inspire and challenge many people who seek to uphold the constitutional values of equality, liberty, fraternity, and justice in India.[13]

Conclusion

Dr. B.R. Ambedkar's views on minorities and social justice reflect his commitment to creating an inclusive and egalitarian society. His ideas on reservation, protection of minority rights, eradication of discriminatory practices, and the transformative role of education continue to shape India's policies and discourse on social justice.

NOTES

1. Upendra Baxi (1992). *Ambedkar and Social Justice* (Vol.1), published by the Director, Publication Division, Ministry of Information and Broadcasting, Government of India, New Delhi, pp. 35-42.
2. Rawls John, *A Theory of Justice: Explained—Sociology Group*. https:// www. sociologygroup.com /john-rawls-a-theory-of-justice-explained/ John, Rawls, *Theory of Justice: Principles of Fairness and Equality*. https:// testbook.com/ias-preparation/john-rawls-theory-of-justice. 09/ 10/23 2pm
3. Upendra Baxi (1992). *Ambedkar and Social Justice* (Vol.1), published by the Director, Publication Division, Ministry of Information and Broadcasting, Government of India, New Delhi, pp. 35-42.
4. G.S. Ghurye (ed.) (1957). *Caste and Class in India.* Popular Book Depot, Bumbay, pp. 4-8.
5. Jaganath R. Sindhe (2019). *Dr. B.R. Ambedkar's Social Thought.* Current Publications, Agra, pp. 82-88.
6. D.K. Baishantry (1981). *Ambedkar's the Total Revolutionary*. Sigment Book Distribution, New Delhi, pp. 28-36.

7. Jaganath R. Sindhe (2019). *Dr. B.R. Ambedkar's Social Thought.* Current Publications, Agra, pp. 82-88.
8. *Dr. B.R. Ambedkar, State and Minorities* (2021 edn.). Gaurav Book Centre Pvt. Ltd., New Delhi, pp. 15-21.
9. Jaganath R. Sindhe (2019). *Dr. B.R. Ambedkar's Social Thought.* Current Publications, Agra, pp.143-49.
10. *Dr. B.R. Ambedkar's Concept of Social Justice and Constitution of India.* https:// www.ijcrt.org/papers/IJCRT2012278.pdf. 10/ 10/23 8pm
11. *Ambedkar's Idea of Social Justice: Some Reflections.* Legal Service India. https ://www. legalserviceindia. com/legal/article-3825-ambedkar-s-idea-ofsocial-justice-some-reflections.html.
12. *Seeing Justice through Ambedkar's Eyes.* Forward Press. https://www. forwardpress .in/2017/08/seeing-justice-through-ambedkars-eyes /.
13. *Social Justice and Ambedkar Into Legal World.* https://www. intolegalworld.com/article?title=social-justice-and-ambedkar.

REFERENCES

Ahir, D.C. (1990). *The Legacy of Dr. Ambedkar.* B.R. Publishing Corporation, New Delhi.

Baxi, Upendra (1992). *Ambedkar and Social Justice* (Vol. l). Published by the Director, Publication Division, Ministry of Information and Broadcasting Government of India, New Delhi.

Dr. B.R. Ambedkar State and Minorities (2021 edn.). Gaurav Book Centre Pvt. Ltd., New Delhi.

Baishantry, D.K. (1981). *Ambedkar's the Total Revolutionary.* Sigment Book Distribution, New Delhi.

Sindhe, Jaganath R. (2019). *Dr. B.R. Ambedkar's Social Thought.* Current Publications, Agra, pp. 82-88.

Ganguli, B.N. (1977). *Indian Economic Thought, Nineteenth Century Perspectives.* TATA McGraw Hill Publishing. New Delhi.

Ghurye, G.S. (ed.) (1979). *Caste and Class in India.* Popular Book Depot, Bumbay, pp. 4-8.

Government of India (1979). *Writings and Speeches.* Vol. I, p. 39.

John, Rawls, *A Theory of Justice: Explained: Sociology Group.* https ://www. sociologygroup.comfjohn-rawls-a-theory-of-justice-explained/

John, Rawls, *Theory of Justice: Principles of Fairness and Equality.* https :// testbook.corn/iaspreparation/john-rawls-theory-of-justice

Kanair, C.S. (1982). *Socio-Economic Transformation of India: Dr. Ambedkar's Vision.* pp. 140-48.

Moon, Vasant (1989). *Dr. Babasaheb Ambedkar Writings and speeches* (From first Vols. 1 to 14). Education Department, Government of Maharashtra, Bombay.

Shabbir, Mohammad (1987). *Dr. B.R. Ambedkar: Study in Law and Society.* Rawat Publication, Jaipur and New Delhi.

Sharma, Kusum (1997). *Ambedkar and Indian Constitution.* Ashish Publishing House, New Delhi.

Srinivas, M.N. (1962). *Caste in Modem India and Other Essays.* Asia Publishing House, Bombay.

Social Justice: Definition, Theories, Examples & Facts. https://www.britannica.com/topic /socialjustice.

Social Justice Meaning and Main Principles Explained—Investopedia. https ://www.investopedia. comfterrns/s/social-justice. asp. I 0/19/2023 Ipm

3

Beyond Classroom Doors

Mapping Intersectionality in the Educational Trajectories of Females in Society

Raja Kourav

Introduction

Education has long been recognized as a powerful catalyst for personal growth, societal advancement, and economic empowerment. It serves as a cornerstone for individual development, shaping future opportunities and trajectories (Goel & Hussain, 2018). However, the journey through the educational system is not uniform for all individuals, and it is influenced by a multitude factors (Evans, 2021). One of the most critical aspects often overlooked in traditional educational research is the intersectionality of gender, race, class, and other social identities, and how these factors collectively shape the experiences and outcomes of students (Tefera & Powers, 2018).

India, as a diverse and culturally rich nation, has made significant strides in expanding access to education, breaking down traditional gender-based educational disparities, and promoting women's empowerment (Jain & Agarwal, 2016). However, within the vast tapestry of Indian society, the education trajectories of females remain deeply influenced by their complex and intersecting social identities. These identities, such as caste, class, religion, region, and ethnicity, intersect with their gender, creating a multifaceted landscape where access to quality education, academic experiences, and career opportunities are far from uniform (Haq, 2023). The historical context of women's education in India, marked by early social reform movements and policy interventions, has set the stage for progress, but disparities persist (Azmitia & Mansfield, 2021). Gender-based disparities are further exacerbated by the intricate web of intersectionality, as female students from marginalized, rural and minority backgrounds face unique challenges in their educational journeys (Careindia, 2023). Understanding these intersections and their impact on the education of females is not only essential for achieving true gender equity but also for addressing broader social and economic disparities in the country (Haq, 2023).

The study aims to explore and analyse the intricate web of identities, experiences, and social structures that shape the educational paths of females. While significant strides have been made towards gender equality in education, the intersectionality framework recognizes that individuals' experiences are shaped not only by their gender but also by a myriad of interconnected factors. Understanding the complex interplay of these dimensions is crucial for fostering more inclusive and equitable educational systems. This research also embarks to investigate the challenges, opportunities, and disparities faced by women across different contexts, stages of education, and geographic locations.

Objectives

- To understand the influence of cultural norms, policies, societal expectations and societal biases on the educational trajectories of women from various backgrounds in India.
- To identify the specific challenges and opportunities faced by women from diverse backgrounds in their pursuit of education and careers within the Indian context.

- To offer evidence-based recommendations for educational policies and practices that can promote gender equity and inclusivity within the Indian education system.

Literature Framework

Theory of Intersectionality

Intersectionality is a critical and influential theoretical framework that emerged within the field of social sciences, particularly in feminist studies and critical race theory. Coined by Kimberle Crenshaw in the late 1980s, this theory recognizes that individuals possess multiple, intersecting social identities and that the convergence of these identities creates unique and often complex experiences (Faham, Davis, and Ernst, 2019). The core premise of intersectionality is that people's experiences cannot be understood by considering a single dimension of their identity in isolation (Evans, 2021). The theory underscores the significance of acknowledging how these various aspects of identity intersect, overlap, and interact to shape an individual's social standing, opportunities, privileges, and disadvantages (Heyl, 2023). This theory has played a pivotal role in promoting inclusivity, social justice, and equity, particularly in fields such as gender studies, social justice, and policy development (Amatya, Tipayamongkholgul and Suwannapong, 2023).

Intersectionality and Identity in Female Education

Intersectionality and identity are critical aspects in understanding female education, as they highlight the intricate web of factors that shape the educational experiences of women (OECD, 2023). In the context of female education, intersectionality refers to the idea that a person's identity is formed by the interplay of multiple social and cultural factors. Understanding the intersectionality of identity is essential because it sheds light on how these multiple aspects of a person's identity can either facilitate or hinder their educational journey (Evans, 2021). For example, a woman's experience in education may be profoundly different if she belongs to a marginalized community, comes from a lower socio-economic background, or faces discrimination based on her religious or ethnic identity (Goel & Hussain, 2018). These intersecting factors can create unique challenges, opportunities, and aspirations, and by these factors researchers and policymakers can develop a more holistic understanding of the barriers and advantages that individuals face in education (Haq, 2023).

Female Education in India

Educational trajectories of females refer to the paths or journeys that women and girls follow through the educational system. These trajectories encompass their experiences, opportunities, challenges, and achievements at different stages of their educational lives (Jain and Agarwal, 2016). According to the UNICEF India, dropout rates of girl students have increased ever since the COVID-19. It is reported that girls who had dropped out of school were engaged in domestic work or got married (Yadav, 2022). As per the unified district information system for education 2021-22, the annual dropout rates for secondary level education stand at 14.6 per cent (Goel and Hussain, 2018, Sharma, 2022). There is difference in the dropout rates, gross enrolment ratio and quality among rural and urban areas (Government of India, 2016). A study says that prevalence of illiteracy among parents in rural areas impedes effective parent-child engagement, and also the economic hardship and social constraints characteristic of rural communities often lead to early child marriages and the pressure for children to contribute financially, hindering their educational opportunities (Kumar, Patel, and Debbarma, 2023). A strong correlation was found between caste and adolescent school dropout, with higher dropout rates among lower social groups. This is supported by UNICEF and UNESCO findings from 2014, which showed higher dropout rates among adolescent girls from low income families in rural areas and of lower caste (Prakash, Beattie, and Javalkar, 2017). Since five years the women enrolment rate have positive change in higher education (TOI, 2021). By mapping these insights into the complexities of gender equity in education and inform policies and practices that promote inclusive and equitable learning opportunities for all (Srivastava).

Methodology

This study employs a mixed-methods research design to comprehensively understand intersectionality in the education trajectories of females in society. The research design combines quantitative analysis of gathered data with qualitative inquiry through interviews and focus group discussions. The questionnaires will gather quantitative data regarding their educational experiences, socio-economic backgrounds, and aspirations. This combination of methods ensures a comprehensive and balanced approach to data collection. For this data collected from 151 respondents with convenience sampling to select female students from diverse geographical and socio-economic backgrounds who are currently enrolled in higher education or preparing for competitive examinations. To ensure a comprehensive representation, participants will be selected from urban, rural, and semi-urban areas, encompassing a wide spectrum of socio-economic strata. A comprehensive review of existing literature and information related to study, with a specific focus on female students in various socio-economic and geographical contexts, will provide a theoretical and contextual framework for the research. Prior informed consent will be obtained from all participants.

Singnificance of the Study

This research is underscored by the pressing need to address persistent disparities in educational outcomes and opportunities for females across the globe. Recognizing the multifaceted nature of identity and the unique challenges faced by individuals due to their intersecting identities is crucial in crafting educational policies and practices that are both responsive and empowering. This study also contribute to the broader discourse on intersectionality, shedding light on the ways in which multiple dimensions of identity interact to shape the lives of women in society.

Findings and Discussion

Demographic Profile

The demographic profile of the respondents, based on a total of 151 responses, offers a comprehensive snapshot of the diverse characteristics within the sample. In terms of age distribution, the majority fall within the 18-22 years range, constituting 62.3 per cent of the respondents, followed by the age group of 23-25 years at 24.5 per cent. Respondents aged 26-30 years make up 9.3 per cent, while those above 30 years comprise 4 per cent of the sample. Sociocultural backgrounds showcase a varied composition, with 45 per cent identifying as General, 33.8 per cent as OBC (Other Backward Classes), 13.2 per cent as SC (Scheduled Caste), 5.3 per cent as ST (Scheduled Tribe), and 2.6 per cent as belonging to minority groups. This diversity highlights the inclusion of perspectives from different social strata. Geographical distribution reveals a mix of rural, urban, and semi-urban backgrounds. Approximately, 31.8 per cent of respondents hail from rural areas, 45 per cent from urban settings, and 23.2 per cent from semi-urban regions, offering a balanced representation across different geographies.

In terms of educational qualifications, the respondents exhibit a range of attainment levels. The majority, 51 per cent, have completed their graduation, while 29.8 per cent hold postgraduate degrees. Those with education up to higher secondary constitute 11.9 per cent, and a smaller percentage, 4.6 per cent, have completed a diploma or equivalent. A minimal 2.6 per cent have pursued postgraduate studies and above. Regarding the present status of education, 42.3 per cent of respondents are currently enrolled in higher education, while 22.5 per cent are actively preparing for competitive examinations. A significant portion, 35.1 per cent, falls into both categories, indicating a dual focus on formal education and examination preparation within the sample. This multifaceted demographic profile provides a rich foundation for exploring the intersectionality in the education trajectories of females within the specified societal context.

Table 3.1: Demographic Profile

Age		**Present level of education**	
• 18-22 years	62.3%	• Enrolled in higher education	42.3%
• 23-25 years	24.5%	• Preparing for competitive examinations	22.5%
• 26-30 years	9.3%		
• Above 30 years	4.0%	• Both	35.1%
Sociocultural background		**Highest level of education**	
• General	45.0%	• Higher secondary	11.9%
• OBC	33.8%	• Diploma or equivalent	4.6%
• ST	13.2%	• Graduation	51.0%
• SC	5.3%	• Postgraduation	29.8%
• Minorities	2.6%	• Postgraduation and above	2.6%
Geographical location			
• Rural	31.8%		
• Urban	45.0%		
• Semi-urban	23.2%		

Challenges and Barriers in Educational Trajectories

The findings from the collected responses indicate that a substantial portion, accounting for 40 per cent, of the participants faced challenges or discrimination during their education journeys. Among those who encountered obstacles, the most prevalent. situation was gender-related challenges, most prevalent situation was gender-related challenges, constituting 38.9 per cent of the reported cases.This underscores the persistence of gender-based discrimination and biases within educational settings. Additionally, participants highlighted other sicant challenges (Fig. 3.1), including those related to caste or class (30%), geographical location (28.7%), and race or colour (11.4%). The findings reflect a complex interplay of factors, illustrating that discrimination in education extends beyond gender and can be influenced bya variety of intersecting identities and societal dynamics. Addressing these challenges requires announced approach that acknowledges the multifaceted nature of discrimination within educational contexts.

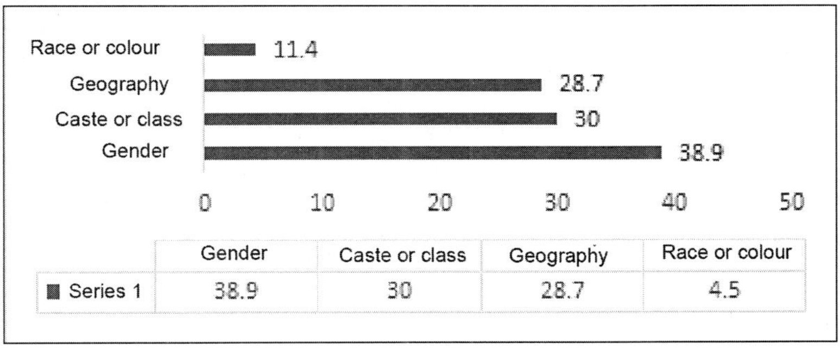

Fig. 3.1: Most encountered discriminations

Table 3.2: Challenger and Barriers

Lack of decision making power within the family for their education	44.90%
Financial access	40.30%
Persisting wrong prejudices	42.20%
Sexual discrimination or harassment	29.40%
Family insecurity	33.90%
Body shaming	31.20%
Eve-teasing	18.30%

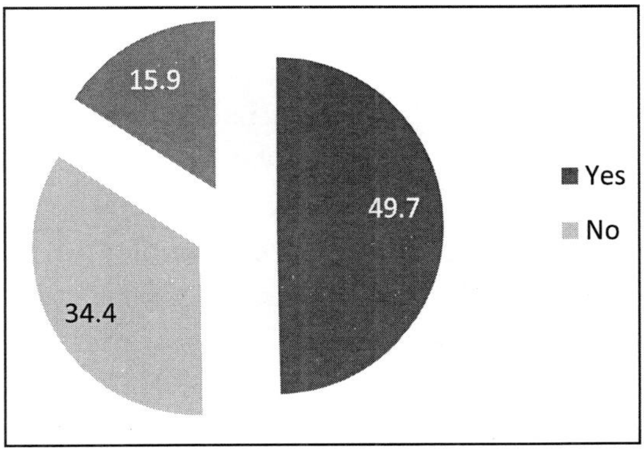

Fig. 3.2: Challenges and barriers as being a girl

In Fig. 3.2, findings from the responses highlight a significant corporation of female participants, 49.7 per cent, who reported facing challenges or barriers specifically because of their gender, and 15.9 per cent are not sure as these challenges are as being a girl. A detailed analysis of 109 responses to specify these challenges revealed a multifaceted landscape. Lack of decision making power within the family for their education emerged as a prominent issue, with 44.9 per cent of respondents expressing this concern. Financial access, a critical aspect of educational opportunities, was identified as a challenge by 40.3 per cent of respondents. This finding underscores the intersectionality of gender with economic factors, emphasizing the need to ensure financial inclusivity for female students. Persisting wrong prejudices in society reported by 42.2 per cent of participants, highlights the deeply ingrained societal biases that continue to affect the educational experiences of women. Tackling these prejudices requires comprehensive efforts at societal and institutional levels to promote gender equity and challenge harmful stereotypes. The findings also shed light on other challenges faced by female students, including any kind of sexual discrimination or harassment (29.4%), family insecurities (33.9%), body shaming (31.2%), and eve-teasing (18.3%). These challenges point to the broader issue of creating safe and supportive environments for female students, not only within educational institutions but also within their families and communities. These findings emphasize the need for targeted interventions and policy measures to address gender-specific challenges in education. This includes initiatives that empower women within their families, ensure financial accessibility. challenge societal prejudices, and foster safe and inclusive educational environments.

The findings regarding the impact of geographical areas on education and career aspirations reveal that 28.5 per cent of respondents felt their geographical location influenced their educational journeys, while the majority 71.5 per cent, believed otherwise. For those who indicated a geographical impact, several significant responses shed light on the specific challenges faced.

Common themes included societal norms that restrict girls' education, the unavailability of higher education in rural areas, and the absence of competitive examination classes. Participants also cited orthodox thinking, leading to judgements based on marital status, feelings of cultural isolation in universities, and limited access to digital or technological resources. The influence of social backgrounds, such as caste-related considerations, emerged as apertinent factor affecting educational and career aspirations in different geographical contexts. These responses underscore the need for targeted interventions to address systemic challenges and ensure equal opportunities for education and career advancement across diverse geographic settings.

Intersectionality and Identity

The findings from the responses shed light on the complex intersectionality experienced by females in their educational and career trajectories. Within the family, 58.2 per cent of respondents indicated that while their family supported them, societal and relative influences their decision. This suggest the complex interplay between individual familial support and external pressures, indicating that societal expectations and influences often impact family dynamics. Additionally, 50.5 per cent highlighted the perception that boys have more freedom to make decisions for themselves, indicating gender-based disparities within familial dynamics. The finding that 28.2 per cent felt that boys consistently received more priority for education suggests the persistence of gender biases even within the family unit. Another 17.1 per cent reported instances where society or community support existed, but their family did not, showcasing the intricate interplay of external influences on family dynamics (Table 3.3).

Table 3.3: Challenges within Family and Society

Challenge Within Family		Within Society	
Family supported but, societal and relative influences their decision	58.2%	Societal perception that girls cannot afford and managed themselves alone out of home	65.1%
Boys have more freedom to make choices	50.5%	Unequal work roles	34.9%
Boys always get more choices and access for their education and career	28.2%	Investing in marriage as dowry instead of education for girls	38.1%
Sometimes society supported but family not	18%	Unproportionate motivation for girl's education	31%

The findings regarding females' experiences within society highlight the prevalence of deeply ingrained gender norms and challenges that impact their educational and career aspirations (Table 3.3). A significant 65.1 per cent of respondents indicated that society perceives girls as unable to afford or manage alone outside of home without any male member. The preference for investing in marriage as dowry instead of education for girls was reported by 38.1 per cent of participants, underscoring the societal prioritization of traditional gender roles and the economic burden associated with marriage. This finding emphasizes the need for challenging societal norms that prioritize marriage over educational investment in girls, hindering their potential for personal and professional growth. Concerns about unequal work roles for males and females in society were expressed by 34.9 per cent of respondents, which suggests that gender disparities persist in occupational opportunities and responsibilities, reflecting a broader societal issue that hinders women's equal participation in various sectors. The unequal distribution of work roles further perpetuates gender-based stereotypes and limits the scope of career options for females. About 31.8 per cent of participants highlighted the disproportionate motivation for female education, indicating that more resources are often allocated to boys' education. This disparity in resource allocation can have long-term consequences, limiting the educational opportunities available to girls and contributing to a cycle of gender inequality. Addressing this imbalance requires a concerted effort to promote equal investment in the education of both genders, fostering a more inclusive and equitable educational environment.

Regarding the influence of gender identities on future educational and career opportunities, 24.3 per cent felt a negative impact. On the positive side, 27.9 per cent of participants perceived that their gender identities had a positive influence on their future opportunities (Figure 3.3). This finding could be indicative of efforts towards gender inclusivity, affirmative action, or supportive environments. Interestingly, 23.6 per cent of participants were unsure that this uncertainty may stem from the complex and multifaceted nature of gender dynamics, where individuals might perceive both positive and negative influences, making it challenging to categorize the overall impact definitively. Equally 24.3 per cent of respondents had no influence, this perception might indicate a level of gender neutrality or a perception that merit and qualifications are the primary determinants of success, irrespective of gender.

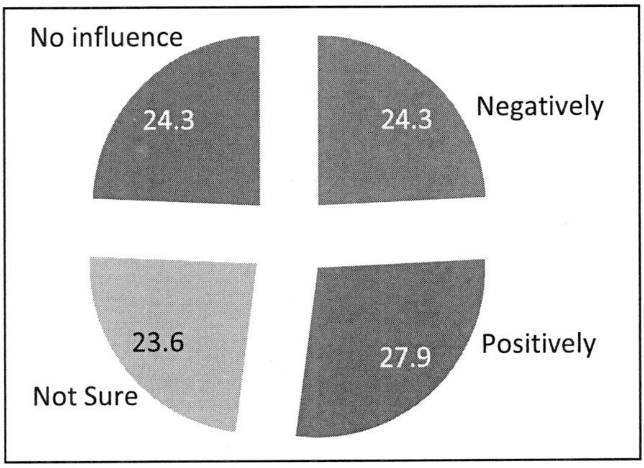

Fig. 3.3: Influence of Gender Identity

These findings could be interpreted a deeper understanding

of the challenges and opportunities faced by females in their educational and career journeys. The intricate interplay of familial, societal, and individual factors underscores the importance cf adopting an intersectional lens to inform policies and interventions aimed at promoting gender equity and inclusivity in education and career opportunities.

Observation

The findings regarding observations of different sociocultural biases within the society offer a comprehensive insight into prevailing attitudes and stereotypes (Fig. 3.4). A substantial 60.9 per cent of respondents highlighted the societal expectation that girls should primarily focus on learning about kitchen-related tasks, reinforcing traditional gender roles. 49.7 per cent of participants noted a prevalent belief that girls should be married early, which not only limits educational and career opportunities but potentially hindering personal development and autonomy. The perception that only males or boys can run a family was nored by 46.6 per cent of respondents, reflecting unequal power dynamics within households, limiting opportunities for women to assume decision making responsibilities. A significant 46 per cent of participants observed a social perception that girls should not go out for education or employment, reinforcing restrictive norm that curtail female mobility and independence. About 41.4 per cent of respondents noted a belief that females have less potential than males, indicating the undervaluation of women's capabilities, hindering their access to equal opportunities in various spheres. The presence of casual sexism, acknowledged by 31.6 per cent of participants, points to the normalization of discriminatory attitudes and behaviours in daily interactions. Similarly, 30.1 per cent of respondents expressed the observation that women are perceived as unable to do meaningful work which diminishes the contributions of women within society. Individual observations and experiences, such as restrictions in higher education, taking girls as debts, the behaviour of male classmates in school, early marriage, and dressing restrictions, provide concrete examples of how these sociocultural biases manifest in individuals' lives. In the discussion, these findings could be contextualized within the broader discourse on gender equality, highlighting the urgent need for targeted interventions to challenge and reshape prevailing sociocultural biases.

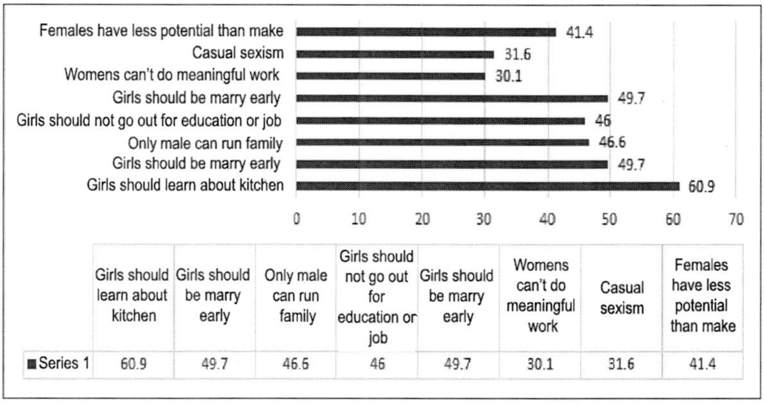

Fig. 3.4: Observed Sociocultural Biases

Support System

The findings regarding support for female students in their educational journey provide valuable insights into the varied sources and effectiveness of support systems (Fig. 3.5). A substantial 74.2 per cent of female students reported receiving support for their edcation. Family support emerges as the predominant source, with a significant 86 per cent of respondents indicating assistance from their families. This underscores the crucial role families play in fostering an environment conducive to female education, emphasizing the significance of familial backing in the pursuit of educational goals. Government support is also noteworthy, with 32.8 per cent of respondents acknowledging assistance from government initiatives. Teachers (29.%), peer groups and friends (20.5%), and civil societies (3.3%) contribute to the overall support network, highlighting the diverse sources that play a role in shaping the educational journey of female students (Fig. 3.6).

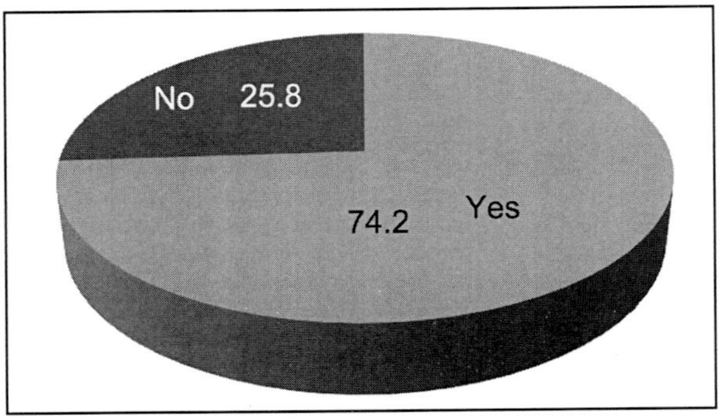

Fig. 3.5: Get any Kind of Support

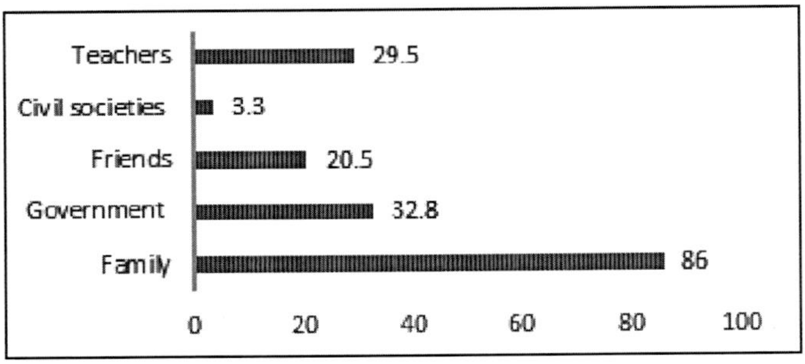

Fig. 3.6: Suppport Sources

Among those who received government support (40.4%), scholarships are the most prevalent form, benefiting 64.5 per cent of respondents. The provision of scholarships indicates a targeted effort to alleviate financial barriers that might impede female students' access to education. Other forms of support from the government include free education (21%), female reservation for jobs and education (8.2%), living allowances (3.9%), and free coaching for competitive examinations (5.2%). These findings underscore the multifaceted nature of government interventions, aiming to address various aspects of educational accessibility for female students (Fig. 3.7).

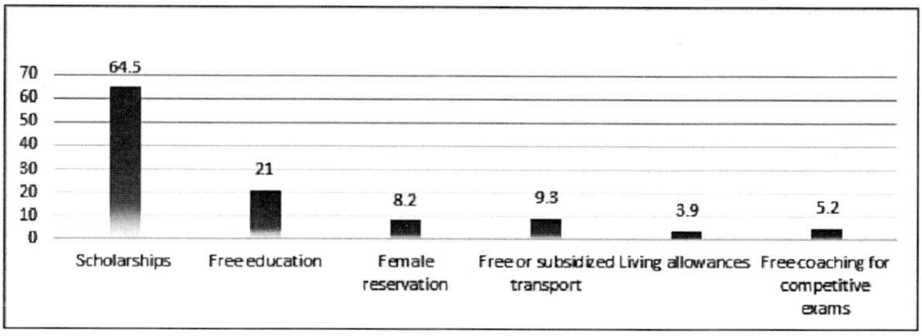

Fig. 3.7: Sources of Government Support

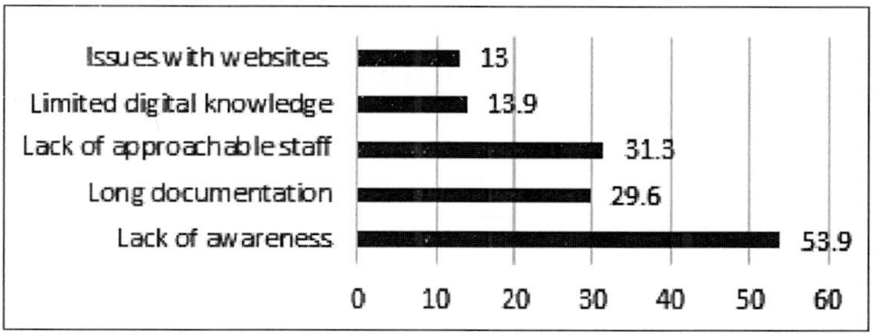

Fig. 3.8: Reasons behind not Getting Benefit of Government Schemes

Despite these positive instances, a major proportion of respondents (83.1%) have not benefited from any government scheme or policy related to female education. Among those who got, policies such as the Post-Matric Scholarship, Mukhya Mantri Medhavi Vidyarthi Yojana, Single Girl Child Scholarship, and Kanya Uthaan were mentioned. The reasons for not benefiting include a lack of awareness (53.9%), lengthy documentation processes (29.6%), a lack of approachable staff (31.3%), limited digital knowledge (13.9%), and issues with websites (13%). Notably, some respondents expressed that scholarships or support were not available for general category students (Fig. 3.8). When asked about the sufficiency of government support, only 13.1 per cent of respondents deemed it sufficient, while 56.2 per cent felt it was inadequate, and 30.8 per cent remained uncertain (Fig. 3.9).

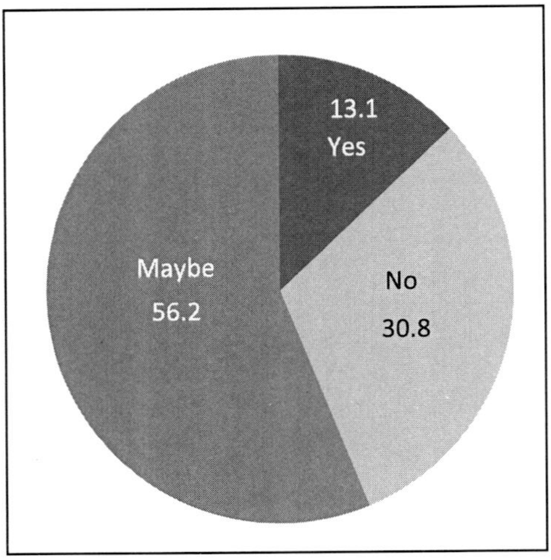

Fig. 3.9: Sufficiency of Government Support

In the discussion, these findings could be contextualized within the broader discourse on female education, emphasizing the importance of addressing barriers and enhancing support mechanisms. Strategies to increase awareness, streamline documentation processes, improve staff accessibility, and enhance digital infrastructure could contribute to a more effective and inclusive government support system. Additionally, the findings underline the importance of considering the specific needs of general category students and ensuring that support is accessible to all, fostering a truly equitable educational landscape for female students.

Major Suggestions

The participants in the discussion articulated several key suggestions to enhance the educational landscape for female students. A prevailing theme was the demand for increased respect for female education, coupled with a specific proposal for free education. The call for government scholarships tailored for general students reflects a broader push for inclusive financial support, ensuring that educational benefits are accessible to all. A crucial aspect emphasized was the need for societal recognition, advocating for girls to be identified on par with boys, accompanied by a commitment to providing equal opportunities without discrimination. The participants underscored the importance of fostering an environment that grants girls the freedom to make decisions, promoting both personal and academic autonomy within educational institutions, family, and workplaces. Transportation barriers were acknowledged, and the suggestion for free or subsidized transport facilities aims to address logistical challenges, particularly for girls in rural areas. The proposal for free coaching for competitive examinations aligns with efforts to level the playing field and encourage diverse career paths. To bridge educational disparities, establishing colleges or schools in rural areas was highlighted as a strategic move. Financial support for female education emerged as a recurring theme, encompassing scholarships, targeted financial aid, and the call for separate schemes and policies specifically designed for the education of female students. The broader societal perspective was addressed with a plea for the recognition of women's personal freedom to decide their aspirations, appearance, dietary choices, and lifestyle without judgement. Participants emphasized the importance of awareness and counselling programmes to empower female students with information and support in navigating educational challenges successfully. Calls for delaying the marriage age for girls align with the recognition that additional time for educational pursuits can contribute to personal development and informed life choices. The advocacy for female reservation in employment and education reflects a commitment to ensuring equitable opportunities and representation.

These suggestions collectively envision a transformative approach, emphasizing respect, equal opportunities, and societal recognition of the autonomy of female students. Through a combination of policy changes, societal shifts, and targeted support, the aim is to create an inclusive and empowering educational environment that enables the holistic development of female students.

Conclusion

The study uncovers a diverse landscape of challenges and aspirations. Advocating for respect in female education, proposals include free education up to higher secondary levels and government scholarships. The overarching theme underscores the need for societal recognition, equal opportunities, and safe educational environments. Initiatives like free transport and addressing financial barriers signify a commitment to accessibility. The research calls for a transformative shift in societal mindsets, recognizing women's autonomy. Proactive measures like awareness programmes, delayed marriage age, and female reservation highlight a commitment to an inclusive educational environment. In essence, the research urges comprehensive changes at societal, institutional, and policy levels for a more equitable and empowering educational landscape for women in Indian society.

REFERENCES

Amatya, R., Tipayamongkholgul, M. and N. Suwannapong (2023). "Matters of Gender and Social Disparities Regarding Postnatal Care Use Among Nepalese Women: A Cross-Sectional Study in Morang District", *Health Equity, 7*(1): 271-79. doi:l0.1089/heq.2022.0186

Azmitia, M. and K.C. Mansfield (2021). Editorial: "Intersectionality and Identity Development: How Do We Conceptualize and Research Identity Intersectionalities in Youth Meaningfully?", *Frontiers.* doi: 10.3389/fpsyg.2021.625765

Care India (2023). *Gender Inequality in the Indian Society.* Retrieved from Care India: https://www. careindia.org/blog/gender-in-inequality/

Evans, J., Sahgal, N. and A. Monique (2022). *How Indians View Gender Roles in Families and Society.* Retrieved from Pew Research Centre: https://www.pewresearch.org/religion/2022/03/02/how-indians-view-gender-roles-in-farnilies-and-society/

Evans, V.E. (2021). *Race and Gender Intersectionality and Education.* Retrieved from Oxford Research Encyclopedias: https://doi.org/l 0.1093/acrefore/9780190264093.013.1345

Faharn, H.A., A.M. Davis and R. Ernst (2019). "Intersectionality: From Theory to Practice", *Annual Review of Law and Social Science, 15*(1): 247-65. doi:l0.1146/annurevlawsocsci-101518-042942

Goel, S. and Z. Hussain (2018). "Gender, Caste, and Education in India: A Cohort-Wise Study of Dropout from Schools", *Research in Social Stratification and Mobility, 58:* 54-68. doi:https://doi. org/ 1 0.1Ol6/j. rssm.2018.10.002

Government of India (2016). *Educational Statistics at a Glance.* New Delhi: Ministry of Human Resource Development Department of School Education and Literacy. Retrieved from https ://www.education.gov.in/ sites/upload_ files/mhrd/files/statistics/E SG2016_0 .pdf

Guy-Evans, O. (2023). *Intersectional Theory in Sociology.* Retrieved from Simplysociology: https://simplysociology.com/intersectional-theory.html

Haq, R. (2023). "Intersectionality of Gender and Other Forms of Identity: Dilemmas and Challenges Facing Women in India", *Gender in Management,, 28*(3): 171-84. doi:https://doi.org/l 0.1108/GM-0 1-2013-0010

Heyl, J.C. (2023). *What is Intersectionality?* Retrieved from Verywellmind: https ://www. verywellmind.com/what-is-intersectionality-7097945

Jain, D. and D. Agarwal (2016). "Women Education in Rural India", *International Journal of Advanced Education and Research, 1*(12): 27-29. Retrieved from www.alleducationjournal.com

Kumar, P., S.K. Patel and S. Debbarma (2023). "Determinants of School Dropouts among Adolescents: Evidence from a Longitudinal Study in India", *Plos One.* doi:ttps ://doi.org/ 10.1371/journal. pone.0282468

OECD (2023). *Intersectionality in Education: Rationale and Practices to Address the Needs of Students' Intersecting Identities.* Retrieved from OECD: https://www.oecd.org /education/ intersectionality-in-education-dbb 1e82l -en.htm

Prakash, R., T. Beattie and P. Javalkar (2017). "Correlates of School Dropout and Absenteeism among Adolescent Girls from Marginalized Community in North Karnataka, South India", *Journal of Adolescence, 61*(1): 64-76. doi:https ://doi.org/ 10.1016/j.adol escence.2017.09.007

Raje, V. and Zeba (2021). "Gender Disparity in Education in India", *International Journal of Research in Social Sciences,* 11(10). Retrieved from https://www.ijmra.us /project%20doc/2021/ IJRSS_OCTOBER2021 /IJRSS20ct21.pdf

Sharma, K. (2022). *School Dropout Rate among Girls Gone Down in 4 yrs Says Modi Govt. Claims Credit for Schemes.* Retrieved from The Print: https:// theprint.in/india/education/ school-dropout-rat e-among-girls-gone-down-in-4-y.rs-says-modi-govt-claims-credi t-for- schemes/ l 058396/

Srivastava, P. (n.d.). "Gender Concerns in Education". In P.G. Srivastava, *Gender Concerns in Education, NCERT.* NCERT.

Tefera, A.A. and Powers, J.M. (2018). "Intersectionality in Education: A Conceptual Aspiration and Research Imperative", *Review of Research in Education, 42*(1). doi:10.3102/0091732Xl8768504

TIME (2023). *What's Intersectionality?: Let These Scholars Explain the Theory and Its History.* Retrieved from TIME: https://time.com/5560575/intersectionality-the ory/

TOI (7 November 2021). *18% More Women in Higher Education in 5 years.* Retrieved from *Times of India*: https://timesofindia.indiatimes.com/education/news/18-more-women-in-highereducation-in-5-years/articleshow/83415039.ems

UNICEF India (n.d.). *Gender Equality.* Retrieved from UNICEF India: https://www.uniceforg/india/ what-we-do/gender-equality

Yaclav, D. (2022). *Increased in School Dropout Rates for Girls Child is Alarming, States UNICEF India.* Retrieved from UNICEF India https://www.timesnownews.com/education/increase-in-school-dropout-rates- for-gir1-child-is-alarming-states-unicef-india-article-90591261

4

Dalit Women Politicians and Social Justice

A Study on the Politics of J. Eshwari Bai and T.N. Sadalaxmi

Vamsi Surapogu

Introduction

According to David Miller, social justice means "how the good and bad things in life should be distributed among the members of a human society" (Miller, 2003: 1) and how to draw boundaries among various communities in order to distribute goods. Social justice also means distribution of goods and bads. For John Rawls fairness is synonym of Justice. He says social justice should be the foundation of any social institution. He proposes a society in which people come together to distribute the burdens and benefits on the basis of equality. Rawls writes

> All social values—liberty and opportunity, income and wealth, and the bases of self-respect—are to be distributed. Equally unless an unequal distribution of any, or all, of these values is to everyone's advantage. (Raphael, 2003: 198)

Miller further questions whether our definition of social justice is confined to the distribution of wealth, income, education, employment, etc. or should we add more to the list. The nineteenth-century political economy textbooks, one of whose major responsibilities was to explain the distribution of the social product among factors like land, capital, and labour, had a significant influence on the early notions of social justice (Miller, 2003). David Miller observes that

> Social justice requires the notion of a society made up of interdependent parts, with an institutional structure that affects the prospects of each individual member, and that is capable of deliberate reform by an agency such as the state in the name of fairness. (Miller, 2003: 4)

This explains that social justice is distribution of goods, both good and bad, among the various sections and communities of the society, and state as an agency acts as distributor of goods in a fair way. The justice for Ambedkar is equality, equality of humans, equality of opportunities, and rights. Dalit emancipation is achieved through the distribution of various social goods among various castes which annihilates caste and brings equality among people of India. He advocated for the distribution of land, equality of castes to enter into temples and equal opportunities for women in general and Dalit women in particular.

The majority of the scholarship on Dalit emancipation focused on the importance of the social. The Dalit experience of everyday caste discrimination, sporadic caste atrocities, and social exclusion happens in the social sphere. Dalit studies have given paramount emphasis on the prerequisites of the social for Dalit emancipation. The Dalit emancipation, among other things, along with social, is contingent upon the state or political. It is evident in history from ancient times to the current times. The ancient Hindu theocratic state synonymous with the king upheld the *varnashrama dharma* which is the exclusion of Dalits from social, economic and political spheres, and any violation would attract retribution. But the secular modern state played a reformistic role enabling Dalit emancipation. During colonial rule, the state played a major role in social reform against caste and gender. The colonial state brought laws banning *sati* (widow burning), restricting child marriages, and allowing widow remarriage (Sarkar and Sarkar, 2007), and temple entry legislations to provide untouchables access to temples (Dirks, 2011).

Dr. Ambedkar, the foremost emancipator of Dalits saw the problems of Dalits as political problems. He saw the modern-secular state as an arbitrator of social reform and social justice. He made several petitions to the British Indian state, submitted reports, gave testimonies, etc. Apart from that Dr. Ambedkar enunciated the importance of holding the political power for social advancement, removal of grievances and Dalit emancipation. Ambedkar speaking at the fifth conference of the Scheduled Castes Federation in 1948 stated "Political power is the key to all social progress and the Scheduled Castes can achieve their salvation, if they capture this power" (Ambedkar, 2019: 388). Ambedkar believed that if any progress was achieved by Dalits it was only possible by making the Dalit problem a political problem and gaining some political rights. For him Dalit interests are better secured with political power of their own and the Dalits cannot exist in the world without political power.

As noted by Urmila Pawar (2018), Dalit women played a prominent role in Ambedkar's movement. But there were also several Dalit women who were greatly inspired by him and continued his legacy and ideology even after his death in post-Independence. The current chapter discusses the social justice politics of two Dalit women—Eshwari Bai and T.N. Sadalaxmi—from the Telangana region during the early decades of Independence. Most scholarship focuses on male Dalit politicians who championed the cause of Dalit emancipation. For example, Kanshiram was given a great deal of attention in studies on Dalit politics. But Dalit women politicians are given less importance. Another reason for not bringing to light these two women is that they are confined to the regional politics of Telangana. Scholars working on Dalit politics of Telugu regions also have ignored the contribution of these two women. So, it is important to bring to the attention of academia the contribution of these two Dalit women politicians regarding the cause of social justice and the emancipation of Dalits.

This chapter is divided into the following way, the introduction deals with the theoretical understanding of social justice, and the first section deals with the Ambedkarite ideological formative years of Eshwari Bai and T.N. Sadalaxmi. The second section deals with social justice and emancipation through land distribution, the third deals with realising social justice through the Telangana state, the fourth section deals with social justice for Dalit women, and the fifth is a conclusion.

SECTION I: Ambedkarite Ideological Formative Years of Eshwari Bai (1918-1991) and Sadalaxmi (1928-2004)

Several women were inspired by Dr. Ambedkar during his heydays. His speeches inspired several Dalit women when he travelled across the country. Urmila Pawar and Meenakshi Moon (1989/2020) describe the influences of Dr. Ambedkar's speeches at different venues at various places that inspired Dalit women.

> Dr. Ambedkar's speech at the Mahaad Satyagraha brought about a revolution among the untouchable women. Their thoughts and behaviour began to change. (Pawar and Moon, 1989/2020: 157)

Similarly, Eshwari Bai and T.N. Sadalaxmi both were inspired by Dr. Ambedkar. Eshwari Bai read Ambedkar's writings, his announcements in newspapers, and his essays. She attended the meetings of Scheduled Castes Federation (SCF) and took great inspiration from the speeches and causes that Ambedkar and colleagues were putting together for the upliftment of Dalits. Eshwari Bai joined the Dalit activists of pre-Independent Hyderabad State like B.S. Venkatarao, J.H. Bucchaiah, Arigey

Ramaswamy, Bhagya Reddy Varma, etc. B.S. Venkatarao is known for his close association with Ambedkar and was called Hyderabad Ambedkar. Later, Venkatarao along with J.H. Bucchaiah formed the Hyderabad Branch of SCF. Eshwari Bai who worked with Bucchaiah great inspired by the work of SCF and became a member of SCF. Later she joined the Republican Party of India (RPI), elected as a Member of the Andhra Pradesh Legislative Assembly (MLA), from RPI. According to her daughter Gita Reddy, she became the President of the RPI, a brainchild of Dr. Ambedkar, and stayed in the party till she died in 1991 (Jaffer & India, 2020).

T.N. Sadalaxmi attended a meeting organized by the SCF in which Ambedkar made a speech. Sadalaxmi, as a young girl, attended the meeting despite the warnings from his family and close associates. Ambedkar's speech in that meeting greatly inspired Sadalaxmi. After she joined Congress which was against Ambedkar, she defied the party's objections to celebrate Ambedkar. She attended Ambedkar's death anniversary despite her party's objection as Ambedkar was anti-Congress and anti-Gandhi. She confronted Neelam Sanjeeva Reddy for attending Ambedkar's death anniversary saying Ambedkar is our caste man. She confronted the Congress stalwarts saying that I would work for my caste, my home first and then party. If you remove me from the party, you all will have to be removed from the party. Masterji, a Dalit poet recalls that she made Ambedkar's statue installed at Tank Bund. Today that statute has become the centre of Ambedkar's celebration. Sadalaxmi in her own way contributed to the spread of Ambedkar and his ideology.

SECTION II: Social Justice and Emancipation Through Land Distribution

The land is a fundamental source of livelihood in India. 70 per cent of its rural households are still dependent on agriculture (FAO, 2023) and its allied activities. The dominant castes in India established their dominance and appropriated surplus, political power as a result of possessing larger acres of land, and this reinforced social reproduction. Several caste atrocities on Dalits happened around land and agriculture. The Karamchedu Dalit atrocity of 1985 happened as a result of the Kamma caste hegemony advanced by the Green Revolution and the political power (Balagopal, 1985; Srinivasulu, 2002). The Dalit atrocity of Laxmimpeta in 2012 happened around the land between the dominant Kapu caste and the Dalit Mala caste. This tells that land is a primary source of self-reliance for an individual or community, and for the dominant castes, it is a source of domination. Dr. Ambedkar expressed his views on the land question of Dalits in the following way:

> In an agricultural country, agriculture can be the main source of living. But this source of earning a living is generally not open to the Untouchables. This is so for a variety of reasons. In the first place, purchase of land is beyond their means. Second, even if an Untouchable has the money to purchase land, he has no opportunity to do so. In most parts the Hindus would resent an Untouchable coming forward to purchase land and thereby trying to become the equal of the Touchable class of Hindus. Such an act of daring on the part of an Untouchable would not only be frowned upon but might easily invite punishment. In some parts, they are disabled by law from purchasing land. For instance, in the Province of Punjab there is a law called the Land Alienation Act. This law specifies the communities which can purchase land and the Untouchables are excluded from the list. The result is that in most part the Untouchables are forced to be landless labourers. As labourers they cannot demand reasonable wages. They have to work for the Hindu farmer for such wages as their masters choose to give. On this issue the Hindu farmers can combine to keep the wages to the lowest level possible for it is to their interests to do so. On the other hand, the Untouchables have no holding

> power. They must earn or starve. Nor have they any bargaining power. They must submit to the rate fixed or suffer violence.

Dr. Ambedkar believed that land is the material basis for caste and social hegemony is maintained through the land. While discussing the economic emancipation of Dalits Dr. Ambedkar says that "They are going to remain slaves, if not slaves, serfs of the landowning classes in the villages" (Ambedkar, 2013: 913). Hence, Ambedkar proposed three solutions to the land issue. He advocated the nationalization of land and collectivization of agriculture, which was to be a state-run sector. Second, he suggested creating distinct Dalit settlements that would grant them autonomy from Hindu village society. Third, he pressed the government to give landless Dalits access to grazing, forests, both cultivable and wastelands. Following Dr. Ambedkar's espousal for land distribution for Dalits, the two women put pressure on the government to distribute land to the Dalits.

RPI which was the brainchild of Ambedkar and formed after his death, took land struggles. It vehemently advocated for the distribution of waste lands, and cultivable lands to landless labourers and Dalits. It took agitation for land distribution in Punjab, Uttar Pradesh, Maharashtra, Rajasthan, and Andhra Pradesh and achieved a significant victory (Narasimharao, 2021). Like Ambedkar who emphasized on government's subsidy to Dalits to purchase lands as Dalits are not equipped to purchase lands on their own and provide capital investments, Eshwari Bai, as a representative from RPI in the Andhra Pradesh Legislative Assembly, persuaded the then Government of Andhra Pradesh to distribute land to landless Dalits free of cost rather than Dalits paying to purchase land to provide capital incentives (Narasimharao, 2021). She asserted that land reforms be brought in and the land reforms should start from the distribution of land of the ministers in the government. She emphasized that the land distribution committees should be constituted by a good number of SCs. Following Ambedkar's idea of nationalization and collectivisation of land, Eshwari Bai stated.

The only supreme remedy, I feel, to all the ills in the country and the state, is to nationalize all the land in the country and make every farmer and agricultural labourer a partner in the joint land cultivation movement in the country and after nationalizing the land, to establish collective farming so that all will work jointly on these collective farms and earn their bread by tilling the soil, to establish grain banks all over the country and distribute grains and money according to the labour put in by each individual on the land. Otherwise all these Land Ceiling Acts and their implementation are only a mere eye-wash (Narasimhan, 2021).

She exposed the bureaucratic and dominant castes' hand-in-glove relationship in confiscating Dalit lands. She argued for the state's protection of such lands from alienating from Dalits.

Sadalxmi being a Cabinet Minister in Andhra Pradesh government led by Indian National Congress could realise the land distribution to Dalits. As a minister, she made temple lands were given to Dalits for lease. During her tenure as an MLA, she advocated for the distribution of land to the Dalits. In the social sphere, temples are the first places of discrimination and violence against Dalits. The caste Hindus perceive that even the sight of the Dalits will pollute the diety and entry of Dalits is denied, even today. Ambedkar believed that temple entry was a point of equality. During his inaugural speech for *satyagraha*, Ambedkar stated "We don't want to go to temples though but we should have rights". But the Kalaram Temple entry movement made Ambedkar to understand that changing orthodox Hindus' mind is impossible. But Sadalaxmi made Dalits and women as members of Temple Trust Committees. Her decision to make Dalit priests became a huge controversy and established a priest training centre in Yadagirigutta. She advocated for 15 per cent Dalit reservation in temples and priests. She decided to utilize temple offers and funds for the welfare of the slum dwellers had become a subject of controversy. Ambedkar also said that wealth in religious organizations should be utilized for people's welfare (cited from B. Vijayabharati on Ambedkar, p. 212).

SECTION III: Social Justice for Dalit Women

The problems of Dalit women were different from the upper caste women. Ambedkar had said that Dalit women had to bear the double burden of caste and gender. Eshwari Bai acknowledged the problems of Dalit women. Dalit women suffer from poverty, malnutrition, and violence. Her daughter Gita Reddy says:

> Though she was known as a Dalit icon, but she was always there for every community, especially women. Even as a child I used to see battered women beaten by husbands sharing their agony with my mother. (Hans, 2020)

Eshwari Bai knows the plight of lower caste women. They were deprived of economic means for mobility and lived in poor conditions to feed their families.

> In those days, she had the foresight of empowering women. She taught these women from poorer and weaker sections candle making, tailoring and other vocations to make them independent. I have seen tailoring and candle-making classes being conducted on our veranda in Chilkalguda states Geeta Reddy. (Hans, 2020)

She argued for the complete banning of alcohol in the state as it was done in Karnataka and Tamil Nadu. She exhorted that alcohol consumption among the poor led to violence against women, throwing families in poverty, and destroying the health of the people. She condemned the government for generating revenue at the cost of depriving people in terms of both health and finance. She staunchly supported and advocated women's education. She firmly believed that education would help ameliorate the social grievances of women. She brought the problems of Dalit girls' education to the forefront and she exhorted that education for Dalit girls is of utmost importance.

Sadalaxmi despite being an Assembly speaker faced caste-gender slurs on her like "She is an arrogant madiga woman". When she offered silk clothes to deities in Tirumala, newspapers wrote sarcastic remarks against her. Being an Endowment Minister, she established SC, BC and women's corporations for their welfare. Sadalaxmi opines that women are greater than men because women can perform all the functions that a man can do and in addition, they can give birth which is the reason for the existence of a society. The intelligence, and physical superiority that a man possesses is because even the male is born out of a woman's womb and a male acquires his characteristics from his mother. Women should be reminded of their power like Jambavanta reminds Hanuman of his powers. By ameliorating the conditions of the women, the world and environment will be better. This resembles the views of Ambedkar where he says that *"I measure the progress of a community by the degree* of progress which women have achieved". She asserted that if a woman is committed to doing a task several of the problems will be resolved. And if political power is invested in the hands of Dalit women, they can do impossible things possible.

SECTION IV: Telangana State as an Answer to Social Injustice

According to Asha Sarangi (2006), Ambedkar argued that linguistic states over a period of time become socially homogeneous and politically democratic. He was of the opinion that one state one language will give freedom, development, justice, and equality. He accorded political and cultural identity to the region. There were several demands from people of different regions to carve a separate State from the earlier state from which they were part of Chhattisgarh, Jharkhand, and Uttarakhand. The demand for Telangana State emerged with similar demands for the first time in 1969. The assertion of separate linguistic identity, culture and region against Andhra. Along with those demands, agitation for separate Telangana was also premised on the economic and political exploitation by the Andhra right from the emergence of Andhra Pradesh in 1956 by merging distinctive Telangana with Andhra. In

1950 N.M. Jaisoorya, an MP from Hyderabad stated that "People have been looted apart from being oppressed and insulted by the outside officials" (Ram, 2007: 90). Eshwari Bai raised several questions pertaining to the deprivation of Telangana during the Andhra rule. She exposed several violations and ommissions by the Andhra ruling classes, ranging from water, and employment to budget allocation. Considering all these injustices done to the Telangana region she ardently demanded a separate Telangana State as a solution of social justice.

Expressing similar views to Eshwari Bai on the exploitation of Telangana resources, Sadalaxmi despite being in the Congress party and its opposition to separate Telangana, she vehemently criticized and confronted the anti-Telangana faction within the Congress. She defied the then Chief Minister Kasu Brahmananda Reddy of Congress. When the government was repressing the movement through violence she took the initiative to gather all the other supporters and fought against the government being a member of the ruling party. Sadalaxmi not only spoke for Telangana agitation but also led the movement from the forefront and contributed a huge amount of finance by selling her gold and silver.

SECTION V: Conclusion

Dr. Ambedkar believed that social reform and Dalit emancipation were possible through achieving political power. Both his writings and speeches and practice. He started three political parties, served as British Viceroy's Executive Council as a Labour Member on 20 July 1942, he was elected to the Bombay Provincial Assembly in the 1937 elections and took initiatives like the abolition of Maharwatan, the Koti system. He joined the Indian National Congress as law minister and brought radical legislation like the Hindu Code Bill. Following his path, Eshwari Bai and T.N. Sadalaxmi took politics for the cause of social justice and Dalit emancipation. T.N. Sadalaxmi asserted that politics is solving the problems. Eshwari Bai as a leader of the opposition—RPI—challenged the party in power to consider the Dalit cause. Sadalaxmi being an MLA and minister from the ruling Congress party took initiatives like leasing land to landless Dalits, making Dalits as part of temple administration and establishing a women's corporation. This tells us that being in political power, be it in a ruling party or opposition party, is important to realize the goals of social justice regarding Dalits. Raising the issues related to Dalits and persuading the governments to implement welfare measures for the upliftment of Dalits is paramount for the politics of Dalit emancipation. These two women politicians set the precedent for the future of Dalit women's politics. Along with the assertion of unity and difference in culture and social spheres among various communities, the two women bring the importance of politics for the emancipation of Dalits in general and Dalit women in particular.

REFERENCES

Ambedkar, B.R. (1990). *Dr. Babasaheb Ambedkar: Writings and Speeches*, Vol. 5. Government of Maharashtra, Bombay, 1137.

Ambedkar, B.R. (1990). *Dr. Babasaheb Ambedkar: Writings and Speeches*, Vol. 15. Government of Maharashtra, Bombay, 1137.

Ambedkar, B.R. (1990). *Dr. Babasaheb Ambedkar: Writings and Speeches*, Vol. 17 Part III. Government of Maharashtra, Bombay, 642.

Balagopal, K. (1985). "The Karamchedu Killings: The Essence of the NTR Phenomenon", *Economic and Political Weekly,* 1298-1300.

India at a glance |FAQ in India| Food and Agriculture Organization of the United Nations. (n.d.). https://www.fao.org/india/fao-in-india/india-at-a-glance/en/

Jaiffer, A. (7 March 2020). The Hans India. https://www.thehansindia.com/featured/womenia/documentary-on-eashwari-bai-to-be-screened-at-world- filmfestival-610224

Jangam, C. (2017). *Dalits and the Making of Modern India.* Oxford University Press, New Delhi.

Miller, D. (2001). *Principles of Social Justice.* Harvard University Press.

Moon, M. and U. Pawar (2020). *We Also Made History: Women in the Ambedkarite Movement.* Zubaan.

Narasimharao, M.L. (2021). *Eshwari Bai: Jeevitamu Udyamamu, Sasana Sabha Prasangam* (Eshwari Bai: Life, Movement and Legislative Speeches).

Ram, M.K. (2007). "Movement for Telangana State: A Struggle for Autonomy". *Economic and Political Weekly,* 90-94.

Raphael, D.D. (2001). *Concepts of Justice.* Clarendon Press.

Sarangi, A. (2006). "Ambedkar and the Linguistic States: A Case for Maharashtra." *Economic and Political Weekly,* 151-57.

Srinivasulu, K. (2002). *Caste, Class and Social Articulation in Andhra Pradesh: Mapping Differential Regional Trajectories.* Working paper: ODI.

Shyamala, G. (2011). *Nene Balanni* (I am the Strength). Hyderabad Book Trust.

Velugu, V. (24 February 2022). (Jetti Eshwari Bai, Voice of the Oppressed). *V6 Velugu.* https ://www. v6velugu. com/jetti-eshwari-bai-fought- for-the-downtrodden-and-women-empowerment

5

Invisible Suffering

Exploring the Plight of Widows in Vrindavan

Shalini Singh and *Pushpender Yadav*

Introduction

Widows in India are living and have been living since time unknown in depressing and oppressing environments. As Indian culture is originally conservative since ancient times, many old norms are still in practice. Many of these widows come to Vrindavan, a city in Uttar Pradesh's district Mathura to find solace and refuge under Lord Krishna, to whom this holy city is dedicated. Vrindavan is a famous holy place in India since ancient times. It is considered a holy place for followers of Hinduism. It is particularly known for its association with Lord Krishna and is home to numerous temples. Vrindavan has become a sanctuary for a large number of widows from various parts of India. These widows often come from disadvantaged backgrounds and choose to live in Vrindavan seeking solace and spiritual refuge. They come to find their final refuge over here that is, by devoting themselves to God. Now, at Vrindavan, although they come here to find peace, instead they deal with a different set of issues. There are near to 30,000 widows residing in the holy city at present. Most of these widows are from West Bengal, which is around 75 per cent. Then from Assam and Odisha (2010).

Widows are considered to be a bad omen for auspicious occasions and pure things. They are shunned because of so many cultural old norms and values. They are blamed for their husband's death and their suffering. They are forced to live an isolated dull life and to be in a state of mourning all the time. They are not allowed to remarry. They are marginalized by society by isolating themselves with these seeptical beliefs. Poor widows in India belong mostly to the states like West Bengal (most), Uttar Pradesh, and Chhattisgarh (NCW, 2010). Widowhood is still considered equivalent to the impurity oneself in many regions of our country. Now widows in the holy city are experiencing problems of different kinds which are unexpectedly almost equal to their old plight which they thought they have left far behind by surrendering their services to the Lord. Shockingly these widows, from which most of them are very old, are experiencing different forms of discrimination like caste, gender, being illiterate, and language barriers. These widows are experiencing intersectionality through different layers of social identities in their lives.

Intersectionality and Widows at Vrindavan

What is Intersectionality?

In 1989, a legal scholar in the US, Kimberlé Crenshaw coined the term "intersectionality" to explain the disadvantages faced by women of colour and how then US legal system was not fit to provide the proper justice (Crenshaw, 1989). She defined the term "intersectionality" in her words as:

> Intersectionality is a metaphor for understanding the ways that multiple forms of inequality or disadvantage sometimes compound themselves and create obstacles that often are not understood among conventional ways of thinking. (Crenshaw, 1989)

Later on, this term came into vogue to analyse how different minority groups around the world are stigmatized and stereotyped in more than one way. It is a concept that diversifies the different forms of discrimination among the people living. Among these people some go through intense inequality, these are those groups that belong to the lowest strata in class and caste-based societies around the globe. The factors in intersectionality are:

- Caste
- Gender
- Ethnicity
- Sexual preference of one
- Class
- Unequal and unfair opportunities
- Other forms of discrimination.

Intersectionality in India is recently added concept in academia, but notion of this concept as existing since many years (Ghosh, 2018). The complexities that Indian marginalities face are reason behind their current shape in the society. The matters like caste, gender, class are intersecting into their daily lives (Foster, 2022).

Intersectionality is the different types of oppression and discrimination experienced by people due to their particular identities established in society. To be more specific, if one of these widows belongs to a lower caste she will face discrimination not only based on her gender but also on her being a widow, illiterate, and a low caste. The widowhood of these marginalized castes or community women turns into a more unbearable social stigma.

A huge percentage of these widows residing in Vrindavan currently belong to the lowest strata of the caste hierarchy of the country, that is, the lowers caste community or Dalits. All the ancient data storage like scriptures, manuscripts, famous texts, and narratives holds proof of how different classes in Indian society suppressed the lowest group monstrously for so long. These low-caste communities have been suffering from marginalization since back then and are somehow still facing discrimination *via* numerous social mores of the past on a daily basis. Widows who belong to these castes face exclusion from different activities and events. They are made to be isolated by discriminating behaviours by other widows and even the caretakers if present in the place. They most surprisingly sometimes had to deal with both physical and verbal kind of abuse too.

Widows in India: An Overview

According to Census 2011, there are around 5.5 crore widowed persons, including both male and females. Among these widowed person women are near to 78 per cent in number (Arora, 2016). India has the largest widow population. Its widow population is 10 per cent of the total female population (Foundation). A recent study conducted in 2021, states that there are near to 4 crore widows in India at present. The number drastically increased due to COVID-19 pandemic emergency (Seven Inhuman Customs that Make the Lives of Indian Widows Go From Bad to Worse, 2021).

In India, which is very well known for its colourful culture and rich ancient traditions. Here, deities and devotion towards the deities are as important as breathing. These deities are of both gender male and female gender. The goddesses are considered as luck bringers, financial gain, protectors, guardians, and even the originator and destroyer of the universe. Contrast to women in Indian culture are considered lower than men since ancient times. Especially the later period of the Vedic period is seen to be the downhill of the status of women in the Indian ethnicity. Respected but low in status to the leader of the house, men. This patriarchic nature in the family system of Indian families is still noticeable.

Widows in the Indian culture are a threat to social gatherings. Ironically, they are females who due to the death of their husbands lose everything including their dignity to live as a normal human. They are not allowed to have ownership of any property. If they bore sons, she is "allowed" to have some measure of secure living. But, once treated as Goddess of the house is now bestowed with new qualities by the society and family members such as evil, bad omen, bad influence, and huge burden in the same household which they used to take care of with so much dedication (Pande, 2020).

Many widows in Vrindavan are of old age group of above 65+ (Study on Widows At Vrindavan, 2010). They face discrimination both gender and age-wise. The Constitution of India also provides for the welfare of the old population of the country. Article 41, provides the right to work, right to education, and assistance to citizens. This article is included in the Directive Principles of State Policy. State governments are meant to make policies by Directive Principles application holistically. Social security is the equal duty of both centre and state governments.

The widows of Vrindavan can be found in several *ashrams* (religious retreats) dedicated to providing them with accommodation, basic amenities, and a community of fellow widows. These *ashrams* are run by charitable organizations, NGOs, and religious institutions. They aim to provide a safe and supportive environment for widows, where they can lead a dignified life and engage in religious activities.

Factors Affecting the Widows of Vrindavan

Vrindavan which was earlier in ancient times commonly known to be the "City of Temples", "The City of Lord Krishna", now has a new name in modern times, i.e. "City of Widows". Other than caste there is another factor that intersects with the life of a widow in the city of Vrindavan. Which is "Class". Class-based discrimination stands next to caste-based unfairness. All the widows residing in the city in homes known as *ashrams* and *kutirs* (spiritual retreats), both private and government owned. Many of them are poor to extremely poor. These *ashrams* provide basic accommodation, food, and medical facilities, allowing the widows to live with some degree of dignity and camaraderie. They came to Vrindavan to find peace and necessities for their survival in the fragile age. In Vrindavan, however, these widows find a supportive environment where they can live together and engage in religious practices. They are dependent on charity for their daily requirements. All these women also face other complications like getting sick and consequently alarming poor health. They have to deal with situations like these hence crushing their desire of living a peaceful life for which they came as their utmost final desire.

Gender discrimination stands in the queue next to the class. Gender-based discrimination in India is age-old. Women are made to live a life lower than men here. Their lives are always considered to be less important than a male. They are discriminated against regardless of their marital status and education too. Their rights are always been put down by the male population most of the time. They are not meant to live freely even in an independent nation. Women are living a biased life in the country without much complaining for a long time. Although, this most current time holds a different perspective now. There are righteous and very much required campaigns going on in the country for the long-lost and denied rights of women. It is essential to raise our voices against the age-old anomalous stand on women in the country. Widows of Vrindavan suffer the same dilemma as those who lack rights and opportunities to live a desirable and respectful life.

Addressing Intersectional Discrimination against Widows

- To recognize the different forms of exploitation the widows are going through.
- To acknowledge their problems and hurdles in their life.
- Their literacy, age, socio-economic background which they belonged to.
- Their life before and after coming to Vrindavan.
- Strategically undertaking the described problems of the widows.
- Alerting them about the rights and wrongs.
- Raising awareness among them and the people surrounding them in the abode.
- Policies and other strategic interventions for specifically to focus on the suffering of the widows.
- Empowerment of these women through educating them,

providing vocational skills, daily wage-based works or chores and giving them financial knowledge too.

Empowering Widows in Vrindavan: Unlocking Economic Independence

Many widows in the Vrindavan are going through financial instability. They come in the city with the state of ill finances to no money security with them. Most of them being illiterate are not able to handle the finance if under their name and further gets into troublesome situations like theft and similar financial frauds. People takes advantage of the women who are illiterate. Many of these women relies on outside aids for the survival. In 2020, COVID-19 pandemic made the hard lives of these widows into more troublesome period. They were due to their old age, made to totally depend on government's and charity based resources. There was no income, only disheartening and worrisome daily routine which they spend in their religious retreats (Chamaria, 2020).

There are many forms of obstacles that widows have to go through daily. Among them there are those widows who suffer from discrimination as explained before in this chapter. Then some widows are dealing with other problems. The experiences of these widows are defined by factors like caste, gender, class, region, disability, etc. All of them are dealing with complex situations varying from individual to individual. But there are some issues that are faced by these widows in a general form. Most of the residing widows have low resources to live upon. They wander in the streets of the Holy City for charity and alms (*madhukori*). Most of the widows staying in the holy city get Rs. 8 for morning *bhajan* rituals and Rs. 12 for the same in the evening. Other than begging and charity, widows are dependent on their earnings of Rs. 20 on a daily basis for survival (Bagchi, 2022). They often gather in temples, singing hymns and engaging in prayers dedicated to Lord Krishna (Bagchi, 2022). These activities provide them with a sense of purpose and spiritual solace. Sometimes, they get abused too. Many of them suffer from exploitation by the public.

Efforts from government and non-government organizations are in motion, to improve the living conditions of widows in Vrindavan. These organizations strive to address the social and economic challenges faced by the widows, advocating for their rights, providing vocational training, and supporting initiatives to enhance their overall well-being. They are working at the forefront since the matter of the sufferings of these widows has been pulled out loud in front of the nation. Providing them with necessities like food, shelter, proper health services, and sanitation facilities, and encouraging them to learn earning skills like embroidery, mask making, toy making, *agarbatti* making, etc. *via* vocational training. Making them alert on their rights and other helpful procedures for their safety and security. Assuring them of their dignity and secure life. According to a sample survey conducted by NCW in 2009, 89 per cent of widows in Vrindavan are illiterate. And a majority of 70 per cent are with no pension and 60 per cent have no ration cards. They are forced to live on alms and charity for the survival (NCW, 2010).

Policies and laws made for the safeguarding and economic empowerment of widows in India are limited but in progressive mode. Over the years, efforts have been made to improve the conditions of widows in Vrindavan. NGOs and social welfare organizations have been working towards raising awareness about the plight of widows, advocating for their rights, and providing them with health care, education, vocational training, and legal support. These initiatives strive to empower widows and help them become self-sufficient, such as:

- Hindu Widow's Remarriage Act, 1956.
- Property rights under Hindu Succession Act, 1956.
- National Social Assistance Programme (NSAP), which includes the Indira Gandhi National Widow Pension Scheme. Under this scheme, widows below the poverty line are eligible for a monthly pension to support their basic needs. The amount of the pension varies across states.
- Being the state where Vrindavan is located, the Uttar

Pradesh government has undertaken several measures to assist widows in the region. The state government operates the Uttar Pradesh Widow Pension Scheme, which provides financial assistance in the form of monthly pensions to widows below the poverty line.

- A Home for Widows (Krishna Kutir) has been set up in Vrindavan city (Schultz, 2019). It has the capacity for 1,000 occupants. This was meant to provide widows a place with safety and security. Also, health care, proper food, physiotherapy, counselling, also legal awareness services.
- The Ministry of Women and Child Development in India has initiated various programmes and schemes to empower women, including widows. These initiatives focus on providing skill development training, financial literacy, and access to micro-credit facilities to help widows become self-reliant.
- NGOs like Maitri India, Sulabh International (Basu, 2019), Veer Nari Shakti Resettlement Foundation, Action Aid Association, Manav Vikas Seva Sangh, RAPID, etc. are vigorously working for the rights of the widows in Vrindavan, and providing proper care, and sustainable livelihood to these women.

Conclusion

In my concluding statement, I would like to shed light on the concept of intersectionality and how this concept is of great importance today to understand the plight of the widows residing in the Vrindavan. How the different types of discrimination that these women had to go through are to the point explainable with it. Pulling out of the weeds of discrimination in this matter is very necessary to provide a dignified and secure life to these women. Hence, to live a life without oppression and suffering. What is more important is a need to make policies for their welfare solely focusing on these widows, which is long overdue. Policies that are in motion at present are not based particularly on the upliftment of these widows. They are included with other populations to have some benefits out of implemented projects. There is an utter need for detailed collected data. Although, NGOs (Radha Seva, Agewell Foundation, Smile Foundation, Maitri India, Sulabh International, to name a few) have initiated much more help towards these women than government itself.

Their voice should be heard, not just for the formality but to provide them with the solid sentiment of being heard and taken care of. These steps will consequently be going to improve their and the country's socio-economic condition more efficiently. Opportunities around will increase, and all of their vulnerabilities including social stigma, caste-class-gender discrimination, literacy, and economic complications, will disappear gradually. They will live a quality life and will become self-sustained.

However, more work needs to be done to improve the lives of widows in Vrindavan. This includes increasing awareness, advocating for policy reforms, and addressing deeply entrenched societal attitudes and practices. It is imperative to continue supporting and expanding initiatives that provide comprehensive support systems, health care, education, and economic opportunities for widows.

By recognizing and addressing the intersectional challenges faced by widows in Vrindavan, we can strive towards creating a more equitable and inclusive society where widows are valued, empowered, and able to lead lives of dignity, respect, and fulfilment. Only through collective efforts and sustained commitment can we make a meaningful difference in the lives of these courageous women and ensure their well-being.

REFERENCES

(NCW), N.C. (2010). *Study on Widows at Vrindavan.*

(2010). National Commission for Women (NCW).

(2010). *Study on Widows at Vrindavan.* National Commission for Women (NCW).

Arora, M. (June 2016). *A Ray of Hope for Widows.* Retrieved from pib.gov.in: https://pib.gov.in/newsite/printrelease.aspx?relid=1

46020#:-:text=Widowhood%20is%20defined %20 as%20the,lakh%20 widowed%20persons%20were%20added.

Bagchi, J. (February 2022). *Irrespective of Who Comes to Power, Life Remains Dingy for Forgotten "Widows of Vrindavan"*. Retrieved from ANI: https://www.aninews.in/news/national/generalnews/irrespective-of-who-comes-to-power-life-remains-dingy-for-forgotten-widowsof-vrindavan202202092 1 1 503/# :-:text=Alike%20her%2 C%2 Ohundreds%20of"/o20others,daily%20eaming%20of"/o20Rs%2020.

Basu, S. (March 2019). *The Widows of Vrindavan.* Retrieved from CNBC TV18: https ://www. cnbctv 18.corn/photos/buzz/the-widows-of-vrindavan- 2537551.htm

Chamaria, P. (12 November 2020). *Life of Widows of Vrindavan.* Retrieved from Transcontinental Times: https://www.transcontinentaltimes.com/life-of-widows-of-vrindavan/

Crenshaw, K. (1989). *Demarginalizing the Intersection of Race and Sex: A Black Feminist Critique of Antidiscrimination Doctrine, Feminist Theory and Antiracist Politics*. University of Chicago Legal Farum, 135-70.

Crenshaw, K. (1989). *Demarginalizing the Intersection of Race and Sex: A Black Feminist Critique of Antidiscrimination Doctrine, Feminist Theory and Antiracist Politics*. University of Chicago Legal Forum, 149.

Foster, P. (September 2022). *What* is *Intersectionality, And How does it Apply to You?* Retrieved from the Organisation for World Peace: https://theowp.org/reports/what-is-intersectionalityand-how-does-it-apply-to-you/

Foundation, K. (n.d.). *The Plight of Widows.* Kamla Foundation.

Ghosh, S.B. (2018). Introduction. "Debating Intersectionalities: Challenges for a Methodological Framework", *South Asia Multidisciplinary Academic Journal [Online}, 19.* Retrieved May 2023, from http://journals.openedition.org /sarnaj/4745; doi: https://doi.org/10.4000/ sarnaj.4745

Pande, R. (2020). "Widows of Vrindavan- Feminisation of Old Age in India", *Pakistan Journal of Gender Studies,* 215-18.

Schultz, K. (August 2019). *India's Widows, Abused at Home, Have Sought Refage in This Holy City for Centuries. Vrindavan: The New York Times*. Retrieved from *The New York Times*: https://www.nytimes.corn/2019/08/27/world/asia/india-women-widows. html

Seven Inhuman Customs that Make the Lives of Indian Widows Go from Bad to Worse. (2021). She the People.

Vaidyanath, A. (August 2012). *Supreme Court Shocked by How Bodies of Vrindavan Widows are Treated.* Retrieved from NDTV: https ://www.ndtv.com/india-news /supreme-courtshocked-by-how-bodies-of-vrindavan-widows-are- treated-495332

6

Women's Empowerment Towards Gender Equality

Rohini

Empowerment means a process through the women able to "take control and ownership of their choices". In other words, it can be said that it is a process that makes women able to take their decision. It is said that women's empowerment is a process in which women increase their choice and freedom to participate, negotiate, influence and hold accountable institutions that affect their lives is a step in the right direction. It leads to the path of gender equality. Gender equality means man and woman should be treated equally. The formal approach to equality says that man and woman are equal so we should give equal legal and political rights to women. It is based on the idea of sameness. We can say that the formal approach to equality neglects the difference between man and woman. On the other hand, the substantive approach to equality says that women are socially disadvantage. Hence, we should provide them special rights to make them equal.

This research paper discusses various plans for women empowerment to achieve gender equality. As these are Beti Bachao, Beti Padhao, Pradhan Mantri Matru Vandana Yojana,

Mahila e-Haat, Ujjwala Yojana, Stand Up India and Pradhan Mantri Kaushal Vikas Yojana, etc. In this context, it also discusses the role of Self-Help Groups (SHGs) in empowering the women socially and economically. SHGs make more cooperation among women and also pave the way for collective saving that encourage the women's group to start their business and encourage their entrepreneurship. It provides them various skills and credits for women entrepreneurship and financial empowerment. SHGs play an important role in empowering the women both socially and economically. After discussing the various programmes it can be said that these schemes not only provide formal equality but make them equal substantially. This chapter will discuss how much the women have been empowered to achieve the gender equality?

Empowerment means a process through the women able to "take control and ownership of their choices". In other words, it can be said that it is a process that makes women able to take their decision. As the World Bank says that women's empowerment should be given more importance. It is said that

> Women's empowerment is a process in which women increase their choice and freedom to participate, negotiate, influence and hold accountable institutions that affect their lives is a step in the right direction.

Kabir says, "The expansion in people's ability to make strategic life choices in a context where this ability was previously denied to them." Gender equality means women should be treated equally. There are two approaches of equality. The formal approach to equality means that all individuals are equal. In this sense man and woman are equal. It ignores the differences between man and woman. Whereas the substantive approach to equality means that man and woman are different as women are disadvantage socially and economically. So, they should be given special rights to make them equal. As Dr. B.R. Ambedkar also argues that women should be given equal rights. In this context he criticizes *Manusmriti* for the degradation of women's position in the society. He says that gender relations are constructed. In his books *Women and Counter Revolution* and the *Riddle of Women,* he argued that women did not have right to property.

He argued that the women should be given equal rights. The Bill tried to provide rights to women. B.R. Ambedkar supported women empowerment, so he emphasizes on education of women for upholding her social status and making them equal. He says:

> it is the education which is the right weapon to cut the social slavery and it is the education which will enlighten the downtrodden masses to come up and gain social status, economic betterment and political freedom.

As we know that Article 14 says that all are equal it means all have equal rights and opportunities in every spheres. Article 14 says, "everyone is equal before law". Article 15 says that "the state shall not discriminate against any citizen on the basis of religion, race, caste, sex, place of birth". Article 15(3) enables positive discrimination in the favour of women. Article 16 provides us equal opportunity in the context of employment. There should not be any discrimination on the basis of religion, caste, creed and sex. Article 39 and 39(d) provides as there should be equal means of livelihood and equal pay for work. Article 42 says that there should be the human condition of work and maternity leave. Article 243D(3), 243(3) and 243R provides for allocation of seats in the Panchayati Raj System.

There are various schemes for example, P.M. Matru Vandana Yojana, Beti Bachao, Beti Padhao, The Ayushman Bharat Programme, National Nutrition Mission, Pradhan Mantri MUDRA Yojana, P.M. Jan Dhan Yojana, and Ujjawala Yojana. P.M. Matru Vandana Yojana provides the financial support to the women during their pregnancy and lactation period. Other programmes are Beti Bachao, Beti Padhao and Sukanya Samriddhi Yojana protect the girl child from female foeticide and provides them the financial security. The Ayushman Bharat Programme, National Nutrition

Mission and Ujjawala Yojana provide the facilities of health and nutritional upgradation.

The Sukanya Samriddhi Yojana was launched in 2015. As we know that by the plan of Sukanya Samriddhi Yojana and P.M. Jan Dhan Yojana provide the banking services to the women who do not have any bank account. Women's share of total saving account increased from 28 per cent in 2014 to 40 per cent in 2017. The Pradhan Mantri MUDRA Yojana provides the credit to the small entrepreneurs. Seventy-five per cent of these loans have been given to women, with 9.81 crore women entrepreneurs already benefiting from this scheme. The Maternity Benefit Act, 1961 was amended in 2017 (Maternity Benefit Amendment Bill, 2017) that increase the period of the paid leave from 12 weeks to 26 weeks. It also emphasizes that there should be creche facility. The Maternity Benefit Act also provides 26 weeks of paid maternity leave to the working women. The Sexual Harassment of Women at Workplace (Prevention, Prohibition and Redressal) Act, 2013, provides safe environment to the women.

There are various government programmes that provide the facilities of entrepreneurship for example, Start-up India'promotes entrepreneurship by mentoring, nurturing and facilitating Start-ups. The Start-up India provides the plans for entrepreneurship. It also provides the facilities of free online classes relates to entreneurship. Start-up India has been launched in 2015 provides institutional credit for the benefit of India's under privileged. The Start-up India portal also acts as a digital platform for small entrepreneurs and provides information on financing and credit guarantee. Start-up India provides institutional credit for the benefit of underprivileged. Its purpose is to encourage their economic participation.The Start-up India portal provides a digital platform for small entrepreneurs and also provides information on financing and credit guarantee.

Support to Training and Employment Programme (STEP) for women provides training to the women especially in the rural areas. It provides skills in several sectors such as agriculture, horticulture, food processing, handlooms, traditional crafts like embroidery, travel and tourism, hospitality, computer, and IT services.

Pradhan Mantri Surakshit Matritva Abhiyan (PMSMA) gives facilities of quality ante-natal care (ANC) to the pregnant women. ASHAs provides various jobs to villages as health care providers such as Auxiliary Nurse Midwives (ANMs). Janani Shishu Suraksha Karyakaram (JSSK) provides all pregnant women for free health care.

Ayushman Bharat Provides Women for Free Health Services

Trade related Entrepreneurship Assistance and Development (TREAD) provides credits to the underprivileged women. Pradhan Mantri Kaushal Vikas Yojana (PMKVY) trains the youth industry—relevant skills to enhance opportunity for livelihood creation and employability. Niti Aayog launched the Women Entrepreneurship Platform (WEP).The purpose of the WEP is to build an ecosystem for women across India to realize their entrepreneurial aspirations. There are three elements of WEP as these are *ichha-shakti* means to encourage the aspiring entrepreneurs to start their enterprise, *gyaan-shakti* means to provide knowledge and eco system support to women entrepreneurs to help them to foster entrepreneurship and *karma-shakti* means to provide hands-on-support to entrepreneurs in sitting-up and scaling up business. MUDRA Yojana Scheme for Women provide loans to small new enterprises and businesses. The schemes have been categorized in three criteria as under *shishu scheme* the limitation of loan is 50,000, *kishor scheme* provides loan amount between 50,000 and 5 lakh and *tarun scheme* provides loans up to 10 lakh. These schemes make them empower that leads to the gender equality.

The Micro, Small and Medium Enterprises Development Organisation (MSME-DO), the various State Small Industries Development Corporation (SSIDCs), the nationalist banks and NGOs provide various programmes relates to Entrepreneurship Development Programmes (EDPs) to encourage women entrepreneurship. It also provides skills to the women to start their business. MSME-DO provides various skills relates to as T.V. repairing, printed circuit boards, leather goods, screen printing, etc. to the women, so that they establish their business and make themselves empower socially and economically. It also gives a special prize for "Outstanding Women Entrepreneur" of the year. The Small Industries Development Bank of India (SIDBI) implement two special schemes for women as Mahila Udyam Nidhi and the Mahila Vikas Nidhi. SIDBI provides training for credit utilization as credit delivery skills.

TREAD programme provides credit to women by NGOs. PMKVY trains youth in industry-related skills. Science for Equity Empowerment and Development (SEED) provides an opportunities to encourage the scientists and the field level workers. It is found that various programme provides credits to women that encourage them to be empower economically and socially also. In such process SHGs play an important role in women entrepreneurship. MUDRA Yojana, priority sector, payment banks and small finance banks play an important role in making them empower. Financial inclusion is also important for women empowerment. It also only includes financial inclusion but also providing opportunities for savings.

India has an 1.053 million Anganwadi centres. They have been provided banking services training.

SHGs are important for making women empower. Women entrepreneurship also plays an important role for making women empower, that help us to achieve gender equality. Here empower means a process that makes the women able to take decision. Micro entrepreneurship also plays an important role for removing gender inequality. Micro credits provide credits to SHGs for example, Abhinav Farmers Cooperative Society, Grameen Bank, Assam Tea Cooperation plays an important role for providing credits so that they could be self-sufficient economically. Here empowerment means a process through the women able to "take control and ownership of their choices". Micro-finance with SHGs play an important role for promoting women entrepreneurship and financial empowerment. SHGs mainly supports the rural women. SHGs not only provides them sufficient income but also upgrade their social status.

It is found that many SHGs as Abhinav Farmers Cooperative Society, Grameen Bank, Assam Tea Cooperation, Indira Kranthi Padhan provide them credits so that women could able to be self-sufficient. Overall, it can be said that these SHGs plays an important role in empowering women and also removing the obstacles for achieving gender equality.

The SIDBI provides two schemes as Mahila Udyam Nidhi and Mahila Vikas assistance pay important role for providing them credit. There are various important entrepreneurship as these are the Micro Small and Medium Enterprises Development Organization (MSME-DO) the various State Small Industries Development Corporations (SSIDCs), the nationalised banks and even NGOs provides various programmes as Entrepreneurship Development Programmes (EDPs) to provide them facilities to women entrepreneurs.

So, it can be said that SHGs can be perceived as "communities for women", that gives social identity to its members. SHGs are important mainly for the empowerment of the poor women. It provides various kinds of entrepreneurship and financial empowerment. It is well-known fact that micro credit encourages that small-scale business enterprises and its major aim to remove poverty by providing them credit to be self-sufficient as "income generating activities".

In Tamil Nadu and Kerala SHGs play an important role. In these states, SHGs encourages women entrepreneurship and micro enterprises. It provides micro finances, capacity programmes by providing them training. Even Reserve Bank of India also recognizes the success of SHGs as it provides finance, loans to women entrepreneurs with the support of NABARD.

As the World Bank says that women's empowerment should be given more importance. It is said that women's empowerment is a process in which women increase their choice and freedom to participate, negotiate, influence and hold accountable institutions that effect their lives is a step in the right direction.

Kabir says,

> The expansion in people's ability to make strategic life choices in a context where this ability was previously denied to them.

SHGs play an important role for the women's empowerment. These programmes provide credits to women that transform the women's condition, in which they not only elevate poverty but also be self-sufficient or it can be said that they transform their economic status. It is found that SHGs make more cooperation among women and also pave the way for collective saving that encourage the women's group to start their business and encourage their entrepreneurship. Overall, it can be said that SHGs play an important role in empowering the women both socially and economically.

Conclusions

SHGs also play an important role in women entrepreneurship. SHGs has been perceived as "communities for women" that gives social identity to its members. After discussing various programmes for the women's empowerment, it can be said these programmes play an important role in empowering women and also for achieving gender equality.

REFERENCES

Chandra, Alka (2019), "Constitutional and Statutory Safeguards for Women in India", in Sunita Mangla and Manisha Tomar (ed.) *Dr. B.R. Ambedkar on Women's Rights and Gender Equality*. Samyak Prakashan.

Chakravarty, Lekha and Piyush Gandhi (October 2018). "Breaking the Shackles of Financial Deprivation", *Yojana*.

Madhuri, N.V. (October, 2018). "Helping Women Gain Control of their Lives", *Yojana*.

Sagla, Sunita and Manisha Tomar (2019). "Exploring Dr. Ambedkar's Ideas on Women Emanicipation", in Sangla, Sunita and Mnisha Tomar (ed.) *Dr. B.R. Ambedkar on Women's Rights and Gender Equality*, Samyak Prakashan.

Sangla, Sunita and Manisha Tomar (ed.) (2019). *Dr. B.R. Ambedkar on Women's Rights and Gender Equality*. Samyak Prakashan.

Srivastava, Nilima, Linda Lane and Sunita Dhal (October 2018). "Meeting the Challenges of Gender Empowerment", *Yojana*.

Sudan, Preeti (October 2018). "Empowering Women through 'Continuum of Care'", *Yojana*.

Tripathy, K.K. and S.K. Wadkar (September 2021). "SHG-led Women Empowerment", *Yojana*.

Vishwanathan, Brida and Sanjana Sharma (October 2018). "In Pursuit of Inclusive Growth in India", *Yojana*.

7

Intersectionality in Casteism

Indian Perspective

Abdul Rahim Wardak

Introduction

Intersectionality is way of exploring a bunch of disadvantages and inequalities existing as a dominant system in a society and creates obstacles and discrimination among different areas.[1] Before Crenshaw, there was a black feminist Combahee River was working with black lesbian socialist feminist organization and she stated the situation of sexism and discrimination against the blacks.[2] Intersectionality is the instrument that is used for achieving human rights and equality and it is monitoring the variant forms of discrimination, disadvantages and abuse; experienced by different categories of people.[3] The policy makers, human rights activists, scholars and writers from different field and disciplines analytically used intersectionality to eradicate and mitigate inequality and promote social equality and justice. Public policy should have sufficient consideration of equal distribution of sources. Intersectionality is also studied to identify whether the governmental agencies take measure and steps systematically against any group, category or no.

Sometimes, the privileges given to someone who is not eligible and it is a big disadvantage for someone who is the eligible. These types of challenges are called structural problems. Intersectional justice analysis helps us to understand that the discrimination and inequality exists is not the result of a single factor and element. Most of the discriminations and inequality come from systematic, structural and institutional outcome. We can reach social and economic justice for discriminated people through institutions that directly and indirectly grants and distribute resources and allocate opportunities. Intersectional justice should be observed and considered in school systems, curriculum, health centers and policies, insurances system and taxation, economic market, media and information releasing centers, banking and loan in the country.

Intersectionality is a framework to assess how the systems of suppression deeply intertwined and affects the experiences and socio-economic, cultural and political opportunities in the society. The Figure 7.1 illustrates that systems shape and form the experiences and cannot be separated from each other absolutely.[4]

Level of Intersectionality

The Figure 7.1 shows that there are four broad categories of intersectionality in general. Intersectionality may work in the individual level and one person may not like and bear the weight, height, color, gender or sex of someone else, in the local level one community may have problem with another community based on their language, educational system, health programs and geographical or territory issue, in the national level there might be party politics, one class might be feeling superior than the other, might have access to some sources, and the religion of some citizens might not be considered significant. In the global level the intersectionality is more complex and there are some elements of racism, faith, colonialism, imperialism and capitalistic which creates intersect differentiation among the human in the world.

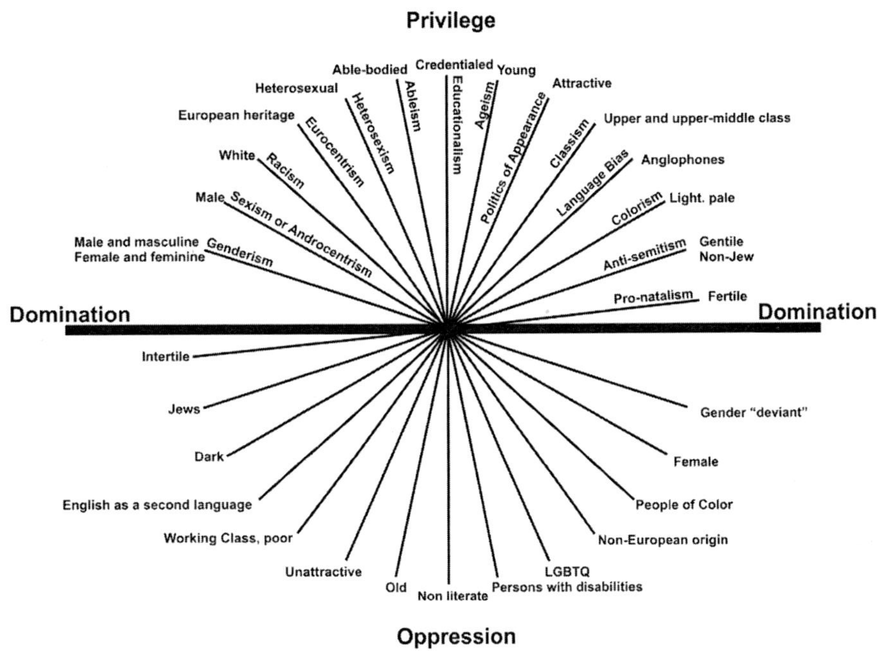

Source: Morgan, K.P. Describing the emperor's new clothes: Three myths of educational (in) equality. In the Gender Question in Education. Theory, Pedagogy, & Politics. Westview Press, Boulder, CO, 1996, 105-122. Used in AWIS' intersectionality fact sheet at https://www.awis.oeg/ intersectionality/

Fig. 7.1: Level of Intersectionality

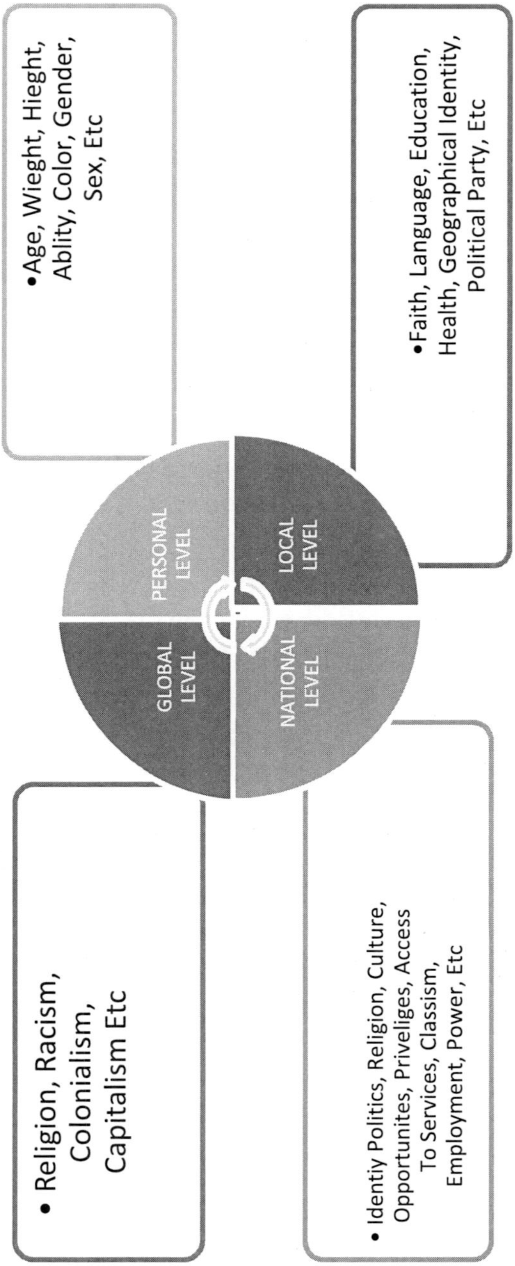

Source: author

Fig. 7.2: Level of Intersectionality

Intersectionality: Indian Perspective

India already was facing Hindu *varna* system, Buddhism, Christianity and Islamism so the condition of untouchables was too worse than the imagination. A flower blossomed in twenty century (Bhim Rao) who shook the Indian unequal systems and ignored theocracy and struggled for secularism whereas each and every community has its own value and identity. He even was vital point and mediator to end disputes between Jinnah and Mahatma Gandhi.[5] Ambedkar is one of the well-known activists who worked hard for equal rights and development of India till his death in 1956. The casteism rooted in *Rigveda* where the nation was divided into four categories (priests, fighters, traders and the workers) and this division based on deeds but later this division remained as an identity among these groups based on birth and the Shudras or the servile divided into different categories and they are counted as poor and weaker section of the society. Followers of one caste cannot marry another caste, restriction on eating and drinking with followers of other caste, there should be specific occupations and the top caste is Brahmin. Baba Ambedkar observed and surveyed nicely the casteism and wrote how to annihilate casteism, to describe who were the Shudras or workers and untouchables. Untouchables were the (Mofles Persian) or broken men who were below the poverty line. Buddhists and Brahmins had enmity and Ambedkar thought, it can cause to create a high level of untouchablity so it is better to ignore casteism.[6] Untouchables were kept outside the castes. The British called them depressed category. Most famous names used for them are (Pariah, Panchamas, Avarnas, Namshudras, etc...). Independence of India just was not an independence from British but also independence from casteism. Untouchables were living a very bad condition where was not clean water, public facilities and even they were forced to leave villages and live outskirt areas. Their children were not allowed to study in villages and they were kept illiterate several decades. In 1935, in a conference Baba Ambedkar advised to the untouchables if leaders of Hinduism persist for no change then untouchables should change their religion. Ambedkar himself hugged Buddhism and his followers also accepted and started following it[7].

Intersectionality: First Decade of Independence

After the Independence rivalry existed among the political leaders. Gandhi had nice friend like Rabindranath, a good comrade like Jawaharlal Nehru and rival as Mohammad Ali Jinnah meanwhile Bhimrao Ramji Ambedkar and Gandhi had a controversial relations and rivalry on the ideological areas. Ambedkar said to BBC Radio in 1955, in New Delhi,

> I know Gandhi better than his disciples". They came to him as devotees and saw only the Mahatma. I was an opponent, and I saw the bare man in him. He showed me his fangs.[8]

Ambedkar refused to call Gandhi to be Mahatma he claimed that Gandhi does not deserve the title. Ambedkar was from Dalit community and came to present his people and untouchables who were broken and had nothing for living good life. Gandhi also wanted to remove social injustice and untouchablity but with maintaining Hinduism and Ambedkar was not in favor of religious supremacy and disputes. He utilized his chairmanship to equalize the rights and privileges among the common by removing the casteism. Sometimes Intersectionality creates a new-born system and caste and may be the reason Mahatma Gandhi was scared of an independent caste generation from Harijans and Untouchables and Hindus will remain alone.[9] Here are some common disputes between Mahatma Gandhi and Baba Ambedkar according to the perception of the writer subjectively.

Table 7.1: Comparison of Mahatma Gandhi and B.R Ambedkar

Mahatma Gandhi	B R Ambedkar
Removing social inequality but meanwhile keeping and maintaining Hinduism and religion.	Removing social inequality and did not accept religious disputes and sectarian life.
Caste system of Hinduism rooted in *Rigveda* was respected and should be remaining untouched and changes to them were not voted.	Ambedkar wanted to remove all castes and had lots of critics on religious leaders who did not work for the life change of Dalits and kept them servants.
He knew casteism is a big problem and still he appreciated a gradual change in casteism.	He was not conservative, he was sharp stable to changes or eradicate casteism and untie the chain of traditionalism.
Gandhi was interested in traditionalism and rural patriot for his country.	Ambedkar was modernist and he wanted to urbanize the country.
Gandhi was faced discrimination by British government and other powers.	Ambedkar was discriminated in his country by indigenous people and British.
Harijan or schedule castes should be helped by the government and should be given equal rights and even some privileges should be given to them.	Dalits are the depressed category and they should be part of government and they should go through election to the parliament and vote their leaders.
Everyone should be in a position where they can survive centuries or several decades.	Schedule castes should be given special attention and besides the morale regeneration there should be economical opportunities.
It is claimed that Gandhi was anarcho-romantic personality.	Ambedkar was anti-romantic personality.
Gandhi was anti-machine and technology.	Ambedkar was pro-mechanistic and technology was preferred
He was accused for anti-modern primitivism.	He was pro-enlightenment modernism in India
Not in favor on positive liberalism.	liberal Democratic and socialist

Source: Author.

Intersectionality: Social justice in India

Social justice as a process of equality emphasizes on allocation and distribution of sources among all the members of a society. Structural inequality also comes from a poor social system that dominant in a society. Those members who are in weaker status must be considered and helped. It is the responsibility of the government and state to take care of the weaker section of the society when they formulate a public policy or passing any Act or Regulation. The inequality existing among the groups of the society should be eradicated. Both the positive and negative liberalism agree on each person of the society should have freedom of self development in the society. If any group monopolized the benefits the state and government should take critical measures to equalize the source distribution among the citizens. A welfare state facilitates for the citizens to develop themselves and the welfare state is not only responsible to provide law and order. To bring social justice a welfare state and democratic government remove deprivation, marginalization and discrimination. Gandhi did not want monopoly of benefits of society by one section but meanwhile he was unlike the supporters of positive liberalism and democratic socialism to eradicate casteism.[10] Ambedkar was supporting equality and rationality in the society so he was against casteism and supremacy among the citizens. He wanted to eradicate the social structure based on caste which causes hatred and separation among the Indians. Ambedkar was not against the *varna* system which was identifying person according to his or her deed and work in the society but he was against caste because it made Indian separated hereditarily. Ambedkar was not too much in worry about the economic because he thought it is not a big factor for social injustice in that time. The role of state was emphasized by him for economic development. Politically, he was in favor of centralized and strong government to guarantee the rights of citizens.[11] When equally wealth is distributed, opportunities allotted to everyone, and no one is inferior to anyone else is called social justice. During Independence of India the writers and policy makers struggled to remove casteism and some of them stood to maintain their religious rituals and culture. India was influenced by Hindu *varna* system predominately and it caused big deals and challenges to arise. The policymakers had to consider the poor classes of the society and distribute equally the sources, grant equal rights, privileges, education, health services, opportunity and economic share. In Indian society social justice is a big challenge and directly concerned with inequality.

Dalit Women

Dalits are the most oppressed heterogeneous entity who are amalgamated from hundreds castes (*jatti*). They are living in different states with different cultures, occupations, rituals and histories. Their geographical and socio-economical status influenced their political situation. Their marginalization from the socio-economic facilities is because of their geographical distribution and political authority. Although, there are some variants and elements which play significant role in the socio-economic condition of Dalits, they, irrespective of those factors have been discriminated and marginalized. Their history and culture is being erased but still there are Dalit and some non-Dalit writers who could awaken the Dalit youth to fight for freedom. Dalit women also played important role in the awakening their community and teach them the lessons of freedom, equality and humanitarian justice. The Legacy from Baba Ambedkar and some other Dalit writers made the community to raise their voice and express their sufferings and inferiority. Dalit after independence could know a little bit about their rights and could participate in the elections to vote their favorite candidate and release themselves from the atrocities of others. The atrocities of others brought a dehumanized form of structure which automatically put Dalits into a religious structure where they have no position and identity. Dalit women, who are educated group and have been influenced by Ambedkarite movement.

Their reactions indicate that Dalit women are facing oppressive system. Dalit women are facing the subjugated and unjust socio-economic situations. They have been exploited in the market and some of them are ready to touch every area of income source. Those women who have been victimized by the cultural and religious categorization system are raped and murdered. Dalit women might be married to rich men of other than Dalits but women of other castes (*jati*) will not be married to Dalits because of social stigma. Dalit women are bored with *varna* system and they demand of equality and justice. They are in struggle of to find a society without discrimination and atrocities. Some Dalit women are writing their suffrage and slavery thorough their poetry and it caused to shaken the conscience of wised humans of the world. Their resistance against the brutal system dominant in the society is appreciated by human rights defenders. Their poetry is a practical presentation of their experiences that they had in their lives. The poetry does not illustrate or celebrate the self presenting in the country but as a whole it present a community with lot of bad experiences from the hegemonic atrocity exists. The poems illustrate the hopelessness of Dalits among the citizens of the country and untouchablity became a case of honor. Dalit women are the strongest ladies of their society as well because they find the food and water of their families and they work harder than some men of Indian society. They raised their voice for equal rights and justice same as other castes who are upper than them. Dalit women are not stick to traditional ways of worships and rituals, in fact they are in search of modern society and they dare to move towards the public space where no gender is differentiated. Not only authoritarianism is not a cumbersome for Dalits but there is a hegemony which oppresses Dalits to bear and tolerate the vulnerability for centuries. It is not a movement of expressing oneself but it is a resistance against the biasness, discrimination, exploitation, massacre, hostility and misery[12].

Intersectionality: Indian Legal Framework

The Indian constitution was written based on secularist nature and meanwhile embracing democracy and socialism. There is ministry of social justice and empowerment in national level and the legislations, policies and special regulations are formulated by. The department watches the implementation of laws which protects the civil rights of Indian citizens, rights and privileges of schedule castes and tribes, maintenance and welfare of parents or senior citizens, transgender and any group which is felt to be vulnerable in India. Part four of the constitution grants power to the state government to formulate policies for the welfare of people. The ministry is the nodal agency dealing with Scheduled Castes. Under the department of social justice and empowerment there a few commissions and committees who work on Scheduled Castes and Tribes.[13] The equality and equity was given special place in in Indian constitution. The rights of Scheduled Castes and Tribes are protected. Intersectionality is being decreased the constitution writers and committee and social, structural, social, political, economical and ritual equalities were specified. The constitution guarantees social justice for the people of India via the below articles.[14]

- Article 15 forbid and prevent offices from discrimination based on religion, gender, geography, caste and sect, ethnicity and race.
- Opportunities should be provided for all without any consideration.
- Article 17 mentions that untouchability has no place among the citizens and it should be removed.
- Article 19 ensures the fundamental rights to all the citizens of India
- Article 23 and 24 prevents the exploitation of Indian citizens and guarantee their rights in the constitutional circle.
- Article 38 hints to the state or government to create a smooth social order and govern based on welfare-oriented policy for the promotion of people.

- Article 41 indicates that Indian citizens have right to work, right to education and other public services.

Intersectionality: Indian Policy Perspective

There are some schemes which can help the schedule castes, back ward class citizens and those who are financially weak in India. Some organizations have schemes to improve the living standard of schedule castes and provide them facilities to boost their capabilities. Normally among the backward class citizens the drugs is inevitably linked so the government of India has some awards and motivational programs which provoke NGOs to campaign against the drugs. In the educational area the government of India has many programs which facilitates for backward classes to start schooling for free and complete their elementary education. The socio-economic condition of schedule castes and backward classes is boosted through some schemes and programs which assist the poor people in the society[15]. The status of Dalits in India should be categorized into four broad parts:

(1) *The Economic Status of Dalits:* There is segregation of gender in job, employment and payment. In spite of many movements and organizations working for gender equality, women empowerment and women education still there are obstacles which do not let the women to express freely and attempt for achieving their rights. The wage gap is still a big issue in India and employment linked with culture is another factor which causes the avoidance of women participation in market. Interaction on the job among the colleagues in organization and between seniors and juniors and this interaction is less considered for women, which causes inequality and improves male domination in the organization.[16]

(2) *The cultural status of Dalits:* It indicates that there is segregation and separation of Dalits in the core Indian core culture. Dalits can go parliament yet but they are not allowed to enter temples. Separation, segregation,

inferiority, degradation and violence against everywhere in India are registered by the government. Marriages between Dalits and non-Dalits are not bearable and tolerated.

(3) *The Political Status of Dalits:* Dalits have rights to stand for elections and they have many representatives in Indian parliament after the independence. Dalits are not disenfranchized and they have rights to vote their favorite candidates. The Indian constitution gives them rights of choice and selection similar to all other citizens.

(4) *Educational Status of Dalits:* Education got better since 2009, after passing the Act of access to free and compulsory education and its enforcement in April 2010. The children can complete their elementary education without passing any board examination or fees tension and it effect positively on the lives of Dalits but the secondary education and higher education is difficult for them. In short, all the above political, economic, cultural and educational dimensions are inter-linked.

Conclusion

The researcher has been in India since 2019 and has reviewed the social structure of the Indian society. I found that still in some states girl child has low value than boy child. Casteism is dominant but the condition is better than the past. Still in India people consider strictly the separation of caste, gender, class and race. The Government of India struggled for inclusion of men and women in social activities, empowered ladies to occupy the governmental posts, girls' education is supported, special scholarships and grants are available for some castes, gender and race but still government could not finish the class and casteism. Intersectionality as tool of critically evaluation of systems whether there is discrimination and biasness based on gender, race, color, sex, ethnicity, ability, and disability, class and religion and how to handle and resolve the obstacles created against social justice. All shapes and forms of inequality should be equalized and resolve the wage gap policy between male and female payment and recruitment should be done based on capabilities rather than the race, color, socio-economic condition, and gender. Justice based on intersectional character and dimension, it is focused on equal and fair distribution of political, social, and cultural rights, wealth and sources existing in the country, and job or other social opportunities among the citizens. Social justice and intersectional justice focus on the advantages and disadvantages of others. Categorization based on economy strengthening the casteism system and it's not a permanent solution for empower Dalits; it is a modern type of improving the Dalitization, Harijanism and Jatism (casteism). Social hierarchy is existed in Indian society put the Dalits in the fifth or the lowest level of social order and economic hierarchy will only made them ready for a short time rather than to get social prestige. Mahatma Gandhi and Ambedkar as political rivals can be evaluated as the completion of each other rather than to see them as not sign or disunity. To stand against the social exclusion, each citizen has to fight against poverty, casteism, religious sacrilege, and supremacy, gender discrimination, ethnicity and abletism, ageism, homophobia and imperialism.

The casteism (Jatism) is predominant feature of Indian society. The *varna* system, namely Brahmin, Kshatriya, Vaishya and Sudra; is the based for intersectionality study. The government instead to touch and remove or annihilate the varna system, it does conservatively focus on the temporary and financial situation of schedule castes. There are dozens of programs and schemes which help the schedule castes and backward classes; however, the solution is not the programs and schemes which help them. To solve the hegemony of suppression and rescue Dalits from the yoke of depression, the way and legacy of B.R. Ambedkar should be pursued. Dalits as Panchamas caste were given the duties of barbering, washing, carpentry, blacksmith, and so on. They were forced to work in the fields of others. In big industries they were exploited and were not paid equally. The exploitation was in both forms mentally and physically. Unfortunately, in many states, burning, raping, land acquisition, trampling their rights by bully persons, physical torture is increasing. Muslim Dalit women are known as Pasmanda (useless or valueless) in social inclusion.

At the international level there is Carta Megna under the charter of United Nations for Human Rights Commission. At the national level in India, there is Human Rights Commission in India and in state level human rights exists to grant justice for Scheduled Caste and Scheduled Tribes. Besides, the laws, Acts and legal framework to protect the rights of schedule castes and schedule tribes still Dalits in India are feeling a disgraceful life. They have cultural problems and a majority of Dalits could not leave the unwanted religious system which was forcibly was written in their documents. Educational and political power should be with Dalits to appoint their future and live the life with honour equally with other citizens.

NOTES

1. Crenshaw, Kimberle' Williams (1989). "Demarginalizing the Intersection of Race and Sex: A Black Feminist Critique of Antidiscrimination Doctrine, Feminist Theory and Antiracist Politics." *University of Chicago Legal Forum* 1989: 139-67, p. 149.
2. Cole, E.R. (2009). "Intersectionality and Research in Psychology", *American Psychologist*, 64(3): 170.
3. Equality and Human Rights Commission (2017). "Measurement Framework for Equality and Human Rights", Measurement Framework for Equality and Human Rights | Equality and Human Rights Commission (equalityhumanrights.com), p. 52.
4. Research Centre, *AWIS*, available at https://awis.org/intersectionality/, reteievred on 20 November 2023.
5. Gurdas Ram Aalam and Chaman Lal (June, 1998). Dr. Ambedkar, Sahitya Akademi , *Indian Literature*, Vol. 42, No. 3 (185) (May-), pp. 19-20, retrieved from ttps://www.jstor.org/stable/23338458
6. M.J. Audi, (September 1989). "Ambedkar's Struggle For Untouchables: Reflections", *The Indian Journal of Political Science*, *50*(3): 307-20, retiereved from https://www.jstor.org/stable/41855436
7. *Ibid.*, p. 8.
8. Ambedkar, Interview on BBC Radio, New Delhi, 31 December 1955. See: roundtableindia.co. in/index.php?option =com_content

&view= article&id=3797:dr-ambedkar-remembers-the-poona-pact-in-an-interview on-the-bbc-&ca tid= l 16:dr-ambedkar&Itemid=128 (accessed on 13 May 2013).

9. Aakash Singh (December 2014). "Gandhi and Ambedkar: Irreconcilable Differences?", Springer, *International Journal of Hindu Studies, 18*(3): 413-49, retrieved from https://www.jstor.org/stable/24713655
10. Shailender Kumar Tiwari, (June, 2009). "Social Justice: Gandhi and Ambedkar", *The Indian Journal of Political Science,* 70(2): 429-39, reterived from https://www.jstor.org/stable/42743907
11. *Ibid.*, p. 436.
12. Kavita B.K. (2016). *Writing Lives: Dialectics of Pathos and Protest in Dalit Women's Poetry*, (Thesis of Doctorate, Department of English Language and Literature), University of Kerala Thiruvananthapuram
13. Department of Social Justice and Empowerment in Ministry of Social Justice and Empowerment, Government of India, Annual Reports 2022-23, available at www.socialjustice.nic.in, pp. 8-12.
14. *Swathi Satish* (29 September 2023). Clear IAS, retierved from https://www.clearias.com/social-justice /#:~:text=Social%20justice%20in%20India,-The%20problem%20of&text=This%20ensures%20that%20the %20 absence,wealth%2C%20pay%2C%20and%20property.
15. Ministry of Social Justice and Empowerment, GOI. Reterievd on August. https://socialjustice.gov.in/scheme-cat
16. Joan Acker (2012). "Gendered Organizations and Intersectionality: Problems and Possibilities, University of Oregon, Eugene, Oregon, USA", *Equality, Diversity and Inclusion: An International Journal,* 31(3): 214-24. DOI 10.1108/02610151211209072.

REFERENCES

Aalam, Gurdas Ram and Chaman Lal (June, 1998). "Dr. Ambedkar, Sahitya Akademi", *Indian Literature,*Vol. 42, No. 3 (185) (May-), pp. 19-20, retrieved from ttps:// www.jstor.org/stable/23338458

Ambedkar, interview on BBC Radio, New Delhi, 31 December 1955. See: roundtableindia.co.in/index.php?option=com_content&view=article&id=3797:dr-ambedkar-remembers-the-poona-pact-in-an-interview on-the-bbc-&ca tid=116:dr-ambedkar&Itemid=128 (accessed on 13 May 2013).

Audi, M.J. (September 1989). "Ambedkar's Struggle for Untouchables: Reflections", *The Indian Journal of Political Science*, 50(3): 307-20, retiereved from https:// www.jstor.org/stable/41855436

Cole, E.R. (2009). "Intersectionality and Research in Psychology'. *American Psychologist*, 64(3).

Crenshaw, *et al.* (2013). "Toward a Field of Intersectionality Studies: Theory, Applications and Praxis", *Journal of Empowering Theory, 38*(4). University of Chicago Press.

Crenshaw, Kimberle' Williams (1989). "Demarginalizing the Intersection of Race and Sex: A Black Feminist Critique of Antidiscrimination Doctrine, Feminist Theory and Antiracist Politics", *University of Chicago Legal Forum* 1989.

Department of Social Justice and Empowerment in Ministry of Social Justice and Empowerment, Government of India, Annual Reports 2022-23, available at www.socialjustice.nic.in, pp. 8-12

Equality and Human Rights Commission (2017). "Measurement Framework for Equality and Human rights", *Measurement Framework for Equality and Human Rights | Equality and Human Rights Commission* (equalityhumanrights.com)

https://socialjustice.gov.in/scheme-cat

Jha, Ankita (2022). "Intersectionality in the Indian Society", *Jus Corpus Law Journal*, ISSN 2582-7820, Xavier University, Kolkata, India.

Joan, Acker (2012). "Gendered organizations and Intersectionality: Problems and Possibilities, University of Oregon, Eugene, Oregon, USA", *Equality, Diversity and Inclusion: An International Journal, 31*(3): 214-24. DOI 10.1108/02610151211209072.

Kavita, B.K. (2016). "Writing Lives: Dialectics of Pathos and Protest in Dalit Women's Poetry", (Thesis of Doctorate, Department of English Language and Literature), University of Kerala, Thiruvananthapuram.

Research Center, *AWIS*, available at https://awis.org/intersectionality/, (reteievred on 20 November 2023).

Singh, Aakash (December 2014). "Gandhi and Ambedkar: Irreconcilable Differences?", *Springer, International Journal of Hindu Studies* , 18(3). retrieved from https://www.jstor.org/stable/24713655

Swathi Satish (29 September 2023). ClearIAS, retierved from https://www.clearias.com/social-justice/#:~:text=Social%20justice%20in%20India,-The%20problem%20of&text= This%20 ensures % 2 0that%20the %20 absence, wealth%2C%20pay%2C%20and%20property.

Tiwari, Shailender Kumar (June 2009). "Social Justice: Gandhi and Ambedkar", *The Indian Journal of Political Science,* 70(2): 429-39, reterived from https:// www.jstor.org/stable/42743907

8

Why is Closing Gender Gap Remains Vast in India?

K. Annapuranam

Introduction

Every year we celebrate International Women's Day on 8 March. It was formally declared by the United Nations in 1977. This celebration is an indicator of women's achievements, equal rights and justice. It also recognizes utmost need of alleviating gender based discrimination, gender bias, and gender-based violence, but issues are not uniform worldwide as it's attributed to indigenous culture.[1] Moreover, several studies widely acknowledged the predominant practice of gender has negative implications on the lives of women and family.[2,3] Nevertheless, the effort of social movements and affirmative action of the state liberates women from social evils, and ensures equality with respect to socio-economic and political freedom. This may make us feel proud of its achievements, and their substantial progress in the field of education, employment, and polity. This has changed the views of scholars as women have enough influence and opportunity so that any observable unequal social position reduced to individuals, not to social structure.[4]

Yet, the efforts are severely lagging in addressing the core issues of women and its punitive consequences in developing countries because substantial proportion of them one or the other way relegated to an inferior social status and marginalized[5].

Gender Marginality

Marginality is mainly observed in the process of development, where women are pushed to the edge of the group or community due to rigid gender norms, unequal distribution of resources and poor representation in the decision making process. This situation continues over a period, and excludes equality and gender justice. As a result, women left with lack of opportunity, poor health status, out of the labour force, poverty, and deprived of minimum standard of living. This adverse condition is pervasive in many developing countries. A wide range of literature found the link between gender, poverty, and poor health,[6,7] but a few made an attempt focusing on women's agency and their achievements on the path of sustainable development. This is a pressing challenge in achieving social development goals.

Asia is the most populous continent, housing more than four billion population in 2024, with India accounting 1.44 billion and China 1.38 billion.[8] In this region, gender imbalance has a long history of higher proportion of males than that of females in the world[7]. One of the reasons is the implication of policy, i.e. one child norm in China and two child norms in India. As a result, the rapid fertility declined. In the areas of less gender equity, it was found that higher decision making on school education, financial contribution, and labour force participation was positively associated with the desire for no more children. A high score on mobility index, ideal family size, wife beating if not justified, and spousal communication, were contributing factors for less preference to have more children and remain subject to the context.[9]

In India, although fertility declines, the culture of son preference still lowers the value of female children in many parts of the country. The sex selective abortion is a common practice until a male child born and is noted as "missing women" by Amartya Sen. Sex imbalance in birth not only distort the demographic trend, but also has an adverse effect on spheres of life, e.g. finding a potential life partner in the marriage market. The ideal situation of demand while scarcity is always valued it is in reverse for instance dowry has been developed as voluntary marriage gift even it is legally banned practice. It reflects the cultural bias of marriage market neglect the value of women. This is also one of the reasons for an insinuation of missing women was 101 million for the world as a whole. It was worse in China, as the figure shows 44 million, which was higher as compared to India indicates 37 million. The recent changes in sex ratio draw attention to girls are outnumbered in some places. The sex ratio is 106.3 males per 100 females in China while inverse with 94.3 males per 100 females in India, in 2015. The scenario is not uniform across states even it shows similar trends in economic growth. The girls are outnumbered in the State of Kerala, while Tamil Nadu shows the low sex ratio, i.e. 995 females per 1,000 males in 2011, within which 16 out of 32 districts females are outnumbered than the males. This difference puzzle when religious background, education, income and economic growth of the state do not explain so it may be more to do with their behaviour and culture.[10]

Gendered Social Status

The practice of taking decisions adhered to in one's own culture signifies women's autonomy because the influence of men makes women to be inferior in the process of decision making. The decision on family affairs remains patriarchal despite increasing educational attainment of male and female in 2011 is 82.14 per cent and 65.46 per cent respectively.[11] Similarly, decisions on health care, major household purchases, and visiting relatives/wife's family are influenced by male because of women's poor access to resources. The states of Karnataka and Jharkhand show more than 60 per cent of women able to access money and can decide how to use, but much lower in other regions of the country.[12] Even if women able to access money and power through their occupational position they lag behind in taking decisions within the ambit of their duties and responsibilities. A marginal representation of women in central government employment such as Indian Administrative Service: 17 per cent, Indian Foreign Service: 8 per cent, and Indian Forest Service: 4 per cent,[13] and it shows an outcome of the policy reservation appreciated. On the other hand, the decision-makers among those in the services were only 14 per cent, 18 per cent and 28 per cent respectively[14] that clearly indicate male hegemony.

The idea of male hegemony legitimates the privilege of men over women and also men who have inferior traits of maleness. As it maintains gender order, and often interwoven with other identities of women causes inequality[15] in spite of the United Nations Human Rights Council and constitution enshrines equal rights for every citizen. The plight of gender disparity is required to be close to 34 per cent in South Asia (2nd lowest region in the world), which is far behind Western Europe: 24 per cent. Within which countries Sri Lanka and Bangladesh are top ranked in comparison to most populous countries in closing the gender gap. Yet, the differences in the sub-index reveal paradoxes within the country. India shows steady progress in closing gender gap in educational attainment, and political participation, but inverse in the labour market (7th lowest country in bridging gender gap), and health (3rd lowest country in bridging gender gap).[16]

Of course, the level of educational attainment shows impressive, but no returns as expected. A nuanced understanding of the scholar indicates that except the basic and middle-level education, has a significant effect on female workforce participation[17] and has a positive effect on family income. Studies say that focusing merely on expansion of school attainment does not guarantee improved economic conditions as it requires skills.[18] This drives emergence of an institutional mechanism for skill development and entrepreneurship in 2015, and its achievement viewed as sustainable employability in the labour market.[19] But, women's participation in the labour market is much lower (32 per cent for female and

85 per cent for male in 2007-08) than that of men and also declined over a period (from 34.1 per cent in 1999-2000 to 27.2 per cent in 2011-12).[20, 21] Consequently, the increase of income and wealth disparity is much higher between male and female even within the same social group.[22]

Outcome of Gender Gap

Poverty rates between men and women are calculated for 89 developing countries, worldwide 104 women living in poor households for every 100 men. Such a difference is statistically significant for South Asia—109 women live in poor households per 100 men. More specifically, the gender disparity with respect to early marriage/widowhood (15-17 age group) and divorced/separated women (18-49 age group) are extremely vulnerable to poverty.[23] Although, the faster reduction of global poverty from 36 per cent in 1990s to 10 per cent in 2015 who lived on less than $1.90 a day. Their proportion is higher in Sub-Saharan Africa (41.1%) and South Asia (16.2%). However, the largest number of them live in the following countries—77.1 per cent of them in Congo in 2012, 53.5 per cent in Nigeria in 2009, 21.2 per cent in India in 2011 and 14 per cent in Bangladesh in 2015.[24] It clearly indicates a substantial proportion of them lack capability to meet their basic needs. If one is not capable of meeting basic needs becoming sick and low productivity.[25] This resulted in increasing inter-group disparity between SCs/STs and other categories in terms of consumption expenditure, the intake of food comes down, in particular, women from Scheduled Castes, Scheduled Tribes, and Muslims, are more malnourished, and anaemic,[26, 27, 28] which has dramatic health effect on physical and cognitive development. The weak body and vitamin deficiency increases the risk of anaemia, affected 1.62 billion people globally, and its prevalence is highest in Africa and South-East Asia in 1993-2005.[29] In India, 53 per cent of women aged between 15-49 years are anaemic while 22.7 per cent found in men in 2015-16. The severity of anaemia is increasing their susceptibility to illness and risk of maternal and child mortality.[30]

It cannot be denied the decline of maternal mortality from 341 in 2000 to 216 in 2015 globally. At country level, Nigeria (19%) and India (15%) are estimated to account for over one-third of all maternal deaths worldwide.[31, 32] On the other hand, non-communicable diseases cause more deaths (mainly cardiovascular diseases, cancer, chronic respiratory diseases and diabetes) and act as key barriers to poverty alleviation and sustainable development. It is projected to increase from 38 million in 2012 to 52 million by 2030, within which 42 per cent of all NCD deaths occurred before the age of 70 years, especially many in developing countries.[33] This would increase inequality between countries as well as affecting men and women invariably. It accounted for two in every three deaths among women each year. Women neglect NCDs as it is defined through reproductive capacity, treated as diseases of men and high income groups. It is estimated at least 25 per cent of premature deaths can be reduced by 2025 if the policies mitigate risk factors such as unhealthy diet and physical inactivity.[34,35]

Closing Gender Gap

The existing institutional mechanisms are unable to deal sternly with gender inequality in the private sphere and the public sphere. The increasing women's vulnerability to health risks, inadequate quality health care services and decreasing productivity are major challenges in achieving sustainable goals by 2030 (alleviation of poverty, good health and well-being, reducing inequalities and promoting gender equality). As it requires an integrated approach to accelerate the process of achieving gender equality, international organizations have extended its support in framing policies, plans, and programmes to many developing nations.[36] The developing countries have made several initiatives to achieve the set goals through various welfare schemes and rehabilitation programmes.

In India, the present government is committed in promoting gender equality for instance Supreme Court declared triple *talaq* is void and unconstitutional while various welfare schemes such as Beti Bachao Beti Padhao to improve the child sex ratio (0-6 years of age) and ensures girl child education. Women specific scheme, i.e. one stop centre was introduced in 2015. It provides an integrated service to distress women through various stakeholders and support agencies. Their work is already underway in rescue and rehabilitates women victim of various atrocities, women who live in difficult circumstances, destitute women, and homeless women across the states with the support of central government.[37] Moreover, States are pioneered in cultivating the savings habit of women and promoting small scale enterprise through SHGs, in which women are from low income group, and a majority constitutes from lower caste groups. More specifically, SHGs, central for the state of Tamil Nadu, have made an effort in creating awareness about health and hygiene (STD/HIV), which in turn, it mitigates, the issue of subjugation of sexuality. Women are also entitled to avail maternity loans from banks through SHGs, and also empowering them by way of giving sustainable employment opportunity at Amma Unavagam—a low cost canteen run by Government of Tamil Nadu from 2013.[38,39]

Way Forward

The convergence model is successful in addressing the issues of women; at times lacks in its coordination between line agencies discern its outcome. Even then, lived experiences of women determine the nature of the schemes that vary according to their needs and context. However, gender equality remains trance unless adopt a unique approach in the process of inclusive development.

NOTES

1. Sylvia Walby (2011). *The Future of Feminism.* Polity, Cambridge.
2. P. Butler Judith (1990). *Gender Trouble: Feminism and the Subversion of Identity.* Routledge, New York.
3. Michel Kimmel (2004). *The Gendered Society.* Oxford, New York.
4. Deborah Frances-White (2018). *The Guilty Feminist: From Out Noble Goals to Out Worst Hypocrisies.* Great Britain, Virago Press.
5. Anwar Alam (2011). *Impact of Gender Discrimination on Gender Development and Poverty Alleviation.* https://www.aup.edu.pk/sj_

pdf/27-IMPACT%20OF%20 GENDER % 20DISCRIMINATION %20ON%20 GENDER.pdf (accessed on 20 November 2018).

6. Deepa Narayan, Pritchett Lant, and Kapoor Soumya (2009). *Moving out of Poverty, Success from the Bottom Up,* Vol. 2. Palgrave Macmillan and the World Bank, Washington.
7. Richard. G. Wilkinson (2005). *The Impact of Inequality*. Routledge, London.
8. World Population Review (2024). https://worldpopulationreview.com/country-rankings/countries-in-asia (accessed on 20 February 2025).
9. U.D. Upadhyay, J.D. Gipson, M. Withers, S. Lewis, E.J. Ciaraldi, A. Fraser and N. Prata (2014). "Women's Empowerment and Fertility: A Review of the Literature." *Social Science & Medicine, 115*: 111-20.
10. Ravinder Kaur (2013). "Mapping the Adverse Consequences of Sex Selection and Gender Imbalance in India and China", *Economic & Political Weekly, 48*(35): 37-44.
11. Soni, S. (2020). "Institution of Dowry in India: A Theoretical Inquiry". *Societies Without Borders, 14*(1): 10.
12. Amartya Sen (2006). *Inequality Re-examined.* Oxford University Press, New York, pp. 109-10.
13. Women and Men in India (2017). *Participation in Decision-Making.* http://www.mospi. gov.in/ publication/women-and-men-india-2017. (accessed on 10 January 2019).
14. Census of India (2011). *Provisional Population Totals India Paper 1.* http://www. Census india.gov. in/2011-prov-results/prov_results_ paperl _india.html (accessed on 10 January 2018).
15. Radha Kumar, Korff Marcel and Sudhir Karthika (2018). *A Gender Atlas of India with Score Card,* Sage Publication, New Delhi.
16. R.W. Connell and J.W. Messerschmidt (2005). "Hegemonic Masculinity: Rethinking the Concept", *Gender & Society, 19*(6): 829-59.
17. The Global Gender Gap Report (2018). *World Economic Forum.* Switzerland. http://reports. weforum.org/global-gender-gap-report-2018/ (accessed on 10 January 2019).
18. Muhanunad Zahir Faridi, Shalmawaz Malik and A.B. Basit (2009). "Impact of Education on Female Labour Force Participation in Pakistan: Empirical Evidence from Primary Data Analysis". *Pakistan Journal of Social Sciences, 29*(1): 127-40.
19. Government of India (2019). *National Skill Development Mission.* https://www. msde.gov.in/nationalskillmission.html (accessed on 25 February 2019).

20. E.A. Hanushek (2013). "Economic Growth in Developing Countries: The Role of Human Capital", *Economics of Education Review, 37*: 204-12.
21. Surjit S. Bhalla and Ravinder Kaur (2018). "Labour Force Participation of Women in India: Some Facts, Some Queries, Asia Research Centre, *Working Paper 40*. http://www.lse.ac.uk/ asia research centre/_ files/ arcwp40-bhallakaur.pdf (accessed on 10 January 2019)
22. S. Verick (2014). "Women's Labour Force Participation in India: Why is it so Low?", *International Labor Organization*.
23. Sunny Jose (2011). "Adult Nutrition in India: Is There a Huge Gender Gap?", *Economic and Political Weekly, XLVI*(29): 95-102.
24. M. Roser & E. Ortiz-Ospina (2017). *Global Extreme Poverty: Our World in data*. https://ourworld indata.org/extreme-poverty (accessed on 12 January 2019).
25. A.M.M. Boudet, P. Buitrago, B.L. de la Briere, D. Newhouse, E.R. Matulevich, K. Scott and P. Suarez-Becerra (2018). *Gender Differences in Poverty and Household Composition Through the Life-cycle: A Global Perspective*. The World Bank.
26. Amartya Sen (2003). "Missing Women—Revisited: Reduction in Female Mortality has been Counter Balanced by Sex Selective Abortions", *British Medical Journal, 327*(7427): 1297-98.
27. Ashwini Deshpande (2000). "Does Caste Still Define Disparity?: A Look at Inequality in Kerala, India", *The American Economic Review, 90*(2): 322-25.
28. Vani K. Borooah, Nidhi, S. Sadana and Thorat Sukhadeo (2012). "Gender and Caste-Based Inequality in Health Outcomes in India". *Working Paper Series,* Vol. VI, No. 3, Indian Institute of Dalit Studies, New Delhi.
29. N.S. Sabharwal (2011). "Caste, Religion and Malnutrition Linkages", *Economic & Political Weekly, 50*:16-18.
30. B. De Benoist, M. Cogswell, I. Egli and E. McLean (2008). *Worldwide Prevalence of Anaemia 1993-2005*; WHO Global Database of Anaemia.
31. International Institute for Population Sciences and ICF (2017). *National Family Health Survey (NFHS-4), 2015-16*, India.
32. WHO & UNICEF (2015). *Trends in Maternal Mortality: 1990-2015: Estimates from WHO, UNICEF, UNFPA*, World Bank Group and the United Nations Population Division.
33. UNICEF (2017). *Maternal Mortality*. https ://data.unicef org/topic/ nmater nal-health/maternalmortality/ (accessed on 3 February 2019).

34. WHO (2014). *Global Status Report on Noncommunicable Diseases 2014* (No. WHO/NMH/NVI/15.1).
35. WHO (2019). *NCD and Women.* https://www.who.int/global-co-ordination-mechanism/ncdthemes/NCD-and-women/en/(accessed on 23 February 2019).
36. United Nations (2018). *The Sustainable Development Goals Report 2018.* New York.
37. Ministry of Women and Child Development (2019). *Women Empowerment Schemes.* http://www. wcd.nic.in/schemes-listing /2405. (accessed on 23 February 2019).
38. Arnma Unavagam (2019). http://webcache.googleusercontent.com /search? q=cache: s-GhRPzBgAsJ:123.63.242.116/tambaram/Newsletter%2520final.pdf+&cd=l 3&hl=en&ct=clnk&gl=in.(accessed on 24 February 2019).
39. A.R. Nithya, M. Bagyalakshrni and R. Karthick (2018). "Linchpins for Sustainability and Scalability of Hotel Industry: Arnma Unavagam An Empirical Research", *Surnedha Journal of Management, 7*(2): 160-70.

9

Sustainable Digital Development and Dismantling Gender Oppression

A Case Study of District Fatehgarh Sahib, Punjab

Diksha Makkar and *Konica Jai Singh*

Introduction

Since olden times, women have been the face of discrimination. Gender inequity has always been a major concern for society. Inequity in any form is harmful and may lead to many consequences including material, socio-psychological, or health-related. The architect of social justice, Dr B.R. Ambedkar was one of the revolutionaries who stood out against socio-economically deprived women to establish solid foundations of society.

In Mexico, 34 per cent of women face sexual violence in the public sphere (UNDP Programme, 2023). According to the Global Gender Gap Index 2023, India ranks 127th out of 147 countries (World Economic Forum, 2023). This shows that pervasive gaps pose a significant barrier to the evaluation of progress in women's lives. Empowerment is a multi-faceted, multi-dimensional, and multi-layered concept. A large proportion of women in India are inadvertently left behind due to digital illiteracy. Ensuring gender justice and empowering women at the forefront of national development is also an important factor in the nation's development. Women are regarded as the foundation of every culture since they can do multiple duties with ease each day. Awareness among women in the families is counted as an elixir for future generations. If our civilization is to survive the technological onslaught of algorithms and artificial intelligence, then every person should be aware of the pros and cons of digital tools. Each of the 17 Sustainable Development Goals (SDGs) depends on achieving gender equality and women's empowerment.

Mehar Baba Charitable Trust, Bassi Pathana, Punjab, India was selected by the Canada Fund for Local Initiatives (CFLI—a High Commission of Canada in India) for the project "Empower Rural Women through Digital Marketing Skills" in Rural Punjab. The project aimed at increasing women artisans' economic empowerment by educating local artisans, small business owners, and individuals on digital tools in Rural Punjab. This project covered 100+ village clusters in the district of Fatehgarh Sahib. So, this study enroutes the road to development to reduce the gender gap and burst myths related to women being at the forefront.

The ancient myths still frighten us not just in the form of nymphs and shepherds but also in many widely held beliefs about how the human experience takes place. The urgent priority is to close the gender gap in the digital sphere and unlock women's potential for emancipation in the twenty-first century. Figure 9.1 depicts the core elements involved in bursting the myths to promote gender equity. There are three elements or parameters on which the chapter is analysed: Gender Discrimination, Digital Literacy, and Access to Capital. It might be challenging to identify the parts of myths that are false because most myths have some elements of reality. Women are expected to be underqualified to thrive in traditionally masculine roles, which is encouraged by gender stereotypes that depict how men and women are different. Gender discrimination occurs when women are treated unfavourably because of their sex which leads to gender prejudice.

Theoretical Framework: Unleashing the Power of Women

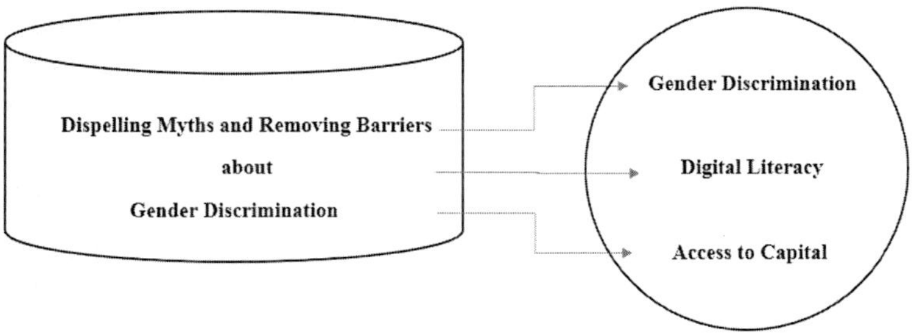

Source: Authors' Compilation.

Fig. 9.1: Model for Dispelling Myths and Removing Barriers for Gender Discrimination

A sizeable portion of the population is still on the wrong side of the digital divide and cannot fully benefit from the revolutionary changes that are occurring. Adaptive administration of resources and their management in the overcrowded world can be possible through sustainability only. Women discrimination is a recurring nightmare as they are the most vulnerable section in terms of access to opportunities, financial freedom, gender equity, and literacy levels especially in the remote areas of the country.

Dr. Ambedkar emphasizes the need to inculcate the spirit of self-help among men and women. Sustainability as the dominant ideology of the time is advocated by a growing number of corporations, civic organizations, political parties, governments, educational institutions and citizens due to its global reach. Digital sustainability is the only solution for the rapid development and enhancement of women's livelihood in present times. Women's empowerment is a vital instrument to expand women's ability to have resources and to make strategic life choices. The Constitution of India expressly reflects Ambedkar's perspective on women. Since, women are essential to human progress, successive governments have introduced a variety of programmes to empower women in societies where men predominate. Start-up India, Self-

Employment Loan Schemes, Support for Women's Education and Employment Programmes, E-commerce, Rural India and Women Entrepreneurship Platform (WEP) are different schemes and provisions to foster women empowerment in India. A plan for progress that is sustainable and leaves no one behind is found in the 2030 Agenda for Sustainable Development and its seventeen Sustainable Development Goals (SDGs), which were accepted by world leaders in 2015. Achieving gender equity and empowering women is an integral part of each of the seventeen goals.

Catalyst: Piecing together the lives: According to Digital Marketing Statistics, the digital marketing and advertising industry in India is currently growing at an annual rate of 25-30 per cent. At once, digital marketing was untapped. But today, it has become an integral part of what the market can be for its customers. However, there is a huge gap in access to resources between urban and rural populations, creating an urban-poor divide. As the internet becomes intertwined with everything we do, the importance of digital marketing becomes crystal clear for a variety of reasons: Efficiency, economy and effectiveness (3Es), hyper-personalization, boosting connectivity, simplification of e-platforms and development of citizencentric framework.

Statement of the Problem

This chapter attempts to find solutions to problems faced in day-to-day lives of women. These problems are related to social issues—psychological, economic, and physical. There are many myths that women must be confined to traditional roles of homemaking rather than entrepreneurial activities. About 56 per cent were homemakers in rural groups due to family responsibility of taking care of small children and, the elderly and due to household work in district Fatehgarh Sahib (Manpreet Kaur, 2023). Women also fall behind in access to adequate resources due to a lack of awareness and a stubborn set of beliefs. This chapter identifies gender disparity to achieve sustainable digital development concerning women and explores the impact in rural areas of district Fatehgarh Sahib.

Objectives of the Study

This chapter attempted to analyse the status of women's empowerment in District Fatehgarh Sahib, Punjab and evaluates the impact. This chapter aims:

- To assess the employment and income generation opportunities concerning rural women.
- To reduce the challenges faced by women which were creating rocks in terms of becoming self-reliant and self-sufficient.
- To explore the growing impact of digital platforms and enable women entrepreneurs to stand on their own feet.
- To develop an inclusive citizen-centric framework with enhanced use of Information and Communication Technology (ICT).
- To encourage rural women to be financially independent and be a part of the decision making process.
- To assess the variations in socio-economic opportunities for women in rural areas of district Fatehgarh Sahib.

Locale of the Study

A city and important Sikhism pilgrimage location, Fatehgarh Sahib is located in Punjab, a state in north-west India. The district's economy is largely dependent on agriculture, industry, and related sectors. Fatehgarh Sahib has earned a noteworthy place in history. The study has covered 105 village clusters in the district Fatehgarh Sahib of north-east and south-west regions and impacted over 1,000+ rural women and men artisans/small business entrepreneurs, etc.

Research Methodology and Sampling

For the entire study, participatory research was used which includes research designs, methods, and frameworks that use systematic inquiry in direct collaboration with those affected by an issue being studied for the action or change. The stakeholders were involved in the entire process from mobilization to evaluation. Mixed method research approach was used. Qualitative Data Analysis included one-to-one interaction, discussions, observations, focus group studies, research studies, field visits, interviews, case studies, record keeping, decoding data, ethnographic research, documentation, and interpretations. Quantitative Data Analysis was done through questionnaires by techniques of data collection and data processing for cross-sectional study. The focus was to know the "What and Why" of the social phenomenon. Handholding as a follow-up evaluation technique was undertaken to trace the impact brought during the training. The data was analysed through a simple percentage method using Excel. Transparency and ethical concerns were kept in mind while dealing with the people of rural areas to ensure that the values of social work were upheld.

Sampling

This study examined sustainable digital development, gender equity, and access to capital in rural areas of district Fatehgarh Sahib. The sample size of this study was taken as 1,195 (1,111 women; 84 men) respondents both from north-west and south-east regions and the training of trainers (TOTs) strategy was built a pool of competent instructors. 18 TOTs (14 women + 4 men) from the north-west and 13 TOTs (12 women + 1 man) from the south-east trained other people using a participatory learning approach. The trainers were also evaluated in this study.

Data Interpretation and Analysis

The analysis is done based on three parameters taken as a model for this chapter:

Gender Discrimination

(i) *Reduced Gender Gap:* The road to development cannot be travelled without women and men walking together. 86 per cent of participants feel that women have equal opportunities concerning business. Rural women are acting as change agents to mobilize the community and lead from the front.

(ii) *Breaking Stereotypes among Rural Women*: TOT allowed the women leaders from community members to take training initiatives. This motivated other rural women to visualize themselves in better roles as community leaders. 83 per cent of women strongly believed that training would get them more work opportunities.

Digital Literacy

(i) *Enhanced Use of Digital Tools*: 61 per cent of participants are more aware of the digital tools which can help to strengthen business online. Ninety-three per cent of people feel more confident after the usage of digital tools.

(ii) *Entrepreneurship among Rural Women:* Today's women seek gender equality and justice at home and workplace because they recognize their value in every aspect. Seventy-nine per cent of women think that they are no longer confined to the four walls of the house.

Access to Capital

(i) *Awareness about Government Schemes:* The government introduces the schemes for the marginalized sections and the irony is that they fail to reach the beneficiaries due to a lack of awareness. Websites for government employment openings have also been made available to young people since India currently benefits from a demographic dividend that should be fully utilized to propel the country forward. Fifty-seven per cent of trainees were aware of government initiatives.

(ii) *E-Participation at Grassroots level:* Consensus-oriented, accountable, transparent, responsible, equitable and inclusive, effective and efficient, rule of law, and participatory are the eight pillars of good governance as described by the UN. Eighty-six per cent of respondents are involved in using e-initiatives by the government.

Miscellaneous

(i) Good Governance is a cornerstone of development—Ninety-six per cent of trainees believed that they have learned about e-governance initiatives and have started getting benefits from e-governance schemes for their personal, familial and community development which is the ultimate goal of their growth.

(ii) Impacted 1,195 (1,111 women; 84 men) from 105 village clusters to grow their businesses on e-commerce platforms of Digital Marketing [Part A: North-west region 620 participants (585 women; 35 men) in 50 village clusters and 575 participants (526 women; 49 men) and Part B: South-east region in 55 village clusters]. 73.73 per cent of trainees understand that digital literacy is a must for achieving a sustainable future (SDG 4). Before training, 79.3 per cent of respondents think that the Internet will open up more opportunities for women (SDG 5). Forty-five per cent of trainees were aware of digital strategies for business growth, highlighting the need to inform people about digital strategies to support their business, and before training, 75.3 per cent of trainees were willing to learn more about e-government initiatives (SDG 8). And 74.4 per cent agreed that women and men have equal opportunities when it comes to entrepreneurship, which is a positive sign for achieving Sustainable Goal 10. The 77.3 per cent strongly believed that digital literacy would help women in self-employment (SDG 12). Five hundred twenty-six participants out of a total of 575 think their lives have changed after the digital empowerment training. Seventy-six per cent believed that doing business online is important in this digital age. Eighty-two per cent of trainees agreed that it is important to commercialize the product for better sales.

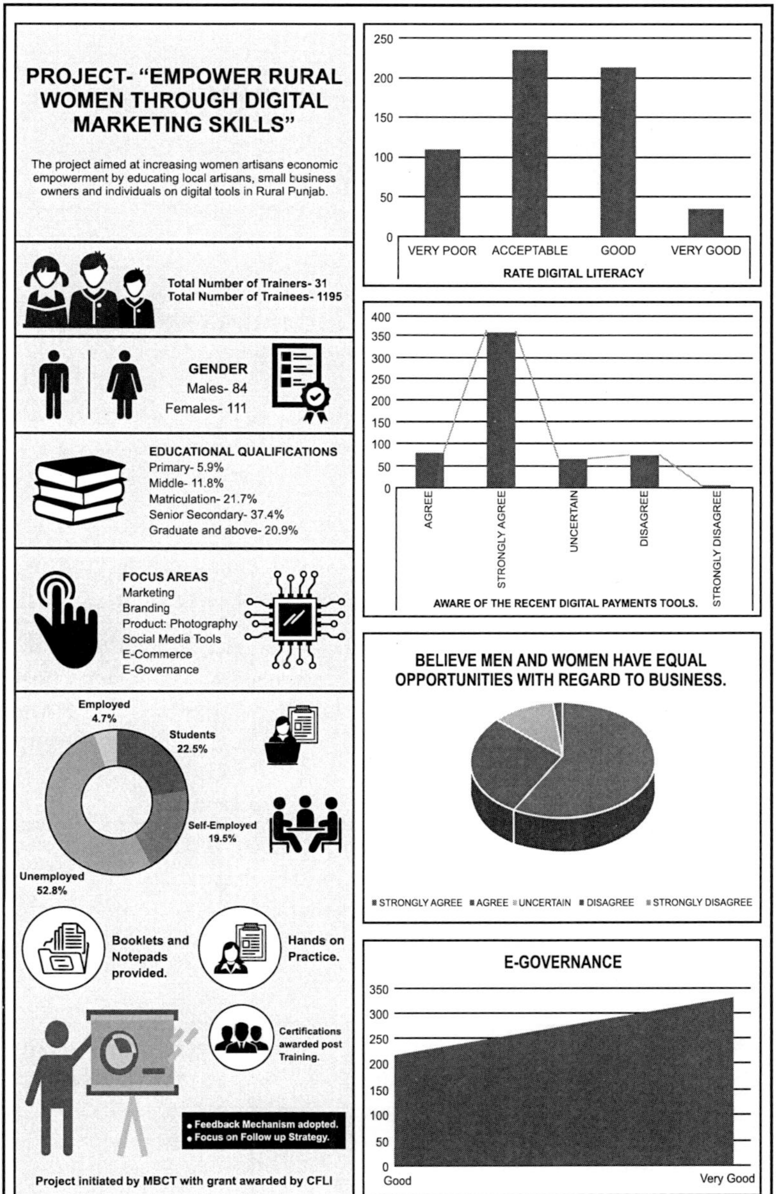

Source: Authors' Compilation.

Fig. 9.2: Infographics of Digital Literacy and Gender Oppression (based on primary data)

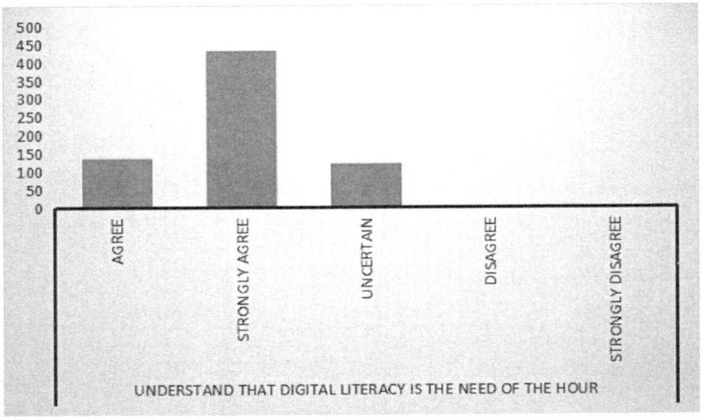

Source: Authors' Compilation.

Fig. 9.3: Digital Literacy is the Need of the Hour

Results and Findings

Parameters	Myths	Bursting Out Myths (Findings)
Gender Discrimination	Women's professional performance is adversely impacted by motherhood.	Regarding the gender gap in society, 445 trainees believed that digital literacy would help self-employed women.
Digital Literacy	Women excel at soft skills more than they do in technical ones.	Due to weak financial standing, women get fewer opportunities but are capable enough to handle both soft and technical skills.
Access to Capital	Younger people (males) are the ones with a future in technology.	Nogawan Village Group: Older women were more enthusiastic to break the shackles of patriarchy and learn more about digital expansion and networking.

Harnessing Mahila Shakti

The grim scenario of women having no voice in their own houses has undergone a major transformation during this project. The 57.8 per cent of women have been playing a major role in household decision making. Around the world, women prepare up to 90 per cent of the meals, but when circumstances are hard, women and girls may be the first to cut back on their food intake. Households headed by women may not eat enough simply because women earn at lower levels, and are less prepared to cope with crisis. Marginalized sections have a relatively inadequate ability to manage technology as a strategic weapon as they have weak financial standing.

Women of village Narsing Pura (Khroda) used to rush back to their homes around noon to prepare lunch but the timing of the session is till 12.30 p.m. Another woman had a degree in Fashion Diploma but was staying home instead of utilizing her skills for the benefit of her family. Women are socially and culturally bound and are expected to behave in a certain way. It is rightly said that women are strongest when they cheer each other. This was well highlighted when mother-in-law(s) sent their daughter-in-law(s) and even joined them during the training. The sales were increased from small digital practices such as adding pictures of the products, adding voice with the products and listing as sellers on e-commerce websites. These were encouraging signs on which further work could be built.

Challenges/Barriers

Due to digital illiteracy the gap between rural and urban areas has expanded rather than contracted. In our system, most of the information is available in the English language creating a barrier for "Diverse Rural India".

1. *Poor Internet Access and Unavailability of Smartphones in Rural Areas:* As an attempt to bridge this gap, trainers facilitated the beneficiaries with hotspots, and internet data packs with good connectivity for practice and learning. The

trainees who owned smartphones shared with the ones who did not possess them.

2. *Limited Resources and Opportunities:* There were space availability issues for accommodating trainees in some of the villages but with strong communications and meetings with the village communities, a few village members facilitated spaces in their homes for conducting the training. Infrastructural requirements were insufficient. All government forms and identification documents are to be made available online as part of Digital India, a government-led programme that was launched in 2015. When rural women cannot connect to the internet, they miss out on services that would improve their livelihood.
3. *Rigid Patterns:* The caste system still prevails in major portions of the rural areas and difficult to break old habit patterns. For this, people belonging to the same caste were clubbed together for smooth functioning. Fear of being a victim of cyber crime and insecurities regarding privacy: healthy discussions and precautionary methods were introduced to establish a climate of trust.

Policy Prescriptions

First, to give rural women a channel through which they can contact the government to claim their entitlements and be given more power through capacity-building and training. Awareness regarding schemes related to skill development and financial inclusion as economic empowerment is central to the overall empowerment of women. Second, with the penetration of the Internet, technology and mobile phones, women's access to employment in rural areas could be leveraged wisely to bring these women closer to the stakeholders in their business ecosystems and bridge the digital divide. The *panchayat* should focus on the regulation of capital, building a resilient digital infrastructure and formation of digital clubs in every village to promote grassroots digital development for democracy and enable them to access a globalized world.

The need of the hour is to introduce soft skill programmes and entrepreneurship development programmes in a time-bound manner to produce greater gender equity and enable globalization for a sustainable world.

To recapitulate the main points, rural people should be encouraged to adapt to the changing world through awareness programmes, highlighting success stories and street-to-street campaigning in the local language for easier dissemination.

Limitations of the Study

During this study, authors came across many limitations. Lack of support from *panchayats* was a major challenge faced and it was dealt with local people consenting to give their personal space for training. There was delay in the registration of participants due to extreme heat from June to August which further caused a delay in the completion of 25+ village clusters training by one month that was covered by speeding up the work from September to November. Timeline Management due to the delay in the registration of participants (Part B of the Project), the team considered decreasing the number of clusters for village training for once but with dedicated efforts, the team was able to achieve the target timely. Lastly, variation in age groups and learning capability—The training module and schedule were tailored according to different age groups and needs of participants. Ice-breaking sessions of basic soft skills were held to build a harmonious environment.

Conclusion

Dr. Ambedkar strongly believed that women's empowerment can be achieved by the welfare of women. Innovation is made possible by technology. Digital marketing training can be the backbone of existing and future high-growth businesses with both foreign and domestic companies investing in the "Make in India" initiative. Digital is the only future because digital cannot only make business more efficient and profitable, but also more agile and smarter, adapting to consumer needs and changing market conditions.

Stepping out, facing a challenge and overcoming fear is victory in itself for the rural people especially women who have been deprived of basic opportunities to work for themselves since ages. With the digital world available in many regional languages, using the English Language is no longer a barrier to use Internet. According to Mnistry of Statistics and Programme Implementation, women constitute 14 per cent of the total number of entrepreneurs in India, and 66 per cent of women remain untapped in rural India.

Even today, Dr. Ambedkar's three-word strategy of "educate, agitate, and organize" is a potent force of social transformation. The findings show that the only way to change is through consciousness, self-awareness, and self-management. The Internet has changed the way we perceive literacy.

> I measure the progress of a community by the degree of progress which women have achieved.—B.R. Ambedkar

Acknowledgements

This work was supported by the Mehar Baba Charitable Trust (MBCT), Bassi Pathana and INUS Global Charity and Canada Fund for Local Initiatives (CFLI)—a High Commission of Canada in India for their contributions to the completion of the project titled "Empower Rural Women through Digital Marketing Skills" in Rural Punjab. The author(s) would like to express special gratitude to Thakur Singh Mejie (trustee of the MBCT), Robin Gupta and Hema Panesar (Managers of the project) and the whole team of MBCT. The authors received financial support for the research by CFLI.

REFERENCES

Amin, S. (2014). *Social Freedom Among Women in Punjab, 5*(6): 745-47.

Azid, T., R.E.A. Khan and A.M.S. Alamasi (2010). "Labor Force Participation of Married Women in Punjab (Pakistan)", *International Journal of Social Economics, 37*(8): 592-612. https://doi. org/1 0.1108/03068291011060643

Cai Li, Naveed Ahmed S.A.Q. (2019). "Impact of Gender-Specific Causes on Women Entrepreneurship: An Opportunity Structure for Entrepreneurial Women in Rural Areas", *Journal of Entrepreneurship & Organization Management, 8*(1).

Dandona, A. (2015). "Empowerment of Women: A Conceptual Framework", *International Journal of Indian Psychology, 2*(3). https://doi.org/ 1 0.25215/0203.044

Dasaria, K. and M.S. Rani (2017). *International Journal of Multidisciplinary Educational Research, 6*(4): 54-69.

Goel, R., S. Sahai, C. Krishnan, G. Singh, C. Bajpai and P. Malik (2017). "An Empirical Study to Enquire the Effectiveness of Digital Marketing in the Challenging Age with Reference to Indian Economy", *Pertanika Journal of Social Sciences and Humanities, 25*(4): 1569-84.

Herman, C. (2003). *Becoming Digital: Empowerment, Identity and Community ICTs*, pp. 237-50. http://oro. open.ac.uk/id/eprint/5638

Jayanthi, M.A. (2023). *A Study on Women Entrepreneurs Challenges in Digital Marketing Technology, 2*(2): 7-12.

Kapila, M., A. Singla and M.L. Gupta (2016). "Impact of Microcredit on Women Empowerment in India: An Empirical Study of Punjab State", *Lecture Notes in Engineering and Computer Science, 2224:* 821-25.

Linda, M. (2000). "Micro-finance and Empowerment of Women: A Review of the Key Issues", In *ILO Social Finance Unit.* http://scholar.google.com/scholar?hl=en&btnG=Search&q=intitle:M icro-finance+and+the+empowerment+of+women+A+review+of+the+key+issues#9

Kaur, M. (2023). "A Study of Women Empowerment in Urban and Rural Area", In Biplab Auddya (ed.) *Research in Multidisciplinary Subjects,* pp. 55-59. The Hill Publication, West Bengal.

Lin, D., X. Li, B. Wang, Y. Hong, X. Fang, X. Qin and B. Stanton (2011). "Discrimination, Perceived Social Inequity, and Mental Health Among Rural-To-Urban Migrants in China", *Community Mental Health Journal, 47*(2): 171-80. https://doi.org/ l 0.1007/sl0597-009-9278-4

Makkar, U. (n.d.). *Achieving Sustainable Strategic Advantage.* www. bhartipublications.com

Roscigno, V. (2007). *The Face of Discrimination,* United Kingdom: Rowman & Littlefield Publishers.

Sharma, P. and S. Nagaich (2014). "Is Literacy a Cause of Increase in Women Work Participation in Punjab (India): A Regional Analysis?", *IMPACT International Journal of Research in Applied, Natural and Social Science IMPACT LJRANSS),* 2(February): 49-56. www. impactjournals. us

United Nations Development Programme (2023). *How Digital Technology and Innovation are Advancing the Sustainable Development Goals.* Retrieved on 20 October 2023. from https://feature.undp. org/ digital-goals/?gclid=CjwK CAjwp80pBhAFEiw AG7NaErSbAS YLKrkGDkiuzqfgudfEpvj_ VXbimgxNmDCHfmLMgBixcmHWmho CEKIQAv D_BwE

World Bank Group (2019). *Sustainable Development Goals.* United States. https ://documentsl . worldbank.org /curated/en/l 06391567056944729/ pdflWorld-Bank-Group-PartnershipFund-for-the-Sustainable-Development-Goals-Annual-Report-2019.pdf

World Economic Forum (2023). *Global Gender Gap Report,* pp. 1-382, Switzerland.

Yeasmin, M. (2018). "Dr. B.R. Ambedkar's Vision for Women Empowerment", *International Journal of Creative Research Thoughts,* 6(2): 1.

10

Role of Digital Technologies in Bringing Inclusive Maternal Health and Gender Equality in Punjab

Vijayetta Sharma

Introduction

Digitization of government health care services has led to greater provision, access, monitoring, evaluation of policy provisions, and removal of service bottlenecks consequently leading to better realization of policy action results. Digitization of services provides impetus to the routine governmental operations and lends innovation in the services by having augmented clarity, transparency, comprehension and better data representativeness. The pervading norm of data directed decisions in governance process and transcending absolute data directed regime in the coming years has made it imperative to take decisions at various levels in the hierarchy incorporating the apps and devices to ameliorate health care delivery and access. Digitization helps in providing reliable, accurate and verified data for policy making at the national and global level. The concreteness and veracity in the data has an inherent advantage of reliability and guarantees accountable results. The national repositories of data provide a database of results and trends in the socio-economic indicators, gendered dimensions of data, inclusive growth indicators, comparative statistics and interactive visualizations. At the structural level, the digitization trigger increased use of health-care services which helps in improving the outcomes of various schemes and initiatives. At the individual level, digitization augments increased use of health-care services and improves motivation and confidence among the health staff to perform health-care roles (Lapao, 2019; Velthoven *et al.*, 2019; Iyamu *et al.*, 2021; Bhavnani 2016; Bhambere *et al.*, 2021).

Digitization helps in bridging the gender gap in the health-care services by providing access to women for their health care needs. The blockages in the gender disparities in the access to health care are resolved by providing them with awareness, knowledge of health care imperatives, linking them to health centres for availing the services, looking at the critical areas in the delivery, institutional coordination measures for improving access, behavioural modification aspects to improve the service outcomes. The achievement of an inclusive growth paradigm and gender equality has been realized with the greater penetration of digital services in the rural areas of the country. Maternal health care services encompassing prenatal, intrapartum and post-natal care has faced a tremendous shift in improvement with the digital integration, digital process execution of services, and digital end point connection.

The benefits of digitization lie in improvement in data integration of routine services, boosting attendance to the health schemes, rendering promptness and representativeness to decision making, value creation by upgradation of services and sustainability of future growth. The digital support to services provided in the form of communication channels such as chat, email, mobile app, social media has augmented maternal health outcomes to a substantial proportion and has brought gender equity in health-care access. Digitization as an improved decision making toolkit and tech-enabled administrative process is espoused by the government as a valuable measure for creating and delivering welfare agendas in multiple domains under different spheres of governance. It is not only marked by process improvement but also fosters gender care and equity leading to better outcomes in the health-care measurement of the population. With the changing landscape of technological and social order, the digital health technologies, mobile applications, and wearable health devices are gradually gaining popularity among the population facilitating in the monitoring and tracking their health-care needs (Agrawal and Manchanda, 2023; Ricciardi *et al.*, 2021; Rantala and Karjaluoto 2017; Gavrilov *et al.*, 2020).

Digital health is an umbrella term which refers to the use and systematic application of information and communication technologies for effective decision making at the structural, operational, and interactional level in an organization. It is used for strengthening the existing operations and make amendments to evolve innovative ways for operational excellence in the health-care processes and policies. Digital technologies have been playing a significant role in making improvements to social indicators and gendered dimensions of health through its novel interventions in making improvements *via* socio-technical integration to policy prerogatives. In the broader sense, the use of information and communication technologies, is sought in supporting health and health-related fields, including health-care services, health surveillance, health literature, and health education, knowledge, and research. Digital technologies have also played a significant role in the provision of health-care services at a distance through telecommunications platforms; remote monitoring of patients' health or diagnostic data enabled by digital technologies; digital therapeutics, i.e. evidence-based treatments delivered using digital technologies. The most commonly used digital health interventions include mobile apps, SMS text messaging, voice messaging, web-based applications, social media, movies and videos, and wearable or sensor-based devices.

Review of Literature

The digital technologies have been playing a tremendous role in the improvement in the service provisions, increasing health staff knowledge, motivation and confidence to perform health roles, correcting gendered distortions in health care, contextual and cultural factors, addressing racial and ethnic health inequalities, etc. Many studies talk about the need for implementing digital technologies in health care, effectiveness of leveraging digital technologies in health care, enabling factors for the implementation of digital technologies, and challenges in digital health care. Studies also highlight that the digital technologies helped in making improvements in the maternal health and building social support to improve the policy outcomes.

The digital technologies have yielded outcomes in the broad spectrum of health-care activities by its diversified techniques such as patient monitoring devices, personal digital assistants, wireless devices, telephone helplines or text message-based health information (WHO, 2016). Digital technologies have made transcending strides at micro, meso and macro level. Studies have shown that at micro or individual level repeated engagement with clinical videos increased health staff knowledge, motivation and confidence to petform health care roles. At meso or organizational level, the trained staff in digital technologies had a greater feeling of empowerment and felt supported to provide an improved management of obstetric complications which triggered the increased use of maternal newborn and child health services. At the macro level, the greater use of reliable and accurate data for policy making was provided by digital technologies (Ebenso *et al.*, 2021). Studies shows that digitization can be used to correct gender distortions in health care (Agrawal and Manchanda, 2023). Digital technologies have been recognized as a potential tool to address racial and ethnic health inequalities in developing nations. Some studies have tried to find the contextual and cultural factors that can inform the design of digital technologies to support ante-natal care services to the refugees (Talhouk *et al.*, 2016). The studies also highlight the effectiveness of leveraging digital health to address perverse nature of Maternal Newborn and Child Health (MNCH) inequities among ethnic minority women in low-resource settings. The digital technologies have provided critical information on the processes of adapting mHealth interventions to respond to uncertain situations (McBride *et al.*, 2023).

The maternal messaging and service providers use of technology has improved the health outcomes at a larger scale in Ghana (Willcox *et al.*, 2019). The routine health processing and its digitization has resulted in far-sighted results in the health outcomes in Tanzania (Unkels, 2023). Some studies highlighted the exclusionary practices of digital health programmes and discussed the vulnerability and exclusion of women at the intersection of gender, literacy, and disability. It has been noted that it is crucial to tackle the exclusionary practices in digital health to ensure that no woman or girl is left behind in the provision of maternal health services (Udenigwe and Yaya, 2022). The digital governance has also been playing a far-sighted role in alleviation of stunting in Indonesia (Lestari *et al.*, 2022).

The studies also suggested the need of implementing e-health technologies in Low and Middle Income Countries (LMIC) countries which would address the barriers and community characteristics of the population and provide positive outcomes in reducing maternal deaths (Tadele, 2019). Digital technologies have potential drawbacks such as accidental deletion of the applications, disconnectivity in certain operations due to lack of electricity, and inability to set up a reminder function which inextricably posed challenges at the operational level (Musiimenta *et al.*, 2021). Some studies highlight that it is essential to implement the e-health programmes across the country through a constructive cycle of policy, execution, and evaluation. In the area of maternal health, the digital technologies have posed enormous scope in making improvement in services in Ghana (Asumah *et al.*, 2023). Studies have shown that maternal and child health using digital technologies has shown steady growth in Africa and other LMIC settings (Till *et al.*, 2023). It has also been noted that telehealth systems have not yet been adopted by low and middle-income nations due to the high implementation costs (Bilal *et al.*, 2022). Further, studies have found that the enabling factors of implementation of digital technologies include community engagement and health worker support, technology adaptation to local context, service integration and health system support. It also came to light that the challenges were mainly infrastructure related such as power supply, network connectivity and mobile phone access in Nigeria (Ekuri, 2020). The digital health practices helped in adopting good maternal health practices, promoting enhanced social support from spouses, provided clinic appointment reminders, and facilitated communication with health-care providers (Musiimenta *et al.*, 2021). The use of big data analysis, artificial intelligence and machine learning focuses on further strengthening and expanding the existing systems by enabling data exchange for health information systems and decision making (Khan *et al.*, 2019).

Research Methodology

The study comprises two districts from the State of Punjab, i.e. district Ropar and district Mohali, Punjab as per the composite health index devised by NRHM. The maternal health beneficiaries belonging to Janani Suraksha Yojana under National Rural Health Mission are selected for the study to assess the impact of digital technologies in maternal health services. A sample of 216 maternal health beneficiaries belonging to Janani Suraksha Yojana were taken from both the districts based on probability proportionate to size sampling. The chi-square test is performed to check the association between different variables. The qualitative interpretations based on individual responses and observations as a method of data collection was relied upon to draw inferences and provide policy recommendations.

Following are the objectives and hypotheses of the study:

Objectives of the Study

- To study the impact of digital technologies in promoting awareness and improving access to maternal health schemes in Punjab.
- To study the impact of digital technologies in improving communication among the community health workers and health officials in Punjab.
- To study the impact of digital technologies on monitoring and feedback evaluation of maternal health services in Punjab.
- To study the impact of digital technologies in promoting gender equality by improving maternal health in Punjab.

Hypotheses of the Study

- The use of digital technologies has resulted in better awareness of maternal health schemes under NRHM in Punjab.
- The use of digital technologies has resulted in faster linking of beneficiaries to the health centres for availing maternal health services in Punjab.
- The use of digital technologies has resulted in improvement in communication among the community health workers and health officials in Punjab.
- The use of digital technologies has resulted in better monitoring and feedback evaluation of maternal health services in Punjab.
- Digital technologies have resulted in bringing gender equity by improving delivery of maternal health services in rural areas in Punjab.

Results and Discussion

The results show that digitization of services has resulted in better awareness, access, integration and delivery of maternal health services at the local level, improvement in communication at the structural level, better monitoring and feedback evaluation at the policy level.

Digital Technologies in Aiding Awareness of Maternal Health Services

The digital technologies such asmobile apps, SMS text messaging, voice messaging, web-based applications, social media, movies and videos, and wearable or sensor-based devices have the potential to revolutionize the health care by generating an improved understanding and awareness of health-care services. Table 10.1 shows the awareness generated by these digital technologies on the different health services among maternal health beneficiaries.

Table 10.1: Awareness on Maternal Health Services with Digital Sources

Maternal Health Awareness	District Ropar		District Mohali		χ^2	*p*-value
	Number	Percentage	Number	Percentage		
Mobile apps	200	92.59	197	91.20	30.22	0.001**
SMS text messaging	216	100.00	216	100.00		
Voice messaging	48	22.22	32	14.81		
Web-based applications	29	13.43	17	7.87		
Social Media	140	64.81	98	45.37		
Movies and videos	197	91.20	122	56.48		
Wearable or sensor-based devices	76	35.19	28	12.96		

**Computed from primary data, *p*-value $\leq$ 0.01 is highly significant to denote.

A perusal of data in Table 10.1 shows that 100 per cent beneficiaries from district Ropar and district Mohali stated that SMS text messaging has led to greater awareness on the maternal health services. The least proportion of beneficiaries, i.e. 13.43 per cent from district Ropar and 7.87 per cent from district Mohali stated the non-usage of web-based applications in spreading awareness about maternal health services. The chisquare result (χ^2 =30.22, p=0.001) is found to be highly significant which reveals that there is an association in the proportion of responses among beneficiaries belonging to district Ropar and district Mohali with the usage of digital technologies in spreading awareness about maternal health services. It implies that there was a difference in the digital awareness provided to maternal health beneficiaries and districts.

Many beneficiaries asserted that digital technologies have led to better awareness about various maternal health service information prerogatives in a speedy, time saving and efficient manner. Many beneficiaries stated that with the integration of digitized medium to health-care services, it is easier to get the complete information and they can clarify their doubts as and when they arise in a phased and easy manner. The awareness spread by way of short videos on health services was noticed to have a lasting impact among the maternal health beneficiaries. Some beneficiaries stated that the wearable devices are picking up in the area of maternal health which can read the text messages more quickly and track location. The voice messages at times have been utilized to save time at the times of emergency by some beneficiaries. Many beneficiaries stated that the social media has been playing a crucial role in spreading awareness about early signs of pregnancy and post partum complications.

Digital Technologies in Improving Access to Maternal Health Services

The information disseminated by the digital technologies has the linkage with the service usurpation on understanding the objective and purpose of different maternal health services. Digital technologies provide a valuable link to bring inclusivity in the range of services offered by the government by proving the worth and desirability of government schemes. Table 10.2 provides the different digital technologies and their role in improving access to health services as perceived by maternal health beneficiaries.

Table 10.2: Improving Access to Maternal Health Service Using Digital Technologies

Maternal Health Service Provision	District Ropar		District Mohali		χ^2	*p*-value
	Number	Percentage	Number	Percentage		
Mobile apps	212	98.15	202	93.52	17.76	0.006**
SMS text messaging	216	100.00	216	100.00		
Voice messaging	56	25.93	48	22.22		
Web-based applications	48	22.22	32	14.81		
Social Media	156	72.22	102	47.22		
Movies and videos	216	100.00	148	68.52		
Wearable or sensor-based devices	97	44.91	56	25.93		

**Computed from primary data, *p*-value $\leq$ 0.01 is highly significant to denote.

A perusal of data in Table 10.2 shows that 100 per cent beneficiaries from district Ropar and district Mohali shows that SMS text messaging has led to improvement in the maternal health services. The least proportion of beneficiaries, i.e. 22.22 per cent from district Ropar and 14.81 per cent from district Mohali stated the non-usage of web-based applications in making improvements maternal health services. The chi-square result (χ^2 =17.76, p=0.006) is found to be highly significant which reveals that there is an association in the proportion of responses among beneficiaries belonging to district Ropar and district Mohali with the usage of digital technologies in making improvements in maternal health services. It implies that there is a difference in the improvements in maternal health services made using digital technologies and districts.

Most of the beneficiaries stated that SMS text messaging has a significant impact on improving the health services provided to them. An advanced messages regarding the services helped them to plan in advance various household activities and visits to their distant family and friends. SMS messages also proved to be a boon in proving the complete information, remembering the dates, and serves as a record for the next scheduled visits. The SMS messaging has led to informed services delivery where the chances of missing the dates were minimal among the beneficiaries. Many beneficiaries stated that the mobile apps proved to be a boon in having a complete information on a single portal which inexcusably impacted their timely visits to the health centres for availing the services. Social media along with movies and videos acted as a motivator in securing attendance to the maternal health services delivered by the health centres by drawing the attention of beneficiaries to the proven benefits of the schemes. Some beneficiaries stated that voice messages were useful during the emergency situations when they were travelling from one health centre to another for intra-partum care. A few beneficiaries stated that visiting the online portals helped them to get complete information about the scheme and establishing authenticity of the provisions which helped in improving access to the maternal health schemes. The wearable devices helped them to monitor their daily health and helped in timely visits to health centres to secure their health.

Digital Technologies in Providing Viable Links between Beneficiaries and Health Centre

The digital technologies play a tremendous role in linking of beneficiaries to the health centres for availing maternal health services. The host of digital technologies has added advantage of providing better information, ensures promptness of service, builds trusted association with the populace, ensures long-term access to records, and lends a superior service comparison. Table 10.3 provides the role of digital technologies in providing viable links to health services as perceived by maternal health beneficiaries.

Table 10.3: Health Care Linking of Maternal Health Services using Digital Technologies

Health Centre Linking	District Ropar		District Mohali		χ^2	*p*-value
	Number	Percentage	Number	Percentage		
Better information	212	98.15	198	91.67	0.40	0.98
Promptness of service	198	91.67	176	81.48		
Trusted association	165	76.39	143	66.20		
Better access to record	212	98.15	198	91.67		
Service comparison	198	91.67	176	81.48		

Source: Computed from primary data, *p*-value > 0.05 is highly significant to denotes.

A perusal of data in Table 10.3 shows that most of the beneficiaries, i.e. 98.15 per cent from district Ropar and 91.67 per cent in district Mohali stated that digital technologies has provided better information and better access to records which served as a linking mechanism to health centres to avail the services in a harmonious way. The chi-square result (χ^2= 0.40, *p*-value = 0.98) is found to be non-significant which reveals that there is no association in the proportion of responses among beneficiaries belonging to district Ropar and district Mohali with different prerogatives providing impetus in linking to health centres. It implies that the difference in the linking to health centres and districts is insignificant.

Most of the beneficiaries stated that digital technologies provided better information which proved to be beneficial in linking to the health centres in a better way to avail the services under the maternal health schemes. A better access to records using the digital technologies serves as a boon in deciding the course of action to be taken for treatment and selecting the right health centre for the visits. Many beneficiaries stated that the promptness of service resulting from the use of digital technologies has attested better linking to the health centres for treatment. The veracity and authentication of services as a result of digital technological use has resulted in trusted association which consequently helped in improving the enrollments to the maternal health schemes. Many beneficiaries liked the component of service comparison offered by the digital technologies which provides them with the decision making alternatives and securing timely visits to the health centres.

Digital Technologies in Improving Health Care Communications Among the Health Staff

Digital technologies have led to improvement in communication among the community health workers and health officials as a result of prompt response for various service decisions, better endpoint service facilitation at the field level, complete and error-free information sharing, adherence to verbal immediacy, language intensity and lexical diversity, and promotion of control, motivation, emotion and expression. Table 10.4 provides the essential improvements made in the health care communication using digital technologies among the health staff.

Table 10.4: Health Care Communication Using Digital Technologies

Health Care Communication	District Ropar		District Mohali		χ^2	*p*-value
	Number	Percentage	Number	Percentage		
Prompt response in routine and emergency cases	50	100.00	50	100.00	1.25	0.86
Better endpoint service facilitation	48	96.00	36	72.00		
Complete and error-free information sharing	50	100.00	50	100.00		
Adheres to verbal immediacy and language intensity and lexical diversity	46	92.00	41	82.00		
Promotes control, motivation, emotion and expression	48	96.00	42	84.00		

Source: Computed from primary data, *p*-value > 0.05 is highly significant to denotes.

A perusal of data in Table 10.4 shows that 100 per cent community health workers from district Ropar and district Mohali stated that health-care communication using digital technologies has led to prompt response in routine and emergency cases, and complete and error-free information sharing. The chi-square result (χ^2= 1.25, p-value = 0.86) is found to be non-significant which reveals that there is no association in the proportion of responses among community health workers belonging to district Ropar and district Mohali with improvements made in health care communication using digital technologies. It implies that the difference in health-care communication and districts is insignificant.

Most of the community health workers, i.e. ASHA (Accredited Social Health Activists) stated that communication using the digital technologies has eased the process of communication in routine and emergency cases by taking prompt action in the interest of providing services to the beneficiaries. Many ASHA stated that health-care communication using digital technologies has resulted in better endpoint service facilitation *via* providing equitable and inclusive service delivery to people at the grassroots level of governance. Complete and error-free information sharing was endorsed by ASHA which improved the service delivery to a large extent in the villages. The use of digital technologies has an added advantage of providing verbal immediacy and language intensity and lexical diversity which enrich the communication parameters and lend an improved velocity of impetus to the provision of services. Most of ASHA are of the opinion that digital services has resulted in devising better coordinates for exercising control, providing motivation, noticing the emotion of stakeholders involved in service dissemination in a better way, and delivery services with an improved expression which has gone a long way in improving the service delivery at the local level.

Digital Technologies in Improving Monitoring and Feed Back Evaluation of Maternal Health Services

Digital technologies have proven to be beneficial in monitoring and feedback evaluation *via* providing better need analysis; superior stakeholder mapping, improving the definition of logic; providing a strengthened theoretical framework and mapping of indicators in a coherent way; improving sustainability and impact; and improving milestone identification, planning and scheduling. Table 10.5

provides essential benefits posed by digital technologies in monitoring and feedback evaluation as elucidated by community health workers.

A perusal of data in Table 10.5 shows that most of the beneficiaries, i.e. 92 per cent from district Ropar and 82 per cent in district Mohali stated that digital technologies leads to better need analysis and superior stakeholder mapping which aid in monitoring and feedback evaluation. The chi-square result (χ^2= 0.76, *p*-value = 0.99) is found to be non-significant which reveals that there is no association in the proportion of responses among community health workers belonging to district Ropar and district Mohali with monitoring and feedback evaluation using digital technologies. It implies that the difference in monitoring and feedback evaluation and districts is insignificant.

Most of the community health workers stated that with the help of digital technologies they can better carry out the health intervention need analysis of the situation in the field and plan their timelines accordingly for visiting the beneficiaries. While doing

Table 10.5: Monitoring and Feedback Evaluation using Digital Technologies

Monitoring and Evaluation	District Ropar		District Mohali		χ^2	*p*-value
	Number	Percentage	Number	Percentage		
Better need analysis	46	92.00	41	82.00	0.76	0.99
Superior stakeholder mapping	46	92.00	41	82.00		
Improved definition of logic, theoretical framework and mapping of indicators	38	76.00	32	64.00		
Improved sustainability and impact	38	76.00	32	64.00		
Improved milestone identification, planning and scheduling	38	76.00	32	64.00		

Source: Computed from primary data, *p*-value > 0.05 is highly significant to denotes.

the need analysis, the digital technologies aid in the analysing the demographic and social factors of the population and helps them in the charting out the inclusive development strategies which percolate in the form of tangible benefits in the form of policy interventions. They stated that with the help of digital technologies a complete information can be extracted from the beneficiaries which helps in having a complete overview of the situation. Stakeholder mapping has become easy with the help of digital technologies as it helps in linking the right beneficiary to the right scheme and helps in tracking the status of the services delivered. The errors are minimal in maintaining the records using the digital technologies. Some ASHA believed that the digital technologies have led to the better mapping of indicators, improved definition of logic and development of theoretical framework for monitoring and feedback evaluation but there is a need of better integration both at the field and institution level to carry out the activities. Some ASHA believed that improved milestone identification, planning and scheduling has become easy with the use of digital technologies which helped the collating the right feedback and also performing the monitoring of the interventions. Digital technologies have helped in augmenting the sustainability and impact of the health schemes due to the added advantage of data led governance and improving the monitoring and evaluation of maternal health schemes. Some ASHA exclaimed that monitoring and evaluation using the digital technologies has aided in bringing the actual situation of the field and the prevalent health interventions which consequently helps in attaining better outcomes to maternal health schemes.

Digital Technologies in Aiding Social and Gender Equity

The digital technologies play a crucial role in improving the delivery of maternal health services and bringing gender equality. Digital technologies have helped in bringing women to the forefront in health care delivery map by aiding in providing them with the timebound services. Digital technologies have the potential to drastically improve the attendance to services at the health centre and bringing social and gender equity in the delivery of health services. With greater access to services to the women by strategic interventions digital technologies can help in reducing the service discrimination in health-care facilities thereby narrowing cultural and social barriers. The empowered women witness improvement in decision making, and there is an enhancement in social indicators such as work and education among women. Table 10.6 provides different forms of gender equity attained in health care as a result of use of digital technologies.

Table 10.6: Gender Equity in Health Care Access

Monitoring and Evaluation	District Ropar		District Mohali		χ^2	*p*-value
	Number	Percentage	Number	Percentage		
Improved attendance in health care service access	216	100.00	202	93.52	5.47	0.24
Reduction in service discrimination in health-care facilities	134	62.04	97	44.91		
Narrowed cultural and social barriers	102	47.22	78	36.11		
Improvement in decision making in households	198	91.67	134	62.04		
Improvement in social indicators such as work and education	78	36.11	65	30.09		

Source: Computed from primary data, *p*-value > 0.05 is highly significant to denotes.

A perusal of data in Table 10.6 shows that all the beneficiaries from district Ropar and 93.52 per cent beneficiaries in district Mohali stated that digital technologies has led to improved attendance in maternal health care services at the health centres. The chi-square result (χ^2= 5.47, *p*-value = 0.24) is found to be non-significant which reveals that there is no association in the proportion of responses among beneficiaries belonging to district Ropar and district Mohali gender equity using digital technologies. It implies that the difference in gender equity using digital technologies and districts is insignificant.

Most of the beneficiaries opined that with the help of digital technologies they can prioritize the usurpation of health services *via* having greater knowledge and better interlinking thereby improving attendance at the health centres. Many beneficiaries revealed that with the greater access to services by the women and efforts of ASHA in taking the women to the health centres for availing the services, there is a reduction in the service discrimination at the health centres to a large extent. The reluctance to visits the health centre among the women have reduced and they readily discuss their problems with the health staff. They also witnessed improvement in decision making in their households due to improved status of their health with the integration of digital services in health care. Some beneficiaries also commented that there is a reduction in social and cultural barriers and improvement in the social indicators such as work and education.

Consolidation of Results and Testing of Hypotheses

The detailed discussion with respect to the use of digital technologies in maternal health revealed that the digital technologies has resulted in creating better awareness of maternal health services in Punjab. The mobile apps, SMS text messaging, social media, movies and videos have proved to be beneficial in dissemination information leading the better awareness of health-care service among the population. It has also come to light that the use of digital technologies has led to faster linking of maternal health services to the health centres in Punjab to avail the services. The use of mobile apps, SMS text messaging, social media, movies and videos have provided viable mechanism to link the beneficiaries to the health centres in Punjab. The detailed discussion also showed that the use of digital technologies has resulted in improvement in communication among the community health workers and health officials in Punjab. The digital technologies have aided the community health workers in getting prompt response in routine and emergency situations, better endpoint service facilitation, complete and error-free information sharing, an enhanced verbal immediacy, language intensity and lexical diversity, exercising an improved degree of control, providing motivation, and incorporating better emotion and expression in their discourses of delivering health care to the doorsteps. The digital technologies have resulted in better monitoring and feedback evaluation of maternal health services in Punjab. The better need analysis and superior stakeholder mapping has taken forefront in the monitoring and feedback evaluation of maternal health services in Punjab. The feedback and monitoring using digital technologies also gained in terms of improved definition of logic, theoretical framework and mapping of indicators, improved milestone identification, planning and scheduling, and improved sustainability and impact. Further, the digital technologies have resulted in bringing gender equity by improving delivery of maternal health services in rural areas in Punjab. The gendered dimensions using the digital technologies improved in terms of better attendance in health care service access, reduction in service discrimination in health-care facilities, and an improved in decision making in households. Table 10.7 consolidates the status of hypotheses as per the preceding discussion.

Table 10.7: Status of hypotheses

Hypotheses	Status
The use of digital technologies has resulted in better awareness of maternal health schemes under NRHM in Punjab.	✓ Validated
The use of digital technologies has resulted in faster linking of beneficiaries to the health centres for availing maternal health services in Punjab.	✓ Validated
The use of digital technologies has resulted in improvement in communication among the community health workers and health officials in Punjab.	✓ Validated
The use of digital technologies has resulted in better monitoring and feedback evaluation of maternal health services in Punjab.	✓ Validated
Digital technologies have resulted in bringing gender equity by improving delivery of maternal health services in rural areas in Punjab.	✓ Validated

Conclusion and Policy Suggestions

The results of the study provide grounds for bringing social equality usmg digitization, inclusive health care growth, and gender equity in rural areas. The digital technologies have resulted in a heightened sense of improvement in bringing awareness of services to the local populace. With the use of digital technologies, the linking of beneficiaries to health centres have improved manifold leading to better usurpation of health-care services. The digital technologies have epic share in bringing inclusive health-care governance in the current age dominated by the use of information technology. The inherent advantage of digital technologies in bridging the communication gaps and smoothening the service intake has resulted in proliferated gains in terms of better coordination, timely service delivery, having better clarity in service provisions, resolution of queries which ultimately affects the service intake. Monitoring and feedback evaluation has become more pronounced with the help of digital technologies and led to enhancement in the provision of services by effectually incorporating the improvements received and strengthening the targets. Gender equity and maternal health services have become two sides of the coin leading to inclusive coverage in the health services fostering SDG 3.

The digital integration of services in the maternal health care can further be improved in attaining the proposed policy outcomes by encapsulating the following policy suggestions. The provision of digital education or digital literacy to the beneficiaries should be strengthened at the grassroots level. The usage of technical devices and their potential benefits shall be covered under the maternal health schemes and disseminated though viable channels. For better linking of beneficiaries to the health centres, the digital technologies should be used for transportation and arranging for escort which was found to be missing at certain places. The clear description of communication channels along with the stipulated timelines for various activities for the use of digital devices will reduce the haphazard nature of services delivery encountered by the beneficiaries as well as the service providers. In order to have better monitoring and feedback evaluation using digital technologies it is crucial to define the logic, theoretical framework, mapping of indicators, identification of different milestones and their mapping to different indicators which thereby would lead to improved sustainability and impact in the field. Further in order to bring gender equity using digital technologies, an integration of social and gendered dimensions should be included in the maternal health policy plan. Finally, the government should invest in the promotion of digital health infrastructure at the different structural levels in the health care hierarchy, sponsor capacity building programmes for community health workers and medical staff, and sensitize the citizenry to take advantage of digital platforms.

The current study provides grounds for bringing social equality using digitization, inclusive health-care growth, and gender equality in rural areas. Hence, we can state that the digitization of services has resulted in better awareness, access, integration and delivery of maternal health services at the local level, improvement in communication at the structural level, better monitoring and feedback evaluation at the policy level in Punjab.

REFERENCES

Agrawal, S. and P. Manchanda (2023). "Can Digitization be Leveraged for Correcting Gender Distortions in Healthcare?". https://ihopejoumalofophthalm ology. com/content/ 132/2023/2/ l/pdfl IHOPEJ0-2-020. pdf

Agrawal, S. and P. Manchanda (2023). *Can Digitization be Leveraged for Correcting Gender Distortions in Healthcare?*. https://ihopejoumalofophthalmology. com/content/132/2023/2/ l/pdfl IHOPEJ0-2-020. pdf

Asumah, M.N., M.Y. Mohammed, A. Abubakari and B.K. Padhi (2023). "Improving Maternal Health Services Utilization in Ghana: should Digital Health be Considered? Correspondence", *Annals of Medicine and Surgery, 85*(3): 557.

Bhambere, S., B. Abhishek and H. Sumit (2021). "Rapid Digitization of Healthcare: A Review of COVID-19 Impact on Our Health Systems", *Int. J. All Res. Educ. Sci. Methods, 9:* 1457-59.

Bhavnani, S.P., J. Narula and P.P. Sengupta (2016). "Mobile Technology and the Digitization of Healthcare", *European Heart Journal, 37*(18): 1428.

Bilal, W., K. Qamar, A. Siddiqui, P. Kumar and M.Y. Essar (2022). "Digital Health and Telemedicine in Pakistan: Improving Maternal Healthcare", *Annals of Medicine and Surgery, 81:* 104425.

Ebenso, B., B. Okusanya, K. Okunade, D. Akeju, A. Ajepe, G.O. Akaba, and M.J. Allsop (2021). "What are the Contextual Enablers and Impacts of Using Digital Technology to Extend Maternal and Child Health Services to Rural Areas?: Findings of a Qualitative Study from Nigeria", *Frontiers in Global Womens Health, 2:* 670494.

Ekuri, S.O. (2020). *Implementing Digital Health for Maternal Health in Nigeria: A Literature Review.*

Gavrilov, G., O. Sirnov and V. Trajkovik (September 2020). "Analysis of Digitalization in Healthcare: Case Study", In *International Conference on JCT Innovations,* pp. 202-16, Cham: Springer International Publishing.

Iyamu, I., A.X. Xu, O. Gomez-Ramirez, A. Ablona, H.J. Chang, G. Mckee and M. Gilbert (2021). "Defining Digital Public Health and the Role of Digitization, Digitalization, and Digital Transformation: Scoping Review", *JMIR. Public Health and Surveillance, 7*(11): e30399.

Khan, M.A.H., V. de Oliveira Cruz and A.K. Azad (2019). "Bangladesh's Digital Health Journey: Reflections on a Decade of Quiet Revolution", *WHO South-East Asia Journal of Public Health, 8*(2): 71-76.

Lapão, L.V. (2019). "The Future of Healthcare: The Impact of Digitalization on Healthcare Services Performance". In *The Internet and Health in Brazil: Challenges and Trends,* 435-49.

Lestari, D., E. Rochaida, R.B. Suharto, S. Mixila and I.N. Sutapa (2022). "In the Era of Digitization, Government's Role in Alleviating Stunting", *Webology, 19*(1): 4925-41.

McBride, B., J. O'Neil, P.C. Nguyen, D.T. Linh, H.T. Trinh, N.C. Vu and L.T. Nguyen (2023). "Adapting and Scaling a Digital Health Intervention to Improve Maternal and Child Health Among Ethnic Minority Women in Vietnam Amid the COVID-19 Context: Protocol for the dMOM Project", *JMIR Research Protocols, 12(1):* e44720.

Musiimenta, A., W. Tumuhimbise, N. Pinkwart, J. Katusiime, G. Mugyenyi and E.C. Atukunda (2021). "A Mobile Phone-Based Multimedia Intervention to Support Maternal Health is Acceptable and Feasible Among Illiterate Pregnant Women in Uganda: Qualitative Findings from a Pilot Randomized Controlled Trial", *Digital Health,* 7: 1-10.

Rantala, K. and H. Karjaluoto (2017). *Combining Digitization with Healthcare Service Processes: Value Co-creation Opportunities Through Standard Work.*

Ricciardi, W., P. Pita Barros, A. Bourek, W. Brouwer, T. Kelsey and L. Lehtonen (2019). "How to Govern the Digital Transformation of Health Services", *European Journal of Public Health, 29* (Supplement_3): 7-12.

Tadele, S. (2019). *Assessing the Impact of Digital Health Technologies on Maternal Health Care in Sub-Saharan Africa.*

Talhouk, R., S. Mesmar, A. Thieme, M. Balaam, P. Olivier, C. Akik and H. Ghattas, (May 2016). "Syrian Refugees and Digital Health in Lebanon: Opportunities for Improving Antenatal Health", In *Proceedings of the 2016 CHI Conference on Human Factors in Computing Systems,* pp. 331-42.

Till, S., M. Mkhize, J. Farao, L.D. Shandu, L. Muthelo, T.L. Coleman, and Network CoMaCH (2023). "Digital Health Technologies for Maternal and Child Health in Africa and Other Low-and Middle-Income Countries: Cross-disciplinary Scoping Review with Stakeholder Consultation", *Journal of Medical Internet Research, 25:* e42161.

Udenigwe, O. and S. Yaya (2022). "Leaving no Woman or Girl Behind?: Inclusion and Participation in Digital Maternal Health Programmes In Sub-Saharan Africa", *Reproductive Health, 19*(1): 54.

Unkels, R. (2023). *On People, Data and Systems: Perspectives on Routine Health Data Processing and Its Digitalization in Tanzania.*

van Velthoven, M.H., C. Cordon and G. Challagalla (2019). "Digitization of Healthcare Organizations: The Digital Health Landscape and Information Theory", *International Journal of Medical Infonnatics, 124:* 49-57.

WHO. Global Diffusion of eHealth. Report of the Third Global Survey on eHealth. 2016. http:// who.int/goe/publications/global_diffusion/en/

Willcox, M., A. Moorthy, D. Mohan, K. Romano, D. Hutchful, G. Mehl and A. Lefevre (2019). "Mobile Technology for Community Health in Ghana: Is Maternal Messaging and Provider Use of Technology Cost-Effective in Improving Maternal and Child Health Outcomes at Scale?", *Journal of Medical Internet Research, 21*(2): el 1268.

11

Study of Gender Disparity in India

Facts and Myths

Special Context of Third Gender in Madhya Pradesh

Manisha Saxena and *Durgesh Mishra*

Introduction

Third gender, an alternative gender role in India, is traditionally perceived as neither man nor woman. Third gender are observed with ambivalence in Indian society and are treated with a combination of ridicule, fear, and shame. Although they have an auspicious presence, they also have an inauspicious potential despite this, Indian society still recognizes them as an important part of their culture and celebrates them on certain days of the year. Third gender people are gradually gaining acceptance in India, but there is still a long way to go to ensure their complete acceptance (Nanda, 1994). They are also vulnerable to violence and discrimination. third gender people are often excluded from access to education and health care. As a result, they face a higher risk of poverty and homelessness.

The Government of India has taken steps to protect the rights of third gender people, but there is still a long way to go. More needs to be done to ensure the safety and security of third gender people, and to ensure that they are able to access the same rights and resources as everyone else. This includes passing more laws that protect their rights, and providing access to education and health care. Additionally, more needs to be done to address the underlying stigma and discrimination that third gender people face. This includes creating safe spaces where third gender people can express themselves without fear of judgement or violence.

Third gender people are denied self-identification and socio-economic and constitutional rights as well. Third gender persons are viewed as untouchables, and they face social marginalization. It also entails offering mental health care and support groups to third gender people moreover it requires making start-ups and educational institutions more inclusive and welcoming for them. It will be helpful to build judicial and societal recognition in the present world, where morality is frequently eroding.

Third gender persons experience an obstruction in stable accommodation, formal and informal education, occupation, approachability in health-care amenities, health-care policies, and accessibility in identical opportunities moreover third gender community is being deliberately deprived of jurisdictional safeguard (Saxena, M. & Mishra, D. 2022). The sexual minority deprived of self-identification and socio-economic constitutional rights. Third gender people treated as untouchables moreover social stigma. Apart from this, it is not the end of unfair treatment. Force to beg on the streets for the sake of survival. The study provides a thorough gap of gender-based disparities, myths, and realities pertaining to the third gender. Numerous non-governmental groups that actively promote the welfare of the third gender population may also recommend the study.

Objective of the Study

As per requirement of the research paper following objectives given bellow:

- To study the gender-based inequality experienced by the third gender in society.

- To ascertain the status of facts and myths related to third gender in present scenario.

Materials and Methods

Research Design of the Study

The methodological approach of this study is based on primary as well as secondary data which is collected from numerous sources such as government survey annual reports, national and global research papers, reputed authorship books and scholarly journals, websites, etc. The presented study is basically based on the third gender community residing in Madhya Pradesh through mixed method research design has been used.

Study Area

Assembly constituencies of overall Madhya Pradesh city has been selected as study area for the study.

Universe of the Study

A total number of populations of third gender reside in the Assembly Constituency of Madhya Pradesh that has been selected as the universe of the study.

Unit of the Study

A selected third gender reside in Assembly constituencies under districts of Madhya Pradesh has been selected as the unit of the study.

Sampling Frame of the Study

Purposive sampling method has been adopted for selection of the respondents from the Assembly constituencies of the district. Data has been collected from total 200 respondents from the study area.

Collection of Data from Study Area

Primary as well as secondary data has been gathered, used and scrutinized for drawing conclusions.

Tools for Data Collection

Standardized self-administered questionnaire has been implemented for the data collection of the study.

Analysis of Data

The collected data is scrutinized, coded for facilitating computerization. Keeping the objective in view a list of the cross and simple tables prepared for analysis of the study.

Findings and Results of the Study has been Presented

It is evident from the data that transgender community is considered discriminatory by the family and society approximately majority of 77.78 per cent respondents admitted they were considered as subject of hatred and shame by the teachers in the school, another 14.81 per cent respondents experience emotional and verbal abuse in school, 4.32 per cent respondents physically and mentally harassed by school teachers remaining 3.09 per cent respondents prohibit to participate in sociocultural gatherings.

It is reflected that the behaviour of other staff was less insensitive compared to teaching staff. While 4.32 per cent of the respondents are considered to be the object of disgust and ridicule, majority of 91.36 per cent respondents experience emotional and verbal abuse, remaining no cases were found who experience sociocultural striations by non-teaching staff of the school. While the behaviour of neighbourhood with respondents was insensitive and cruel. Another 25.93 per cent respondents had to face disrespectful, ciuel and derisive behaviour by their neighbourhood along with that 72.22 per cent respondents confess that they were brutally emotionally and verbally maltreated by their neighbourhood, merely 1.23 per cent cases suffered from physical and mental abuse by their neighbouthood.

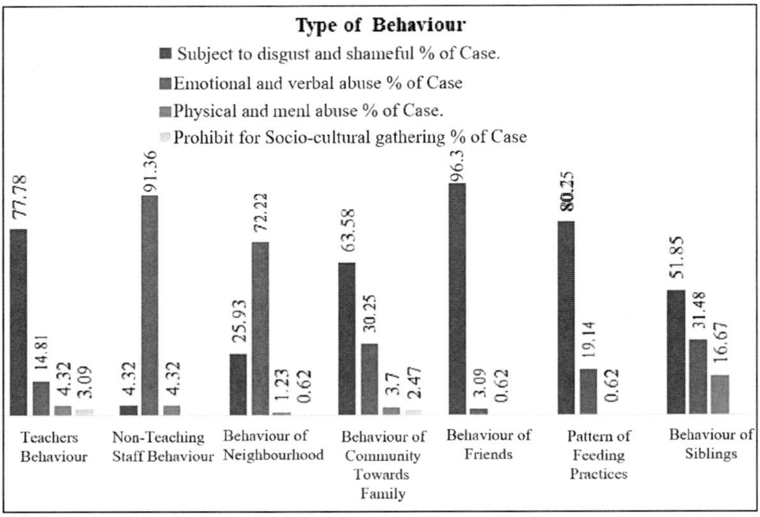

Fig. 11.1: Level of Discrimination with Transgender in Society

The statement is absolutely unequivocal that when transgender children born in a family, the most difficult situation is that of parents who become insensitive and harsh with their children out of the threat of social exclusion. 63.58 per cent respondents reveal that their family had to receive disgustful and witty behaviour by their community because their gender.

The remaining 30.25 per cent of the respondents disclosed that their family members were subjected to emotional and verbal abuse by their community; merely 3.70 per cent respondents confess that their siblings were physical and mentally harassed by their community and 2.47 per cent of the respondents admitted that their family members were intentionally excluded from sociocultural gatherings. It is represented in the above table that the behaviour of friends with respondents was unfriendly and unpleasant and 96.30 per cent of the respondents reported that they were treated with hatred and disdain by their friends.

Apart from this merely 3.09 per cent respondents were encored with brutal emotional and verbal abuse by their friend's merely 0.62 per cent respondents expensed from physical and mental exploitation by their friends. None of the respondents were prohibited from attending the sociocultural event by their friends and above data clearly underline the pattern of feeding practices within family of respondent majority of 80.25 per cent of the respondents faced biased food practices within the family. It was found that 19.14 per cent respondents become malnourished; due to indecent behaviour they feel emotionally sick. Apart from this merely 0.62 per cent respondents were confessing about physical and mental abuse to meet out dietary needs in the family.

Data reveal that behaviour of siblings with respondents was discriminatory and nasty. It is underlined in the above data that 51.50 per cent of the respondents stated that they were treated with hateful and unkind behaviour by their siblings another 31.48 per cent respondents were encored with taunting and ridicule by their siblings, another eye-opening data reveal that 16.67 per cent respondents experience physical and mental assault by their elder siblings. No cases are recorded as prohibiting attending the sociocultural events in the community.

Human Rights Campaign Foundation, U.S.A. (2021) study concluded that youth who identify as third gender are more likely than their classmates of other genders to commit suicide as a result of rejection, bullying, and other forms of discrimination.

Tanveer Abbas *et al.* (2014): The study found that children of higher age categories (third gender) had better social adjustment than children of lower age categories (third gender). Additionally, third gender individuals with female bodies adjusted to society better than third gender individuals with male bodies.

Khan, A. *et al.* (2008): According to the study, mothers and sisters tend to be more understanding of gender-dysphonic family members, but male family members are typically the ones who victimize them. Not a single respondent disclosed experiencing familial sexual abuse.

Ministry of Social Justice and Empowerment Report (2013): The report concludes that most third-gender college dropouts are caused by the physical, sexual, and emotional abuse they experience in educational institutions, leading to stigma on all fronts.

Table 11.1: Status of Hazards Faced by Transgender

Hazards	Yes	% of Case	No	% of Case
Deprived of proper motherhood during childhood	150	75	50	25
Ever faced hatred and Shame by the family	130	65	70	35
Family ever treats you as stigma and curse	180	90	20	10
Ever had to suffer discrimination in relation to food and shelter	120	60	80	40
Denied proper health services	170	85	30	15
Kept away from social acceptance and freedom	160	80	40	20
Excluded from the right to ancestral property and resources	190	95	10	5
Social exclusion by the society	190	95	10	5
Denied livelihood opportunities	180	90	20	10
Do you ostracized by family after Sex reassignment surgery	200	100	0	0

Study found that majority of the transgender population involved in the study faced harassment within family and society. Almost 75 per cent of the respondents experienced a lack of proper motherhood during childhood, another 65 per cent faced hatred and shame by the family members, despite this, 80 per cent of the cases felt as a subject pf stigma and curse. While 60 per cent cases were considered as a curse in the family. Approximately, 60 per cent cases admitted that they had suffered discrimination regarding food and shelter. It is evident from above data that all the majority of them denied proper health services by their families.

Data reflected that 80 per cent of respondents confess that they were kept away from social acceptance and freedom in society. About 90 per cent of respondents reveal they have been excluded from the right to ancestral property and resources in the family because of their gender. While 95 per cent of them admit that they were socially excluded by society and also deprived of employment opportunities in society. Followed by the research study 100 per cent of respondents disclosed that they were face huge humiliation and rejection by their family and society after sex reassignment surgery. In fact, the total population of the study area confesses that they were sufferers of all these hazards. The findings and responses of the study reflect the intensity of disparity experienced by the transgender community in the society.

According to B. Fraser, *et al.* (2019) study, a large number of transgender women were either forced or voluntarily left their homes as teenagers, which raised their risk of homelessness, poverty, and other unfavourable outcomes.

According to study by Boss *et al.* (2013) when family members learn about a transgender person's gender identity, their perspective toward them shifts. Family strife can occasionally escalate to the point of cruelty and lead to various forms of harassment. After coming to terms with their sexual orientation, transgender youth depart from their families.

Concluding Remark

It is summarized that discrimination against transgender people starts right after their gender recognition. They have to face tyranny and discrimination throughout their life, this mindset is not limited to discrimination rather has to be faced in the form of social stigma throughout life. Although transgender community still faces considerable stigma after being called as mentally ill, misogynistic, and sexually predatory for more than a century. Study concluded that the transgender community has to face discrimination from the biological family as well as from the society. Their basic civil and fundamental rights were highly compromised. Even though their socio-economic, socio-educational, sociocultural and civil-political rights were highly compromised, which is very unfortunate for the progressive society in the present era. Transgender community is considered discriminatory and physically and mentally harassed by the family and society. They are treated with hatred and disdain although they were not even given adequate food by their family members due to indecent behaviour they feel emotionally sick. It is explicit from the findings that discrimination against transgender people starts right after their gender recognition. Transgender persons have to face tyranny and discrimination throughout their life, this mindset is not limited to discrimination but they are also seen as social stigma.

Suggestions of the Study

- The study recommends that transgender parents and society be made aware of social justice issues in order to create awareness of transgender children.
- The study recommendations that should be endowment of free education from primary to higher education to promote family acceptance.
- The study recommends that the parents should be rigorously tackled who for their biological distinction neglect accuse or abandon their transgender children.
- The study recommends that the government and society must plan and adopt an inclusive attitude to transgender. policies are, however, structured but not enforced adequately.
- The study recommends that the persons who commit violence towards transgender at workplace or educational institution should be counsel and punished by discipline authorities.
- The study recommends that the for the transgender society the provision of free legal assistance must be assured and made easily accessible.

REFERENCES

Abbas, T., Y. Nawaz, M. Ali, N. Hussain and R. Nawaz (2014). "Social Adjustment of Third Gender: A Study of District Chiniot, Punjab (Pakistan)", *Academic Journal of Interdisciplinary Studies*, *3*(1): 61-71.

Bandura, A. and R.H. Walters (1977). *Social Learning Theory* (Vol. 1). Englewood Cliffs: Prentice Hall.

Census of India (2011). *District Census Hand Book Indore*, Series 24, Part XII A, Directorate of Census Operations, Madhya Pradesh.

Census of India (2011). *Houses, Household Amenities and Assets Data- 2011*, Registrar General and Census Commissioner, India.

Jay, Brown (2021). "Reports on an Epidemic of Violence 2021. Fatal Violence against Third Gender Andnon-Gender". *Human Rights Campaign Foundation*, *42*(1): 74-94.

Khan, A.A., N. Rehan, K. Qayymn and A. Khan (2008). "Correlates and Prevalence of HIV and Sexually Transmitted Infections among Hijras (Male Third Genders) in Pakistan", *International Journal of STD & AIDS*, *19*(12): 817-20.

Lamon, Carol (2013), *Psychology of Lifespan Development*. Boundless Psychology.

Ministry of Social Justice and Empowerment (2013). *Report of the Expert Committee on the Issues Relating to Third Gender Persons.*

Nanda, S. (1994). "Hijras: An Alternative Sex and Gender Role in India". In G. Herdt (ed.), *Third Sex, Third Gender: Beyond Sexual Dimorphism in Culture and History*. New York, NY: Zone Books, pp. 373-417.

Rumjaun, A. and F. Narod (2020). "Social Learning Theory-Albert Bandura". In *Science Education in Theory and Practice*. Springer, Cham, pp. 85-99.

Saxena, M. and D. Mishra (2022). "Impact of Dr. Ambedkar's Philosophy of Social Justice on Legal Emancipation of Third Gender." A Book entitled *Dr. B.R Ambedkar Education, Equality and Empowerment*, Vol. I, pp. 30-39, Gujarat: Krishna Publication House.

Seifert, Kelvin (2013). *Theories of Human Development*. Boundless Psychology.

12

North-Eastern Spectrum of Gender Equity

A Myth and Reality?

Phulrani Gogoi and *Raktima Goswami*

A society can be best defined as a dynamic concept with fluidity. With due course of time society witnesses various changes and created a space for adoption and adaptions that makes the whole concept of society a flexible in nature. One of the wrong notion that is prevailing in the society since then, till the date is the clubbing of two terms into one, i.e. "gender" and "sex". Whereas, gender is an outcome of the social construction and sex is biological. One is born with "XX" and "XY" chromosome is sex where as the "masculinity" and the "feminine" is gender. Gender is the social cleavage of the society which determines different roles in respective to their sex. Which is known as gender roles. Anna, Senden, and Renstrom elabourately discuss how the concept of gender may be operationalized by considering several dimensions, which can be categorized into three primary facets: (a) physiological or biological features, often referred to as sex; (b) gender identity or an individual's self-perceived gender; (c) legal gender, which pertains to the gender associated with gender. Various feminist scholarships draws attention bringing light on nation and ethnicity with the concept of gender (Anna, Senden & Renstrom, 2021). In the past two decades, feminist work has critically examined various aspects of universalism, such as the belief in a gender revolution leading to complete social transformation. It has also questioned the explanatory goals of second-wave feminism and the effectiveness of certain analytic categories, particularly the concepts of "women" and gender. However, it is important to note that within the realm of social sciences, there exists a strong emphasis on the pursuit of explanation as an intellectual endeavour.

While making an attempt on dealing with the gender-based violence, we should not tend to fail in focus on the *cult of silence*. Violence can be best defined as a process of instilling fear psychophysics within the mind of individuals. Women often experienced violence in various forms as physical, mental and financial. Though in the recent times the society is able to break the cult of silence but that too limited to the physical violence, whereas the mental and financial violence are still under the cover. A violence is the only key to maintain the stronghold in a gender based stratified society, where women are always considered to be a second sex in a patriarchal society. North-east is not an exception too. Geographical canvas of the north-east supports a feudalism with agriculture as the backbone of the economy. In order to maintain a hold over the land and its production, women must be convinced as a reproductive agents to procure labour to the land in this process of reproduction women often faced physical and mental violence either initially in the domestic sphere and gradually in the public sphere as well, if we broaden the lens of the violence, it would be crystal clear how the cult of silence worked as a catalyst in encouraging this crimes even for a long time period.

While making an attempt on dealing with gender equity as a myth or a reality, one must first be clear with the concept of gender and how does both the terms related to one another in the contemporary times. Gender is a social construction which is framed to meet the social expectation that associated with the characteristics of "being a man" or "being an women" in the society in the contemporary times a gender issue emerged as an intense topic of debate and discourse in terms of equality and equity in the society. The notion of gender is often clubbed with the sex and one is trained in a particular way to behave since the time of birth. These treatments not only confined within the behaviours but also in their tastes, choices in everyday, life, i.e. an woman is asked to be conscious about her skin tone, obedient with a chaste character where as a man is asked to be strong, brave and a productive one.

Since the time immemorial, women are often deprived from certain privileges that could change her position from a reproductive agent to a productive asset, the expected gender roles confines their physical and mental mobility within the four walls. In other words equity was a completely an alien concept for the women, i.e. this prevailing deprivations for a long time eventually give rise to the concept of *equity* more of *equality*. Equity is a treatment that is offered as per the requirement which make a fair play.

The geographical canvas of the north-eastern region is surrounded by hills and rivers leads to a distinguished form of physiographic condition to support a typical form of livelihood to this region This bifurcation was historically enhanced by the chicken neck corridor which eventually develops an unique cultural background to the region in reference to the pan-Indian level. People of north-eastern region are mostly dependable on agriculture as a main source of income back then till the date along with some other occupations like fishing, pottery and so on. Though gradually the scenario experiencing some changes but the hardly a few changes is noticeable in the gender engagement over these areas.

An attempt has been made in this work to throw light on "does the region is still lagging behind in maintaining a balanced gender involvement culture or in other words a gender-neutral society".

The idea of gender equity is an intense topic of debate and discourse in a global level and many of the scholars postulated various theories or evidences to support the gender equity as a reality. But while making a microscopic analysis to this aspect in reference to the north-eastern region the picture is yet quite doubtful. Though in comparison to the pan-Indian level this area has a fair representation of women gradually in the overall frame, but the voice of patriarchy is still audible, which made the picture of gender equity a feeble one. Though in the recent times government sponsored various women centric schemes, the question is to what extent women enjoys those privileges if it is so, then why the picture is so blurry yet so far.

In order to make a deep analysis to the above concerned issues, we adopted various parameters such as education, health, violence to study the status of women in the north-eastern region as our area of interest.

Despite of various other practices prevailing in other parts of India such as, *sati* practice and wearing *burkha* and female infanticide, dowry death, status women in this concerned area is slightly better off but historically north-east India is bounded up with various customary laws which acts like an invisible force to make a distinct stratification within the society on the basis of gender. These customary laws acts as a catalyst in forbidding the movement of an women. "One is not born, rather, one becomes a woman." She argues that it is not the case that women were naturally inclined to do childcare or housework as was earlier assumed, but rather that females were held back by their upbringing, or by social and cultural expectations from them or by the limited educational or job opportunities available to them. Hence this gender-based division put the women just as a bearer and rearer of child, which eventually make her being a second sex: an unproductive and submissive to the first sex, i.e. male. The customary laws which is prevailing in the concerned areas which not only framed women as a secondary option but also further proceed in the process of "reification of women". North-east India has an unique practice of "bride price", where the groom had to pay a price in order to marry the bride for her absence in her natal home. But the question is does this practice uplift the status of an women as an asset? With a deep analysis, it could be visible that instead of recognizing her as an asset, this is more of a reification of women, where her worth is measured with money and paying the price to her family is like making her an object which could be exchanged for transaction. "The Zemei Naga males are forbidden to touch the meat of an animal killed by a woman, as it is 'considered that touching the meat would be below their dignity because bravery is a quality of men and docility that of women", this could be also seen as a how women were pushed away from the mainstream of economic earning to a home maker, where she is just being a reproductive agent than being a productive asset.

North-east also had the practice of matriliny prevailing amongst the Garo and Khasi communities, where the offspring bears the maternal linage and also younger daughter holding the property of the deceased parents, but only as mere custodian of the property, as she could not sell off the property on her own even in this matrilineal society dominance of man is still prevalent while making any of the decision, maternal uncles holds a louder voice in any of the processes. Thus, it can be said that its just a transition of power from the males of the typical paternal order to the maternal patriarchal order.

Often an widow and a barren women's presence is considered to be inauspicious invarious rituals within the Brahmanical fold, thus this shows how society perceived women not as an women but more of a wife and a mother, society framed women as an object which needs to be either guarded or bearer of a child, while doing so society made a successful attempt in this process of manipulation.

The treatments in respective to the gender happened right after the birth of the child, the birth of a boy is more welcome than a girl in the family.

Thus, these customary laws portrays the status of the women in the north-east platform and how these laws act as a pulling force from achieving gender equity.

Though in the contemporary times, certain changes can be observed in the concerned area, but still it is yet so far from achieving a gender equitable society. Education is still a dream for the many of the girls. Though government sponsored schemes like, Sarva Shiksha Abhiyan to ensure education for all, but the parents reluctance to send off their daughters to the school is its biggest flaw of the concept. Hence this deprivation further enhanced the employment gap between male and female. Though few women are successful in imbibing higher education and getting enrolled in a job, in a corporate sector the preferences are generally more open for men in comparison to women, like a company prefers more male employees in the field of marketing and executives, while women are mostly welcomes in the advertising field.

Even in the field of health, women often ignored her own health issues in order fulfilling her household chores, maximum women in India suffers from various health issues like low bone density, fatty liver, miscarriage, economic inefficiency of her own and dependency on the male partner to undergo a proper medication treatment is an another curse on women mobility.

So, while moving back to the main concern of the proposed topic gender equity as a myth or reality within the north-eastern spectrum is a broad area for various new issues to be focused.

Even though from an outer space north-east is often portrays as a epitome of gender equity since a long back in the paper works. But reality is quite contrasting to it, even after a numerous efforts, women are still considered as second sex, who is incapable of dealing with things other than the kitchen, i.e. from Sharmila who went on a hunger strike for sixteen years from November 2000, to protest against the AFSPA Act failed to gain the confidence of the people as a leader. Thus, this shows the picture where the general notion of gender division of labour is deeply rooted. Political participation of women is still very countable, idea of equity is still remain a partial reality in the north-eastern spectrum.

The eight states located in the north-eastern region of India are characterized by a mostly tribal population, resulting in a distinctive and intricate social environment. The task of comprehending the north-eastern states of India from a gendered perspective is of utmost importance. An investigation conducted by the north-east network examined a sample of 152 Naga women belonging to various tribes. This study sheds light on the enduring influence of customary rules within the Naga community, which perpetuate a patriarchal world view and normalize violence against women. A multitude of emerging inquiries have characterized the mindset of contemporary individuals. Is the stratum of their belief system and insecurity regarding their culture the only factor at play, or is the politics of power the driving force behind these inquiries? Could the recent appeal from the All Nyishi Youth Association to all political parties in Arunachal Pradesh, discouraging the issuance of party credentials to Arunachalee women married to non-tribal men in *panachayat* and municipal elections, be rationalized? The impediment to their release is the potential erosion of the rights, integrity, progress, and well-being of the indigenous population in the state of Arunachal Pradesh.

It is postulated that the current ethnic conflict between the Meitei and Kuki communities in the state of Manipur is predominantly driven by political factors rather than just rooted in ethnic differences. During an interview, a representative from the National Federation of Indian Women emphasized that regardless of ethnic groups such as Meiteis and Kukis, it is evident that women and children bear the brunt of the suffering. This particular scenario bears a striking resemblance to the ongoing Israel-Palestine conflict. Revisiting the topic of the weaponization of women's bodies, it is important to note that the issue is situated within a context characterized by disturbance and violence. The protest by twelve Imas* against the Indian Army's actions under AFSPA and the incident involving two Kuki tribal women being paraded naked and assaulted by a mob of men are closely related. The context of the situation varies, but it is important to identify who the victims and agents are in each scenario. The Meira Paibis, a collective of Manipuri women self-identified as "Women with

*In Manipuri, "Ima" means "mother", symbolizing respect and reverence for women who have significantly contributed to the state's history and social movements. A notable example is the historic protest by a group of mothers, known as the "Imas", against the Armed Forces Special Powers Act (AFSPA) in the year 2004.

Torches", spearheaded several remarkable peaceful protests across a range of concerns. But the reconfiguration of this group's identity as the instigator of violence within the framework of two distinct ethnic groups serves as a significant indicator of the power dynamics inherent within the governing body.

Extensive research has been conducted on the limited involvement of women in political activities within the north-eastern region. The gendered lens reveals the evident lack of women's political participation in electoral politics. The lower levels of political participation cannot solely be attributed to the behaviour of political parties; there are other significant factors at play. Is it possible to overlook the attitudes of women towards being in a domestic environment, their acceptance of being a homemaker, or the dominance of their male counterparts in the decision making process? The Indian government's recent policy on reservation for women, the Nari Shakti Vandan Adhiniyam (Salutation to Women Power Bill), the 128th Constitutional Amendment Bill seeks to reserve 33 per cent of seats in the Lok Sabha (which would amount to 181 of the total 543 seats) and in state legislative assemblies, including the Delhi Legislative Assembly, and is definitely a positive outlook in political sphere. It would be an interesting journey to assess in near future. The world is waiting to see the spillover effect of this promising development in the realm of politics. In the contemporary times, works done by various scholars often ended up in focusing on the unavailability of exposures either in political or economic terms to women in maintaining a gender equitable society, the recent political exposure of the 33 per cent reservation of women would be a basic drift to make a study on the topic how women can access to this to make this a provision a fruitful one.

Women of north-eastern region is closely linked to the region's peace process. Most of the researches attributing women in promoting peace. While women in the north-east have played a significant role in the peace process, their involvement has been limited to specific peace initiatives and has not translated into broader political power or influence. Despite their efforts to prevent the breakdown of society, women's peace activities have been hindered by ethnic divisions and a focus on their respective communities (Bhattacharya, 2010). Additionally, their rise in the peace process may be driven more by changing circumstances than a genuine desire for societal transformation, leading to their exclusion from decision making and participation. A lot of scholars highlight that both state and non-state actors contribute equally to the destabilization of the situation for women residing in north-east India.

If the question is about gender, the views held by women regarding traditional practices comes in between. These beliefs may exhibit a profound level of internalization, which can be shaped by various cultural, religious, and societal influences. Alternatively, they may undergo transformation and adjustment in light of evolving circumstances and individual encounters. Acknowledging the plurality of these belief systems and the autonomy of women in determining their engagement with customary rituals is of utmost significance. Furthermore, it is essential to comprehend and uphold these values in order to advance gender equality and foster cultural variety throughout society.

Even after a numerous efforts made by various pioneers for eradicating the various disparity prevailing within the society, but none of these attempts include the concept of gender in their motives. In context of Assam, Sankardeva initiated a Neo-Vaishnavism movement, to established a *eka-saraniya-dharma,* with the believe of maintaining equality among the people, but gendering alienation is clearly visible till the date, in various *satra*s women are strictly prohibited from entering the same. This is a clear juxtapose to its own concept of an equal society.

The north-east area of India lacks a forum to address women's issues, including domestic and ethnic violence. Although external social organizations provide training and confidence development, creating a constituent base is crucial for gaining public support for tackling gender-based violence. Creating networks of women promotes regional interaction on gender equity, women's rights, and empowerment. The network can facilitate partnerships between domestic violence and sexual assault activists/organizations. They can also act as pressure organizations to promote women's rights at regional and national levels. All of these might help women live violence-free.

REFERENCES

Banerjee, P. (2014). "Women, Violence and North-East India", *Economic and Political Weekly, 49*(43/44): 3940. http://www.jstor.org/stable/24480991

Bhattacharya, J. (2010). "Gender, Peacemaking and the Case of North-East India", *The Indian Journal of Political Science, 71*(1): 233-39. http://www.jstor.org /stable/42748384

Das, J.K. (2003). "Reflections on Human Rights and the Position of Indian Women", *The Indian Journal of Political Science,* 203-20.

De Beauvoir, S. (2023). "The Second Sex", In *Social Theory Re-Wired,* Routledge, pp. 346-54.

Irengbam, A. (2000). *Between the Lines: Streotypes and Prejudices Opinion-1*, January Issue, Vol. I, Issue II, January.

Lindqvist, A., M.G. Senden and E.A. Renstrom (2021). "What is Gender, Anyway: A Review of the Options for Operationalising Gender", *Psychology & Sexuality, 12*(4): 332-44.

Menon-Sen, K. and A.K. Shiva Kumar (2001). *Women in India How Free?: How Equal?* Report commissioned by the Office of the United Nations Resident Coordinator in India.

13

Overcoming Gender Disparities in Eminent Indian Educational and Research Institutions with Ambedkar

Mehboobun Nahar Milky

Dr Ambedkar said, "I measure the progress of a community by the degree of progress which women have achieved". Unfortunately, the Global Gender Gap Index Report, 2020 ranks India 112th out of 153 countries, with a score of 0.668, indicating a decline from the 2018 ranking of 108th with a score of 0.665. Across different aspects of society including culture, social interactions, politics, economy, and the education women often face multiple challenges, discrimination, and exploitation. Studies indicate that gender-based division of labour leads to women's exclusion from high-status occupations (Kaur, 2021; Bal, 2005; Cronin, 1999). For instance, while examining India's leading engineering institutions, the IITs, I have noticed a significant gender gap. On average, only 11.24 per cent of the faculty members are women. Similarly, the NITs have an average of 17.75 per cent women faculty, and the IISERs nationwide show a gender distribution of 15.47 per cent (Swarup & Dey, 2020).

In research institutions, especially those focusing on biological sciences like the National Centre for Biological Sciences (NCBS), Institute of Life Sciences (ILS), and Indian Institute of Chemical Biology (IICB), a consistent pattern emerges. These institutions have 23.12 per cent women scientists, whereas male scientists make up a much higher percentage at 77.49 per cent (Swarup & Dey, 2020).

However, this trend is persistent across various research and teaching establishments in India, irrespective of factors such as establishment year, prestige, and geographical spread. In summary, these institutions consistently maintain a pattern of employing women faculty and researchers, making up only 10.20 per cent of their overall workforce. The growing gap in opportunities and representation within both institutions and society is a significant problem today. Scholars have started examining this issue, as seen in works by Kaur (2021), Jaganathan, Bawa & Rai (2020) and Bal (2005).

Attempts have been made to understand the low representation of women in pursuing a high-status research and teaching career (Cronin, 1999). Scholars have referred to a few models (Western Models), such as the "leaky pipeline effect", "glass ceiling at workplace" and "Matilda effect" to explain the low representation and/or the loss of female representation in eminent educational institutions throughout the country (Bal, 2005; Swamp & Dey, 2020; Kaur, 2021).

However, the focus on factors like caste, community, and religion has been limited. It is noteworthy that non-Western concept such as caste have not received enough attention in this domain. This is concerning because there is substantial and long-standing evidence of the exclusion of individuals from lower and untouchable castes from various aspects of society, education, and the economy, leading to their classification as "subaltern" or "Dalit". Drawing on the ideas of the Italian theorist Antonio Gramsci and subsequent neo-Gramscian scholars, the term "subaltern" is used to describe individuals who are dependent, marginalized, and powerless due to their caste, as well as their occupational and class status (Gramsci, 1971; Guha, 1988; Srinivas, 2013).

While, 'Dalit' is primarily a political term, representing a quasi-class identity born during the Ambedkarite movement in India and the term is used to characterize the marginalized "untouchables" who suffered oppression at the hands of the dvija (Brahman, Kshatriya, and Vaishya) castes (Teltumbde, 2017).

1. The fundamental issue of inequality is thus tied to caste. However, we also have to remember that in India, along with caste, deeply rooted patriarchal norms subtly coerce women into enduring discrimination and limited rights, perpetuating the belief that women's primary domain is the home and marriage is their ultimate destiny. Hence, this paradoxical position of Indian women persists, and particularly, it is far worse for Dalit.
2. It is a metaphor describes the way in which women become underrepresented minorities in the STEM fields. Often depicts women passively leaking out of STEM careers with no discussion of why those leaks occur, but, in fact, the cracks and gaps caused by the biases and barriers are a major cause of the leak of women and minorities out of the STEM pipeline.
3. The notion of glass ceiling effect implies that gender or other disadvantages are stronger at the top of the hierarchy than at lower levels and these disadvantages become worse later in a person's career.
4. The Matilda effect is bias against female accomplishments in science and one manifestation is fewer citations when compared to male authors women who bear the triple burden of caste, class, and gender. Dalit women navigate unique challenges, experiencing the compounded oppressions of being both Dalits and women.

Doubly marginalized these women endure subjugation, degradation, and marginalization, underscoring the imperative for a more comprehensive examination of such disparities in our society. In this chapter, I will try to understand the gender disparities by drawing inspiration from the insights of Dr. B.R. Ambedkar. I will explore the life and contributions of Dr. Bhimrao Ramji Ambedkar, referred to as Ambedkar hereafter. I believe embracing an Ambedkarite framework with an emphasis on state-driven institutional reforms guided by the subaltern has the potential to address the issues of inequality and gender disparity in organizational and institutional settings. I will focus on Ambedkar's critical examination of the Indian caste system, his proposal for comprehensive reform, and his advocacy for representational opportunity as a means to achieve equality. Ambedkar argued that the Indian caste system hindered the lower castes in India from achieving socio-economic mobility. This system establishes a hierarchy in society, where the socio-economic rights of different caste groups are predetermined solely by their birth and heredity, not by their abilities (Ambedkar, 1936).

Despite efforts like constitutional reforms, affirmative action, and long-standing socio-political movements for equality, a rigid economic system based on caste still persists (Thorat & Newman, 2007). Ambedkar's writings and philosophy hold significant relevance for all oppressed and socially disadvantaged groups in India. In his works, he provided a framework for mobilization, organization, and the demand for equal citizenship rights.

This chapter aims to highlight the enduring relevance of Ambedkar in addressing gender disparity. First, Ambedkar's insights offer valuable perspectives on Indian society, where he consistently critiqued mainstream practices that perpetuate inequalities, leaving an indelible mark on the struggle for sovereignty (Vajpeyi, 2012). Second, although Ambedkar's focus was on India and its caste-based disparities, the principles he championed hold universal significance. By challenging entrenched systems of inequality, such as caste and patriarchy, Ambedkar advocated for the equality and dignity of all human beings, particularly emphasizing the rights of marginalized population, including women and, more specifically, Dalit women.

This chapter delves into the intricate ways social, cultural, and political disparities contribute to gender inequalities, with a particular focus on the impact on women. It explores Ambedkar's potential to reshape institutional and organizational structures to foster subaltern equality, drawing from a comprehensive understanding of interconnected inequality systems. The subsequent sections follow a structured approach, commencing with a brief biography of Ambedkar to provide readers with a contextual understanding of his life and work. Subsequently, I will discuss the key aspects of Ambedkar's perspectives: a critique of caste-based gender inequalities in Indian society; and his advocacy for comprehensive reforms across various institutional realms and organizational spaces emphasizing on pursuing justice and equality, especially women's equality.

B.R. Ambedkar: A Brief Bio-sketch

Widely recognized as Babasaheb, meaning a revered father, Ambedkar was born in a Mahar family on 14 April 1891, in Mhow, a small town in central India. Traditionally, the Mahars categorized as an untouchable caste in India, worked as village servants for the dominant groups within the village. Throughout the history, it is evident that a person's caste has played a crucial role in defining the various forms of capital they inherit or have the opportunity to access and accumulate. This includes economic, social, cultural, and symbolic capital (Bapuji & Crispal, 2020).

During British colonial rule, the social status of the Mahars underwent a positive transformation, attributed to emerging opportunities in road and rail construction, factories, and service in the British Indian armies (Zelliot, 1970). Despite the traditional denial of education to untouchables, Ambedkar's father, Ramji, a British Army officer, was committed to providing his son with appropriate education. In 1913, Ambedkar earned his BA in English and Persian from Mumbai's Elphinstone College.

Following this, he ventured to New York for further studies. While at Columbia University, he delved into various domains of social sciences and was influenced by figures like John Dewey, whose ideas shaped Ambedkar's perspectives on democracy in twentieth century India (Mukherjee, 2009), and it was during this period that he authored the essay "Castes in India: Their Mechanism, Genesis, and Development", challenging prevalent caste theories by suggesting its origin as a class system characterized by endogamy, reinforcing a rigid structure and perpetuating inequalities. Despite earning two economics doctorates and being called to the bar at Gray's Inn in London, Ambedkar encountered ongoing caste-based discrimination upon returning to Bombay in 1924. Hindered in establishing his legal practice, he founded the Bahishkrit Hitkarini Sabha, initiating his role as a mass organizer for social, economic, and political reform. Inspired by personal experiences, this marked the beginning of Ambedkar's advocacy for the welfare of excluded peoples (Ambedkar, 1990).

In 1926, Ambedkar joined Bombay's Legislative Council, challenging both the colonial government and Indian nationalists for oppressive practices. He advocated for subaltern masses, demanding provincial autonomy, adult suffrage, and a reform of representation system. Ambedkar emphasized the link between literacy and franchise, asserting that denying the illiterate the vote perpetuates their disenfranchisement (Ambedkar, 1928). In 1927, Ambedkar initiated the Mahad Satyagraha, denouncing *Manusmriti* as the "Bible of slavery" and calling for a new code to end caste and gender-based inequalities. In 1928, he advocated for the abolition of class and communal electorates, proposing general electorates with seat reservations, particularly for Dalits. Founding the Independent Labour Party in 1936, Ambedkar later formed the Scheduled Caste Federation in 1942, dissolving the former due to lack of socialist support. Appointed as the Labour Minister in 1942, he expanded his views on industrialization and economic planning. His 1945 works criticized Gandhi and Congress, offering an alternative economic model based on "state socialism" for independent India, emphasizing nationalization, planning, and human rights while rejecting untouchability (Thorat, 1998).

In July 1947, Ambedkar joined India's Constituent Assembly and later became the Law Minister in the first post-colonial cabinet after India gained Independence on 15 August 1947. He played a pivotal role as the chair of the Drafting Committee, earning the title of the "chief architect" of the Constitution of India (Brecher, 1959). In 1952, Columbia University conferred upon him an Honorary Doctorate in Law. Disheartened by Hindu leaders' indifference to caste-based inequalities, Ambedkar converted to Buddhism in 1956, asserting that leaving the dominant religion was the only path for social mobility.

In 1990, he posthumously received the Bharat Ratna, India's highest civilian honour, being the sole recipient from an untouchable caste. Caste-based Gender Inequalities in Indian Society: Ambedkar's Critical Examination, Dr. Ambedkar strongly emphasized the pursuit of equality for the oppressed classes, particularly the Dalits, who were often labelled as untouchables and marginalized within the Hindu caste hierarchy. In the initial phases of his advocacy, he employed *satyagraha*, a non-violent resistance approach inspired by Gandhi, to challenge and protest the caste-based restrictions and promote access to public spaces for untouchables. Additionally, Ambedkar recognized the intertwined dynamics of gender and caste in the Indian society. He believed women were victims of the caste system and emphasized the "double burden" borne by women.

In this section, I will attempt to look into the connection between caste and gender, examining the role of the caste system and its impact on the oppression of women within caste and patriarchal structures. An analysis of Dr. Ambedkar's perspectives on the caste system, which systematically excluded women, will be provided. Additionally, I will explore Dr. Ambedkar's advocated rights aimed at promoting women's equality in India. In his seminal anthropological paper, "Castes in India: Their Mechanism, Genesis, and Development", published in 1916, Dr. B.R. Ambedkar delves into the theoretical and practical implications of caste oppression on people's lives. Focusing on Indian castes, he identifies endogamy as a pivotal factor in perpetuating the caste system among various social groups in India. Ambedkar contends that the juxtaposition of endogamy upon exogamy is the fundamental mechanism behind the formation of castes. He argues that exogamy is the natural state of communities, leading to integration and amalgamation, culminating in a homogeneous civilization. The practice of endogamy, or arranging marriages within the same caste, plays a vital role in the caste system as it functions as distinct units within a broader production system. Ambedkar suggests that endogamy serves as a method for expressing, maintaining, and reproducing caste and gender subordination. Furthermore, he highlights the patriarchal system's role in safeguarding land, women, and rituals, emphasizing their significance in preserving the closed structure of Indian society. The control of women's reproductive abilities by the upper castes becomes essential in maintaining this closed structure, positioning women as gateways into the caste system within the context of Hindu and Brahmanic patriarchy. Shifting to historical context, in ancient Indian society, women initially experienced freedom, autonomy, and rights during the pre-Vedic period characterized by a matriarchal system. However, the advent of Aryan or Vedic culture led to a shift towards a patriarchal society, though women retained some autonomy, rights, and educational opportunities.

The later Vedic period witnessed a decline in women's status due to increasing gender differentiation, leading to socio-economic marginalization, loss of rights, autonomy, and property rights. This decline worsened with stringent rules imposed by the lawgiver Manu, exacerbating challenges faced by women in ancient Indian society. In his book *Manusmriti*, Manu organized societal issues into accepted norms rather than addressing their elimination (Kumar, 2016), leading to the subjugation of women to various deprivations in property ownership, education, and access to knowledge. The concept of restraining women's freedom and subjugating them to male dominance became deeply ingrained.

However, the advent of the British Raj brought a ray of hope for Indian women, with enlightened reformers like Swami Vivekananda, Raja Rammohun Roy, Jyotiba Phule, Ishwar Chandra Vidyasagar, and Mahatma Gandhi working tirelessly to eradicate social evils. Ambedkar's vision of women's rights, advocates for the equal treatment of women alongside men, emphasizing their right to education, property, and political inclusion. Drawing from J.S. Mill's philosophy, Ambedkar condemns the subordination of women as a crime and stresses the need to empower half of the world's population for the realization of a developed world committed to human rights. Through his literary contributions, Ambedkar opposed societal norms that advocated submission for women, challenging male dominance and stereotypical feminine behaviour. He highlighted the interconnectedness of caste and gender, asserting that the eradication of gender disparities is inherent to eliminating caste distinctions (Kumar, 2016).

Ambedkar attributed the emergence of caste to growing differences within groups, emphasizing how castes controlled women's sexuality through endogamy. He accused the caste-gender nexus of being solely responsible for various forms of exploitation. Ambedkar, drawing from his theoretical knowledge and personal experiences of caste-based humiliation, understood the intrinsic link between caste and gender. He believed that political democracy could only thrive with the foundation of social democracy, promoting a way of life based on equality, liberty, and fraternity. Viewing the elevation of women's rights and status as a crucial step towards achieving this vision, Ambedkar emphasized the urgency of ensuring gender equality (Dhara, 2016).

Ambedkar's Vision

Advancing equality through comprehensive reforms Ambedkar stands out as a pioneering Indian scholar and social reformer who was among the first, if not the very first, to articulate the impact of layered patriarchy on women, especially on Dalit women. His ideas highlighted the vulnerability of Dalit women within the vertically structured caste system, emphasizing the detrimental effects of both endogamy and exogamy. His influential journals *Mook Nayak* and *Bahishkrit Bharat* was the mouthpiece to speak out against gender inequality. Ambedkar strongly believed in the importance of women's rights, supporting their right to vote and recognized the crucial role of women in political discussions, understanding that their active participation was key to challenging their subordinate status (Kumar, 2016).

He emphasized that without women's input, efforts to eliminate gender inequity and achieve women's liberation would be incomplete. Ambedkar expressed his confidence in women's organizations, stating that they could significantly contribute in improving societal conditions by eradicating social evils. Actively engaging in events and organizing women, Ambedkar advocated for gender equality and sought equal opportunities for women, especially Dalit women, aiming for their self-sufficiency akin to their upper caste counterparts. He emphasized on the education of women, and believed that it would benefit the entire family. The teachings from Ambedkar's perspectives were intended to benefit women universally, transcending caste boundaries. Ambedkar's speeches and ideas had a profound impact on women. Notable initiatives, such as the Mahad Satyagraha in 1927, the burning of *Manusmriti* in the same year, the Kalaram Temple Entry Satyagraha in 1930, and the formation of women's associations in 1928 in Bombay, were steps towards organizing and empowering women. As a strong advocate for women's strength, Ambedkar said:

> I measure the progress of a community by the degree of progress which women have achieved. Let every girl who marries stand by her husband, claim to be her husband's friend and equal and refuse to be his slave. I am sure if you follow this advice, you will bring honour and glory to yourselves. (Singariya, 2014)

Ambedkar aimed to bring about a significant lifestyle change, urging women to live lavishly and avoid clothing or ornaments that indicated lower status. Ambedkar sought to liberate women from traditional customs, rituals, and superstitions, encouraging them to embrace modem values and a progressive outlook (Babare, 2016).

Recognizing the challenges of child-rearing, Ambedkar advised women to limit childbirth and engage in other tasks. He emphasized women's education, equal treatment with men, property rights, and political involvement. As a member of Bombay Legislative Council, Ambedkar advocated for family planning and introduced the Maternity Benefit Bill. He emphasized the importance of providing mothers with adequate rest during the prenatal period, stating, "It is in the interest of the nation that the mother ought to get a certain amount of rest during the prenatal period" (Kumar, 2016).

His consistent efforts resulted in the passage of the Maternity Benefit Act by the Madras Legislative Council in 1934, followed by other provinces. Ambedkar's efforts extended to the national level between 1942 and 1946, leading to the enactment of the Mines Maternity Benefit Bill for women across the entire country. Subsequently, in 1961, the central government passed a unified Maternity Benefit Act applicable to the entire nation. Ambedkar also played a key role in advocating for equal wages for women, aligning with the principle of equal pay for equal work, as stipulated in Article 39(d) of the Directive Principles of State Policy. The Constitutional provisions, such as—Article 14 (ensures that everyone in India is treated equally under the law), Article 15 (prohibits discrimination based on religion, race, caste, sex, or place of birth), Article 15(3) (empowers the state to implement positive discrimination in favour of women and children), Article 16 (ensures equal opportunities in public employment), Article 23 (prohibits human trafficking and forced labour), Article 39(a) and (d) (obliges the state to provide equal means of livelihood and equal pay for equal work), Article 42 (mandates the state to ensure fair and humane working conditions and maternity relief), Article 51A(e) (imposes a fundamental duty on citizens to reject practices that demean the dignity of women), Article 243D(3) (reserves not less than one-third of the total seats in every *panchayat* filled by direct election for women), Article 243T(3) (reserves not less than one-third of the total seats in every municipality filled by direct election for women), Article 243T(4) (provides reservation for Scheduled Caste and Scheduled Tribe women in the office of chairpersons in municipalities) and most importantly, the Hindu Code Bill reflects Ambedkar's attempt and commitment to advancing the rights and status of women in the India Society. In 1952, four crucial components of the Hindu Code Bill received approval, transforming into laws in 1955 and 1956. These enactments were the Hindu Marriage Act, Hindu Succession Act, Hindu Minority and Guardianship Act, and Hindu Adoption and Maintenance Act. These legislative measures have played a crucial role in transforming the legal landscape and empowering women within Hindu family structures (Omvedt, 2008; Babare, 2016).

Dr. B.R. Ambedkar's concerns extended beyond Hindu women to encompass the well-being of Muslim women as well (Babare, 2016). In his book *Pakistan or the Partition of India*, Ambedkar articulated apprehensions about various aspects of Muslim women's lives, including the wearing of veils, religious traditions, and marriage practices. He ardently opposed any form of discrimination against them. Ambedkar not only voiced these concerns but also took concrete actions by formulating legislation aimed at improving the status of women in India. Some of these legislations include the Women Labour Welfare Fund, Women Labour Protection Act, Maternity Benefit for Women Labour Bill, Leave Benefit to Piece Workers, Revision of Scale of Pay for Employees, and the Restoration of Ban on Women. His efforts aimed to address and rectify various challenges faced by women, irrespective of their religious affiliations (Babare, 2016).

Ambedkar's writings emphasize that inequalities are complex and harmful to individuals and societies. To overcome these problems completely, it is important to make changes to ensure fairness in all aspects of life for those who are disadvantaged. One crucial way to achieve equality for marginalized groups is through representation and reservations, which give them the right access to opportunities. Representation helps reduce differences in wealth and status. However, it is not enough. Even when marginalized people getjobs, they often face discrimination in various forms like bullying, bad job assignments, lower pay, and slower career growth, especially because of things like gender, caste, and religion (Noronha & Sharma, 2002; Pandey & Varkkey, 2020; Noronha, 2019).

To change these unfair attitudes, we need to follow Ambedkar's advice to educate, agitate, and organize. Ambedkar wanted marginalized groups to be represented in different sectors. Recent research shows that inequalities still exist in organizations and institutes because of biases in selection, cultural fit assessments, and reference practices that favour privileged individuals (Ajit, Donker, & Saxena, 2012).

Ambedkar suggested using reservations, similar to affirmative action, to address grievances and ensure fair representation, especially in public services, where many marginalized people work (Ambedkar, 1928). The Hindu Marriage Act, especially through Sections 5, 11, 17, 25, and 26, has significantly impacted Hindu Matrimonial Law, benefiting Indian women by emphasizing monogamy and providing post-divorce relief. Notably, Section 5 raised the marriage age for girls from 15 to 18, while Sections 11 and 17 enforce monogamy. The Act also addresses nullity, divorce, and maintenance, with Section 26 specifying child custody. The Hindu Succession Act of 1956, through Section 14, elevates women's property rights, placing them in a superior position. The Hindu Minority and Guardianship Act, particularly Section 6a, ensures custody with the mother for minors below 5 years, while Section 6b covers custody of illegitimate children. Section 9 grants the mother the authority to appoint a new guardian. The Hindu Adoption and Maintenance Act empowers women in adopting children, respecting their decision making autonomy. However, Ambedkar's plan for representation, using quotas for disadvantaged sections, is different from Western diversity initiatives like affirmative action. While the latter relies on indirect methods, Ambedkar's plan is more direct and measurable, making it easier to monitor and evaluate achievements. In today's Indian institutions, there is resistance to quotas based on meritocracy, leading to certain genders dominating top positions. Even though there are more women in the country, their representation in academic positions is only 12-20 per cent, showing the need for a strong implementation of state-mandated representation methods for true equality.

Conclusion

Dr. B.R. Ambedkar was a strong advocate for changing Hindu society to promote equality. As the Law Minister and Chairman of the Drafting Committee, he worked to free women from long-standing social restrictions by reforming laws influenced by Manu (Singariya, 2014). Through his writings and activism, Dr. Ambedkar made significant contributions in advancing women's empowerment.

The National Policy for the Empowerment of Women in 2001 acknowledged that gender inequality was largely influenced by social and economic structures, a view anticipated by Ambedkar earlier years (Shukla, 2011). Government initiatives, such as women's education, support for SHGs, capacity building, skill development training, emphasis on women and child development, employment opportunities, and the establishment of the National Commission for Women, aim to empower women (Babare, 2016). Despite progress in social, economic, legal, and political empowerment, there remains insufficient awareness of women's rights. Indian women still face numerous social challenges, including issues like harassment, violence, and discrimination. The prestigious research and teaching institutions of India consistently employ a low percentage (10-20%) of women faculty, mirroring trends in organized sectors like judiciary, defence, business, and management. However, exceptions exist in "feminized" sectors such as school services and nursing. To ensure equality, it is imperative to safeguard women's representation in these fields through quotas or reservations. Ambedkar emphasized the need to eliminate patriarchy and the caste system deeply rooted in society for transformative change. Genuine emancipation, beyond constitutional provisions, requires a shift in people's hearts and attitudes. Dr. Ambedkar's vision for empowering women can be realized through representation and collaborative efforts between women and the government, overcoming obstacles on the path to their development (Swant, 2019).

REFERENCES

Ajit, D., H. Donker and R. Saxena (2012). "Corporate Boards in India", *Economic and Political Weekly*, *47*(32): 39-43.

Ambedkar, B.R. (1928). "Dr. Ambedkar with the Simon Commission (Indian Satutory Commission". Report Containing Views and Recommendations Regarding the Constitution of the Bombay Presidency), *AWS,* Vol. 2.

_____ (1936). "Philosophy of Hinduism", *AWS*(03).

_____ (1990). "Waiting for a Visa. Manuscript as Part of People's Education Society, Mumbai Collections", *AWS*, Vol. 12.

Babare, S. (2016). "Ambedkar and Women Empowerment in India", *Research Front*, *4*(1): 23-26.

Bal, V. (2005). "Women Scientists in India: Nowhere Near the Glass Ceiling", *Current Science*, *88*(6): 872-78.

Bapuji, H. and S. Crispal (2020). "Understanding Economic Inequality through the Lens of Caste", *Journal of Business Ethics*, *162*(3): 533-51.

Brecher, M. (1959). *Nehru: A Political Biography*. Oxford: Oxford University Press.

Chandra, T. (October 2019). *Literacy in India: The Gender and Age Dimension*. ORF Issue Brief No. 322.

Cronin, C. (1999). "Theorizing Progress: Women in Science, Engineering, and Technology in Higher Education", *Journal of Research in Science Teaching*, *36*(6): 637-61.

Dhara, L. (14 April 2016). *Ambedkar's Understated Feminism*. Retrieved in 10 November 2023, from https://www.forwardpress.in/2016/04/ambedkarsunderstated-feminism/

Gramsci, A. (1971). *Selections from the Prision Notebooks of Antonio Gramsci*. (Q. Hoare, & G.N. Smith, eds.). New York: International Publishers.

Guha, R. (1988). "Preface". In R. Guha & G.C. Spivak, *Selected Subaltern Studies*, Oxford: Oxford University Press, pp. 35-36.

Jaganathan, S., A. Bawa and R. Rai (2020). "Narrative Worlds of Frugal Consumers: Unmasking Romanticised Spirituality to Revael

Responsibilization and De-Politicization", *Journal of Business Ethics, 161*(1): 149-68.

Kaur, R.P. (2021). "Gender Issues in Science and Technology", *Asia Pacific Journal of Health Sciences, 8*(3): 119-22.

Kumar, B. (2016). "Liberating Indian Women from Slavery: An Analysis of Dr. Ambedkar's Contribution for Uplifting", *International Journal of English Language, Literature and Humanities, IV*(1): 212-19.

Mukherjee, A.P. (2009). "B.R. Ambedkar, John Dewey, and the Meaning of Democracy", *New Literary History, 40*(2): 345-70.

Noronha, E. (2019). "Caste and Workplace Bullying: A Persistent and Pervasive Phenomenon", In P.D'Cruz, E. Noronha, C. Caponecchia, E.D. Salin, and M. Tuckey (eds.), *Dignity and Inclusion at Work Handbook of Workplace Bullying, Emotional Abuse and Harrasment*. Singapore: Springer.

Noronha, E. and R.N. Sharma (2002). "Indian Industry and Ethnicity: A Study of Two Organizations in Mumbai", *Global Business Review, 3*(1): 153-70.

Omvedt, G. (2008). *Ambedkar: Towards an Enlightened India*. New Delhi: Penguin.

Pandey, J. and B. Varkkey (2020). "Impact of Religion-based Caste System", *Business & Society, 59*(5): 995-1034.

Shukla, D. (24 October 2011). *Dr. B.R. Ambedkar's Vision Towards Gender Equality*. Retrieved from https://www.lawyersclubindia.com/articles/dr-b-r-ambedkar-vision-towardsgender-equality-4144.asp

Singariya, M.R. (2014). "Dr. B.R. Ambedkar and Women Empowerment in India", *Quest Journals, Journal of Research in Humanities and Social Science, 2*(1): 1-4.

14

Reforms in Marriage and Divorce Laws and the Role of Ambedkar

Swati Pandita

The life of a Hindu woman was governed by heterogeneous customs which varied from region to region. The interpretation of these customs and rites, which were a result of divine revelations, were heavily influenced by the individual commentators. Public and procedural laws were already codified in the beginning of the nineteenth century; however, Hindu family law somehow escaped the ordeal. Sir C. Ilbert was of the opinion that the only way to codify customary laws is to have "generations of Indian lawyers" on the team.

In 1921, a resolution was introduced in Central Legislative Assembly asking for governments support in implementation of codified Hindu law. T.B. Sapru requested the withdrawal of the resolution on the assurance that the government would informally look into the matter after taking into consideration opinions of various legal bodies. Two decades later, in 1937, Hindu Women's Right to Property Act was introduced to "amend the Hindu law to give better rights to women in respect of property". The statute provided widows with claim over property of husband dying intestate.

In 1941, B.N. Rau Committee was for formed with the objective of resolving ambiguities created by the 1937 Act and to modernize the Hindu Law. The members were in favour of removal of provisions upholding polygamy, exclusion of female heirs by male, and limited estate of women. The committee was directed by the authorities to draft a code based on the report. Author in his book remarked that

> It argument was cautiously lawyer-like and scholarly. In content its specific reform proposals were, in direction if not exact degree, congenial to official opinion.

However, the report received opposition from members of the Legislative Assembly, who were mostly scholars of Sanskrit or *panditas*, on grounds that it was highly influenced by the Western culture. Amongst them the most prominent was V.V. Deshpande, Professor of Hindu Law in Banaras Hindu University, who informed various orthodox organizations about the Rau report violating the sayings of the Vedas.

The 1947 report went few steps further and gave the following recommendations:

- the joint family property system to be abolished;
- daughter's right to succession similar to son's rights;
- abolition of barriers serving as an impediment in inter-caste marriages;
- assimilation of civil and sacramental marriages; and
- introduction of divorce for oppressor castes (so-called higher castes) too.

By this time, Dwarkanath Mitter, who had contributed to the 1941 report as a former judge and scholar of Sanskrit, started vehemently opposing the 1941 and 1947 reports. He remarked:

> Hindu ladies and gentlemen representing the public spirit of this country are almost unanimously in condemning the code while only a microscopic minority is favouring codification.

The orthodox Hindus wanted any change in the Bill to be made and approved by a Pandit Parishad and not by lawyers or members of legislature.

The 1947 report also mentioned that the general public is divided into three factions. The first one being extreme right and opposing it, the other being extreme left or liberal who are supporting it and asking for uniform laws to be applicable to Muslims and Christians too and the third, which constitutes majority of the population, was somewhere in the middle, agreeing to nearly every reform with minor disagreements. It was also noted that the report had strong support from bulk of the women associations.

The Bill was referred to the Select Committee on 17 November, 1947 comprising eminent jurists and parliamentarians, viz. Sir Alladi Krishnaswami Ayyar, Bakshi Tek Chand, Shri H.V. Kamat, Smt. G. Durgabai and many others.

By 1948 a rift was created in the Assembly between traditional Congress leaders lead by Sardar Patel and progressive faction lead by Babasaheb Ambedkar. He was aware of the deplorable condition of Hindu women owing to these conservative customs and believed that ideally a political democracy should transform into social democracy for the country to progress. This ideology propelled him take measures to reform the Hindu law and work steadily towards the enfranchisement of women.

Babasaheb believed that,

> No law passed by the Indian Legislature in the past or likely to be passed in the future can be compared to it (Hindu Code) in point of its significance. To leave inequality between class and class, between sex and sex which is the soul of Hindu society, untouched and to go on passing legislation relating to economic problems is to make a farce of our constitution and to build a palace on a dung heap. This is the significance I attached to the Hindu Code.

Provisions in the Hindu Code Bill Regarding Marriage

Who is a Hindu?

The Bill has a broad definition of the Hindu which included any person born in the Hindu religion, or converted to it, or is a Sikh, Buddhist or Jaina. Any child, irrespective of their legitimacy, if born to a family where both or one of the parents were following Hinduism or was brought up following the Hindu religion shall also come under the ambit of this definition. It also included Virashaivas, Lingayatas and followers of Brahmo Samaj and Arya Samaj. It essentially included everyone who was not a Muslim, Jew, Parsi or Christian.

The present legislation adopted the same definition.

Types of Marriage

The Code varied from the current laws as it recognized a new kind of marriage, civil or registered marriage. The Act mentioned that,

> no marriage between Hindus shall be recognized as valid unless it is solemnized—(a) as a Dharmik marriage, or (b) as a civil marriage, or (c) in accordance with the provisions of section 24A.

However, the essentials of a dharmic marriage were quite similar to that of the sacramental marriage, as it barred marriage if one of the parties was below the legal age of marriage, within prohibited degrees of relationship, lunatic or already married. The Bill stated that, dharmic marriages would be considered solemnized with the final step of *satapadi* (seven rounds in front of the sacred fire) and the state government might make it mandatory to register it as a proof of its validity.

For civil marriages, there would be a registrar appointed for each district and parties have to submit a written notice. To decide territorial jurisdiction, one of the parties to the marriage should have resided in that district at least thirty days prior to serving of the notice.

It also provided that, general public could object to the marriage within thirty days, if the said marriage violated any of the essentials under Section 8 of the Bill. However, if the objection was not bona fide, a fine would be imposed on the objecting party. Later, Special Marriage Act, 1954 was passed which provided for a notice to be given to the marriage Officer by the parties intending to marry, which shall be published by him for general public to raise objections.

Similarly, for Hindu marriage, state government can make registration mandatory as a proof of solemnization of marriage. However, a non-obstentate clause is added later to specify that omission of registration shall not affect the validity of the marriage.

Sapinda and Prohibited Degree

The term *sapinda* is derived from Sanskrit, where *sapinda* means "having a common ancestor" or "related by blood". The concept is rooted in the idea of maintaining social and familial harmony by avoiding unions between individuals who are too closely related.

Under Hindu Law, a person is said to be in the *sapinda* relationship with another if they share a common ancestor. This means that marriage between individuals who fall within the *sapinda* relationship is generally prohibited, as it is considered too close and could lead to potential issues related to consanguinity.

The Hindu Code Bill allowed parties to marry despite similarity in *sapinda*s or *gotra*s, or dissimilarity in caste or sub-caste, two barriers for sacramental marriage. Later on in the subsequent statutes, *sapinda* and marriages within prohibited degrees are allowed if each of the parties are governed by customs that permit it, otherwise such marriages are void.

Similar provision is enacted under Special Marriage Act, where, it shall be allowed if any one of the parties comes under such custom.

Maintenance

Under the customary Hindu Law, a legally married wife was not allowed to claim maintenance from the husband if she was not living in his company in the matrimonial house. The Bill included provisions for right to claim separate maintenance if the wife was suffering from some loathsome disease; the husband had a mistress; he committed cruelty against her; deserted her for two years or more; converted to any other religion without her consent, etc.

The Bill acknowledged the fact that wife might be living separately ineluctably and the present statute was narrow in not providing her maintenance.

Hindu Marriage Act under Section 24 clearly mentions that if the court thinks that one of the parties does not have independent income to sustain themselves or for the legal proceedings, it can order the husband or the wife to pay interim maintenance during the course of proceedings to their partner. Later, HMA 1955 added Section 24 where it was established that if wife or husband, during the course of the proceedings, do not have any independent source of income to support the expenses incurred on the proceedings, the court may grant them interim maintenance.

In addition to this, the court may also grant any spouse permanent maintenance till their lifetime, until they re-marry or indulge in sexual intercourse outside marriage.

Polygamy

The Bill called for the abolishment of polygamy. Babasaheb Ambedkar observed that in Hinduism only men had the right to marry more than once but that right was not absolute according to our Shastras. Nattukutai Chettiyars in south did not allow the husband to marry twice unless the first wife permits and after she is given a share in property. Similar provision was visible in *Arthashastra* by Chankaya.

Rau Committee report observed that the public opinion was in favour of monogamy but experts and some members of legislative assembly were apprehensive on grounds that it might lead to men converting to Islam to practice polygamy; weavers, cultivators and other working communities felt the need of multiple working hands, hence they prefer more than one wife; for monogamy to be practised, divorce would be allowed, which is opposed to Hindu orthodox sentiments; and, it would also lead to men keeping concubine.

Babu Ram Narayan Singh objected to the idea of monogamy and said,

> one woman may be divorced today; other women may be coming for marriage the next day. Monogamy may mean many-gamy; you won't allow a man to marry a second wife.

Similar sentiment was reflected in the joint parliamentary committee report on Hindu marriage and divorce where they held it to be arbitrary as

> the so-called monogamy is only a misnomer for a regularly unprincipled polygamy and polyandry, as both the men and women are permitted to divorce and remarry even hundred times.

Section 5 of the HMA, 1955, prohibits marriage if any of the parties have any living spouse at the time of the marriage. Any marriage solemnized in violation of this provision shall be considered void and punishable with imprisonment till seven years under Sections 494 and 495 of the Indian Penal Code.

Child Marriage

Child marriage was then also recognized as a human rights violation as it deprived children, especially young girls, of their childhood, education, and future opportunities.

Babasaheb Ambedkar remarked that,

> *Sati*, enforced widowhood and girl marriage are customs that were primarily intended to solve the

> problem of the surplus man and surplus woman in a caste and to maintain its endogamy.

Shrimati Hansa Mehta suggested in the assembly to include the provisions stringently dealing with child marriage. She opined that Sarda Act, 1929 was not sufficient in curbing the menace. Hence, the Hindu Code Bill should include the age of marriage as a criterion to deicide validity. However, Shri V.S. Sarwate had an opposing view and commented:

> when you once admit that sacramental marriages are sacramental, then let religion be the test for providing the conditions for such a marriage. If religion allows child marriage and marriages of minors, let it be allowed.

The present legislation prohibits child marriage and specifies that both the bride and bridegroom should be of legal age, that is, 18 years and 21 years respectively, for the marriage to be considered valid.

However, the Hindu Marriage Act, allows wife to present a petition for dissolution of marriage, if she was married before the age of 15 years and has repudiated the marriage before 18. This makes child marriage voidable not void.

To cure this discrepancy, legislature of Haryana amended the Prohibition of Child Marriage Act, 2006 in 2019 to make child marriage *void ab initio*.

Inter-Caste Marriage

In ancient India, marriage where a man of higher caste married a woman of lower caste was labelled as *anuloma*. When a woman of higher caste married a man of lower caste it was called *patriloma* marriage. Both kinds of marriage were looked down upon by the society.

The Hindu Law at that time barred inter-caste marriages between Hindus, Sikhs, Jainas, etc. and was strictly endogamous. The State of Bombay allowed *anuloma* marriages but *partiloma* was prohibited. Many High Courts described both of them to be invalid.

Arya Marriage Validation Act, 1937 did allow Hindus to marry outside caste but then a person need to claim to be a Arya Samaji. Pandit Bhargava Dass highlighted this issue in assembly:

> Supposing a person does not belong to Arya Samaj why should he have recourse to falsehood to effect his purpose? Therefore, the thing which the law should care about is that persons be enabled to do things in a legal manner.

Special Marriage Act, 1872 also allowed such marriages if the person declared himself to be a non-Hindu. This provision was created ambiguity in the mind of people and H.S. Gour in his commentary "Hindu Code" mentioned that,

> It will thus be seen that the Special Marriage (Amendment) Act has created a paradox. If the Hindu declares himself to be a non-Hindu and marries, he remains subject to Hindu Law. If he does not so declare, he ceases to be subject to Hindu Law, giving rise to a conundrum: When is a Hindu a non-Hindu? The answer is: When he marries as a Hindu under the Special Marriage (Amendment) Act.

Babasaheb Ambedkar contended that,

> The *vydhikas*, the orthodox, are left free to do what they think is right according to their *dharma*. The reformers who do not follow *dharma* but who follow reason, who follow conscience, have also been left to follow their reason and their conscience.

Hindu Marriage Act, 1955 and Special Marriage Act puts no bar of caste on marriages. It mentions that any two Hindus can marry if they satisfy the conditions provided.

Conclusion

Rajendra Prasad, S.P. Mukherjee, Pandit Malviya and many other orthodox members of the assembly were of the opinion that the Hindu Code Bill interferes with the religious belief and personal laws of Hindus and would cater to only a few progressive citizens. They also had apprehensions that it will lead to a string of suits in the court over inheritance rights and many poor parties would find it difficult to bear the expenses. Additionally, few members raised concerns over the religious obligation of a Hindu man to have a son, as he would be prohibited under new laws from marrying again.

The Hindu Code Bill was an earnest attempt by Babasaheb to correct the wrongdoings of Manu and reform the laws regulating Hindu marriages. Nehru in one of his speeches remarked that,

> I will get the Hindu Code Bill passed, whether I win or lose the election. I am prepared tofight the election on the issue of the Hindu Code. I can give this in writing to Brahmachariji.

However, his efforts were not completely wasted as his vision reflects in other statutes dealing with women rights like Sati Prevention Act, 1987; Dowry Prohibition Act, 1961; The Family Courts Act, 1984; Protection of Human Right Act, 1993; The Maternity Benefit Act, 1961; Immoral Traffic (Prevention) Act, 1956; The Child Marriage Restraint Act, 1929; The Equal Remuneration Act, 1976; The National Commission for Women Act, 1990; Protection of Women from Domestic Violence Act, 2005; etc.

Henceforth, it would not be wrong to conclude that Babasaheb Ambedkar played a pivotal role in emancipation of Indian women.

15

Dr. Bhimrao Ambedkar's Discussion on Women

With Special Reference to Dalit Women

Uday Bhan Singh

Introduction

Decades ago, Babasaheb had called upon women "not to marry early and not to be slaves to their husbands" for women empowerment.

The hallmark of Ambedkar's thinking regarding women empowerment was seen in a conference of women from the exploited class in the year 1942, when he said, "The progress of a community is measured by the progress of women".

Well-known Dalit thinker and writer Chandrabhan Prasad says that in the first part of Dr. Ambedkar's 17th treatise, it is mentioned that on 20 July 1942, Babasaheb had organized the "All India Depressed Classes Women's Conference" in Nagpur. In this conference he had said that "the progress of any community is measured by the progress of women".

Prasad said that in the same conference, Dr. Ambedkar had called upon women not to marry early and not to be slaves to their husbands. Babasaheb had said these things at a time when male chauvinism was very dominant.

Anita Nayak, president of the women's wing of "Dalit Indian Chambers of Commerce and Industry" (DICCI), says that Ambedkar's economic philosophy is very important for all the exploited classes. His economic philosophy is very important. Our effort is that women should get involved in employment and business along with education in large numbers. Prabuddha Kumar Omi, head of the non-governmental organization "Bahujan Samaj Parishad", says that Babasaheb not only talked about the upliftment of Dalits but also emphasized on the empowerment of all the exploited sections of the society and especially women. It was the result of the consciousness raised by him that in independent India, many women from the Dalit class achieved great heights in different fields. Omi says that Dr. Ambedkar's basic *mantra* regarding women empowerment was education. He described women's education as very important for the development of the society. Ambedkar, born on 14 April 1891 in Mhow (Indore district) of Madhya Pradesh, received education from prestigious institutions of the country and the world like Mumbai University, Columbia University and London School of Economics playing an important role in the freedom struggle, Ambedkar raised the voice of rights for the Dalits and the exploited sections of the society. Babasaheb, who became the first law minister in the government of Independent India, said goodbye to the world on 6 December 1956.

Review of Literature

Chandrabhan Prasad says that Ambedkar's personality cannot be limited only to Dalit consciousness and Dalit upliftment.

According to him, intellectuals of a particular section of the society have deliberately tried to associate Ambedkar only with Dalits. The real thing is that Ambedkar's personality is very broad. He was the voice of all the exploited people of the society. All sections of the society will have to accept that Babasaheb was the leader of the entire nation. Till now the Dalit women's movement believed in joining non-Dalit women's movements and working together with them. But the women leaders of the non-Dalit women's movement, suffering from upper caste mentality, discriminated against Dalit women. This discrimination emerged more clearly when in December 1937, in the session of "All India Mahila Parishad", Hindu women insulted the famous Dalit community writer and Dalit women leader Jaibai Choudhary by making her sit away from the dining place. Angered by their discriminatory behaviour, on 1 January 1938, Dalit women organized a massive meeting at Dharam Peth in Nagpur in which thousands of Dalit women participated.

Objectives

We can discuss the objectives of this theory-based studies according to following points:

- To understand the ideologies of Dr. Bhim Rao Ambedkar about women.
- What was the thinking of Bhim Raw Ambedkar on Dalit women of the society?
- Efforts of Dr. Bhim Raw Ambedkar for upliftment of women specifically Dalit women.
- Draw attention regarding laws which advocated by Ambedkar for the welfare of women, etc.

Hypothesis

Following hypothesis were surrounded when researcher was thinking to write this research paper:

- Dr. Bhim Rao Ambedkar nothing done any thing for the upliftment of women.
- He was not aware of the problems of the women.
- Dr. Ambedkar done only for the Constitution of India.
- He never efforts for the Dalit women in the society, etc.

Study

The ill-treatment, untouchability and discrimination against Dalit women by the upper caste women was strongly protested.

Dalit leaders Anjani Bai Bhratar and Sakhubai expressed their anger by strongly condemning these Hindu women by calling them"shameless" and "having low behaviour" and taught Dalit women to live a self-respecting and self-reliant life. Ramabai Ambedkar Mahila Sangh was established in the council. This Mahila Sangh decided to start a night school for Dalit women (*Itihas Ghadwala*—Urmila Pawar, Meenakshi Moon). Twenty-five thousand women participated in the All India Dalit Women's Conference held on 20 July 1942. Dr. Ambedkar himself was present in this conference. The special thing about this conference was that Dalit women representatives from all over India participated in this conference. This conference was presided over by Sulochana Dogre and the Chief Secretary of the meeting was Indira Patil and the welcoming guest was Kirti Patil. In 1942 itself, the All India Dalit Women Federation held a convention on the political and social status of Dalit women, in which Federation Secretary Indira Patil, while throwing light on the deplorable condition of Dalit women in the society, said in her passionate speech, "The rights of their male colleagues are being denied to them". Behind us in the fight Don't want to stay. We have to live with them. Generally, household chores are the responsibility of women, but we should not stick to them. We are also anxious to get the same freedom as men and that is our right. We can get this right only through movement and our efforts. Only those who are suffering need freedom. The literacy rate among our Dalit women is very low. It is our duty to awaken their passion for education. At the same time, with the help of our illiterate and clumsy sisters, we will be ready to fight for the rights of the untouchables by sacrificing our lives under the leadership of our leader Babasaheb Ambedkar. We have to work together to eliminate our backwardness. To carry out these tasks, I propose to open a central institution and its branches in all the provinces. General Secretary Indira Patil laid emphasis on the education of Dalit women. Criticizing the Hindu religion for being responsible for the deplorable condition of women, she said, "It is because of the Hindu religion that we consider it our duty to bow before our husbands and take care of the house and children. The most important task before us is to remove the slavish thinking of Hindu religion from the minds of our sisters." In the same meeting Sulochana Dogre said that "We will destroy the monster of untouchability with Babasaheb" (*Itihas Ghadwala*—Urmila Pawar, Meenakshi Moon).

This council raised many important issues which were invaluable in improving the conditions of Dalit women. Getting the government to make a law regarding the right of husband and wife to divorce, opposition to polygamy, twenty-one days leave for labourers, farmers and women working in coal mines and other unorganized sectors, injury. Compensation on arrival, at least Rs. 15 per month to every woman after twenty years of service. Proposals were passed in the interest of working women by providing pension scheme, health, entertainment facilities and fixed working hours. The issue of reservation of Dalit women in District Taluka Local Board and Legislature was also raised loudly in this meeting. Babasaheb was very happy to see the thoughts and intellectual vision put forth fearlessly by the Dalit women and their leaders and after seeing the huge gathering of Dalit women and their free discussion, Babasaheb praised the Dalit women and said,

> Women when I woke up, I became a big supporter of the untouchable society. There may be a revolution. I have unwavering faith in the existence of an organized organization of women. Women can make a big contribution in destroying social evils. I am telling you from my experience that when I took up the work of Dalit community, I had decided that along with men, women should also be taken forward. That is why along with our own council, a women's council is also formed. I count the amount of progress that the women's society has made in the progress of the Dalit society. I am satisfied to see the participation of women in large numbers in this council and am also happy that we have made progress. (We have also Created History, p. 78 quoted)

In this meeting Dr. Ambedkar appealed to the Dalit women not to marry their daughters at an early age and emphasized on educating them to stand on their own feet and giving the message of having less children and living cleanly, the level of equality of women in the families. Yes, we talked about this also. While instilling self-respect in women, he said that you should live in an equal relationship at home, not as your husband's servant, but as your husband's friend. After the establishment of Scheduled Caste Federation in Nagpur in 1942, Shanta Bai Dani was made the District President of the party in the meeting of Scheduled Caste Federation in Nasik. In 1944 also, in the second session of the Dalit Federation in Kanpur, women held their own independent session and similar resolutions were passed as in Nagpur. It was headed by Ms. Shanta Bai Dani did it. While participating in this convention, Babasaheb said, "You move forward, a golden morning has dawned in your life". On 6 May 1945, the third session of the All India Untouchable Women's Council was held in Mumbai. In which thousands of Dalit women participated. The meeting was presided over by Meenambal Shivaram, a prominent activist of the then Madras State. The main speakers of this meeting were Shanta Bai Dani, Sarojini Jadhav, Mukta Sarvgaud, Ms. of Hyderabad. Rajmani, Godavari Rokar, etc. of Mumbai expressed sharp views on male-female inequality. He said that he guided the women who are victims of male inequality as to what steps should be taken for their liberation. In the presidential speech of the council, Sarojini Jadhav said that "The untouchable woman is dependent in every respect. If she has to achieve freedom, then a movement of untouchable women should be formed. Expressing his views, Minabal Shivaram said that

> Untouchable women, despite being free from these practices like widow remarriage and divorce, are still burdened with the rules and regulations of Hindu religion. Because of this his situation has become tragic. Dalit women should abandon Hindu religion. Dalit women should stop removing their veil and live with confidence without fear.

Mukta Sarvgaud, who wrote the *Dalit Autobiography*, expressed her revolutionary thoughts by giving a speech like "Men and women are equal and the responsibilities of both are equal" (we are history stick).

Maharashtra Chamar Dhor Parishad was held in Pune on 29 May 1956. In this session also, both Mrs. Savitri Bai Boradai and Gunabai Waghmare of Seva Sadan gave speeches. In her speech, Savitri Bai Borade said,

> Girls need education more than boys. There is a need for women's education to avoid the misfortunes of future generations. Children's education depends only on mothers. We should eliminate the begging attitude of being dependent on others. Cleanliness, good health and hygiene all require education.

After this Gunabai baghmare said that women should study. If a woman is educated, she will impart good values to her children. We will make our future generations smart and cultured through education. Therefore, it is important for women to be educated.

The agreement made for separate representation and separate constituencies is called Poona Agreement. All the promises made by the government and Gandhi to the Dalit community under that Poona Pact turned out to be false. Therefore, on behalf of the All India Dalit Federation, it was decided to hold a *satyagraha* in front of the Indian Legislative Assembly. Thousands of Dalits from Bombay, Poona, Kanpur, Uttar Pradesh participated in this *satyagraha*. Dalit leaders like Sitabai, Geetabai Gaikwad, etc. played an important role in this *satyagraha*. Kashinath Gaikwad, brother of the famous Dalit leader Bhaurao Gaikwad, was beaten badly by "non-violent" Gandhians, mistaking him for Bhaurao, in which one of his ears was also broken. Seeing this form of Dalit oppression, Dalit *satyagrahis* started the jail-wide movement. In this Jail Bharo movement, many Dalit women along with their small children remained imprisoned in jail, hungry and thirsty. There is a very interesting incident when the *satyagrahis* were raising slogans in the form of a procession to fill the jail, then the one and a half year old girl of Dalit activist Barada was also raising slogans. On being told by Chalo Pukaron Jai Bhim, she used to say "Chalo Pukaron". Hearing his "Chalo Kaparo", a wave of happiness and enthusiasm ran among the people. Dalit activists like Manorama Bai, Tulsiram Dhotre, Kashibai Jaitapkar, etc. went to jail after participating in *satyagraha*. Manorama Bai remained in jail for fifteen days. Mrs. Varadai was imprisoned with her small children. The judge showed pity on her small children and said, "Sister, your child is very small, confess your crime and ask for forgiveness and go home". On this, Mrs. Varalai told the judge,

> The day we left the house, we thought carefully. Had left the tax. Still, we are not going to back down. If I have committed a crime then punish me. After being released from jail, a very long and thought-provoking interview of the fearless and brave Mrs. Worade was published in *Janta Patra*. (*Aamii Itihas Ghadwala*, pp. 82-83)

Thus, in the beginning of the Dalit women's movement, by making efforts to impart knowledge through welcome songs, by symbolizing the issues like temple entry, water, equal pay, untouchability, freedom from male slavery, etc. Dr. Holding Ambedkar's hand, gradually fighting exploitation at all three levels —equality, untouchability and poverty, building his ideological understanding and walking on the path of liberation, he became the lifeblood of the Dalit movement and a source of inspiration for other movements. Passing through the rough and tough path of freedom and identity struggle, the Dalit women's movement entered the realm of Dalit feminism. Thousands of Dalit women joined this movement everywhere in India, went to jail, sat on hunger strikes day and night and struggled to fulfil their demands with courage, bravery, patience and dedication. The Dalit women's movement kept sharpening the weapon of education to destroy the fort of untouchability, gender discrimination and inequality. Many

Dalit women, along with opening schools, colleges, hostels for the Dalit community, started writing and editing newspapers and magazines. Also started publishing. Many Dalit women established themselves as famous writers in the field of social work as well as writing. Hundreds of Dalit women came out in the Dalit women's movement during Ambedkar's time and took charge of the struggle for Dalit liberation. Ramabai Ambedkar, Tulsi-Bansode, Geetabai Gaekwad, Anjani Bai Desh Bhartar, Shanta Bai Dani, Jaibai Chaudhary, Sita Bai Gaekwad, Indira Patil, Kirti Patil, Sulochana Dogre, Radha Bai, Lakshmi Nayak, Surabai Mohite, Venubai Bhatkar, Rangbai Shubhakar, Tanubai Kamble, Radha Bai Varalai, Mitaleli Kawade, Kaushalya Baisantri Baby Tai Kamble, Meenabal Shivram, Shanta Bai Sarode and many other anonymous Dalit women who were hidden in the depths of history, all of them came out of their homes, families, factories, fields and mines and hoisted the flag of Dalit women's liberation in all directions.

Why Hindu Code Bill?

Dr. Ambedkar wanted revolutionary changes in the social, economic, and political condition of Indian women, especially Hindu women, including both the upper castes and Dalits. To improve their condition, he wanted to make a law which would purely act as a lifesaver in improving their social and legal status. That's why he made "Hindu Code Bill" in favour of 100 per cent women. Both this Hindu Code Bill and Dr. Ambedkar had to face fierce opposition from fanatics. Dr. Ambedkar had to face personal insult many times in protest against the Hindu Code Bill. Even stones were pelted at his house and he was also boycotted in the parliament. Along with Dr. Ambedkar, many Dalit and non-Dalit women have fought the social and economic battle of Indian women to get the "Hindu Code Bill" passed. On "Hindu Code Bill" Durgabai Deshmukh, Member of Lok Sabha, Smt. Padmaji Naidu, Rajshree, Ms. Chandrakala, Urmila Mehta, Mrs. Mithan, Mahila Congress Minister Kumari Mukul and her group of women met Dr. Along with Ambedkar, he travelled from village to village, town to town and drew pictures of the socio-economic plight of Indian women in meetings and public meetings.

Often the Hindu Code Bill discussion meetings organized by Dr. Ambedkar and his female colleagues were directly attacked by fanatics, and the discussion meetings were forcibly closed. The newspapers of that time were also publishing many inflammatory articles against the "Hindu Code Bill". At that time the atmosphere of the country had become toxic against Dr. Ambedkar and his women colleagues. But they all stood firm. Finally, when the "Hindu Code Bill" could not be passed in the parliament, Dr. Ambedkar resigned from the parliament in protest.

The more progressive steps Babasaheb took for the progress of Indian women, the more the radicals tried to hold him back. Angered by progressive steps like the Code Bill, the fundamentalists spread a web of animosity, hatred and tension all around against Dr. Ambedkar. Attacking the patriarchal culture, this Bill glorified Indian women by giving them equal legal rights as men. Because of this Bill, Hindu women were given the same rights as men in marriage, divorce, etc. Nine Acts were made in this Bill:

- Hindu Marriage Act.
- Special Marriage Act.
- Adoption Short-Life Protection Act.
- Hindu Succession Act.
- Maintenance Act of weak and resourceless family members.
- Act related to minor protection.
- Succession Act
- Hindu Widow Remarriage Rights Act.
- Rights in father's property, etc. in Hindu Code Bill.

> The marriage of a girl or a boy of any caste was not illegal by the Hindu Code Bill. According to Hindu Code, a wife and husband could marry only one person at a time. If a husband marries his first wife and the wife marries his first husband, he will be punished legally. In the Hindu Code, after the death of her husband,

> a rule was made to give a Hindu woman a share in her husband's property equal to that of his children. In Hindu religious scriptures, there was no provision for second marriage for a widow, nor did she get any share or share in any property. By the grace of Hindu Code, after the death of the father, the daughter was also made the heir of the property on an equal basis with the brothers. Similarly, the right of adoption was available only to the child born in one's own family, but according to the code, a girl or boy born in any Hindu family could be adopted and that boy or girl could belong to any Hindu caste. If they belong to any family, they become heirs to the property of the person being adopted. The interesting thing was that now not only a boy could be adopted, but a girl could also be adopted. Therefore, it can be said in short that the Hindu Code had destroyed the old religious stronghold of the Hindus. (*Hindu Code Bill and Ambedkar*—Sohanlal Shastri Vidyavachaspati)

By passing these nine Acts in the Hindu Code Bill, Dr. Ambedkar wanted a radical change in the status of women legally. In order to strengthen the social and economic status of women in the family and society through the Hindu Code Bill, they kept the status of the daughter equal to that of the son and the status of the wife equal to that of the husband in the family. In case of divorce, the husband will have to pay maintenance to the wife and in the division of property, the daughter will get an equal share as the son. Women can also adopt a child as per their wish. By getting the right to adopt a child, the women who did not have children will be freed from the mental and physical harassment given by the family and society. On Hindu Code Bill Dr. Ambedkar believed that he wanted to provide welfare to all the women of India by passing the Hindu Code Bill. During the days when the Hindu Code Bill was being considered, he had seen many young women and mature women abandoned by their husbands who were cruel, tyrannical, drunkards, barbarians, etc. belonging to the upper castes, whom their husbands had abandoned for their livelihood. A nominal monthly maintenance allowance of Rs. 4-5 was tied often the husband did not even give that much allowance. These abandoned women were forced to live a life of slavery and poverty. Seeing such pitiful condition of these women, their parents and brothers were also sad. Because there was no law to end the suffering of these abandoned women. The Hindu Code Bill could have been the only law that could have stood in favour of such destitute, distressed women. What is meant to say is that Hindu Code Bill was a law that brought a radical change in the perceived condition of Indian women. In which there was a provision of punishment for the culprits in favour of women who were oppressed in any form and situation in the society. Through this Bill, Dr. Ambedkar and his female companions were making efforts for legal improvement and rights in the status of women. In support of the Hindu Code Bill, a council was organized at Bhandari Hall in Dadar on 21 August 1949 in which twenty women's ten organizations and social organizations submitted a demand letter to the government in support of the Hindu Code Bill. On 19 January 1950, in Wilson College, Urmila Mehta and Mrs. Mithan strongly supported the Hindu Code Bill through their powerful speeches. This movement lasted for about five years in which many Dalit and non-Dalit women joined. The purpose of this movement was to provide social justice which was being violated for years.

Conclusion

In this way Dr. Ambedkar believed that this Bill (Hindu Code Bill), while opening new avenues of progress, is not against religious rituals. The purpose of this Bill is to legalize and reform certain branches of Hindu Law and to provide deprived rights and representation to women. So that the uniformity of the country is maintained, because the social and religious life of Hindus should be governed by the same law. What he said was that it is not that this reform is happening now (in the present time), it has happened before in the Hindu scriptures and is not because the Hindus are reviving themselves. The weak people were in stopping but so that they bring uniformity wanted. This Bill is a right step in the direction of equal civil law. In any case, the law should be such that it should be easily understandable and applicable to the entire society without regional barriers.

But, after widespread protest and criticism due to the misuse of majority, fundamentalist, conservative, patriarchal power, this Bill had to be withdrawn. Due to which Dr. Ambedkar was hurt and saddened. Ambedkar, while resigning from the cabinet on 27 September 1951, said,

> When the society is leaving behind its past and anticipating the future, then only.... It is the only criterion on which anything should be judged. Therefore, the very soul of the Hindu society, the disparity between classes and men, cannot be shaken without being shaken if we keep making one law after another on the economic aspect only. So, this is like making a mockery of the constitution, or a castle on sand. There is an attempt to stand up.

In this way Dr. Ambedkar for the social progress of women which religious laws create hindrances.

REFERENCES

Barua, H.M., *Dalit Women: Social Development and Dr. Ambedkar.*

Bharti, Anita, *Dr. B.R. Ambedkar the Savior of Indian Women* (Anita Bharti is a famous Dalit writer and social worker).

Keer, Dhananjay, *Dr. Ambedkar: Life and Mission.*

Medhwal, Kusum, *Dalit Women: Yesterday, Today and Tomorrow: An Analysis.*

_______, *Mahad Satyagraha.*

_______, *The Savior of Indian Women: Dr. B.R. Ambedkar.*

Mohan Manju, *Dalit Women*, Samyak Prakashan.

_______, *Dalit Women: A Discussion*, Samyak Prakashan.

Naimish Rai, Mohandas, *Contribution of Dalit Women's in the Women's Movement.*

_______, *Slap on both Cheeks/Dalit Women: Double Exploitation, Double Struggle.*

Nayak, Abhimuk (December 2004). *Samman Ki Awaaz*, Special Issue.

Pawar, Urmila and Meenakshi Moon, *Our History Ghadwala*, pp. 70-94.

Shant, Shant Swaroop, *Illustrated Bhima Biography Creator.*

Shastri, Sohan Lal (Legislative Assembly), *Hindu Code Bill and Dr. Ambedkar.*

Shri, Geeta, *Women's Liberation and Women's Movement.*

Verma, Brajlal, *Social Justice awardees Dr. Bhimrao Ambedkar.*

Index